AT ANY COST

AT ANY COST

How Al Gore Tried to Steal the Election

Bill Sammon

Since 1947
REGNERY
PUBLISHING, INC.
An Eagle Publishing Company • Washington, DC

Cataloging-in-Publication Data on file with the Library of Congress

Published in the United States by
Regnery Publishing, Inc.
An Eagle Publishing Company
One Massachusetts Avenue, NW
Washington, DC 20001

Visit us at www.regnery.com

Distributed to the trade by
National Book Network
4720-A Boston Way
Lanham, MD 20706

Printed on acid-free paper
Manufactured in the United States of America

10 9 8 7 6 5 4 3 2 1

BOOK DESIGN BY KASHKA KISZTELINSKA
SET IN SABON

Books are available in quantity for promotional or premium use. Write to Director of Special Sales, Regnery Publishing, Inc., One Massachusetts Avenue, NW, Washington, DC 20001, for information on discounts and terms or call (202) 216–0600.

To my wife, Becky, and our children,
Brittany, Brooke, Ben, Billy, and Blair

CONTENTS

SPOILING FOR A FIGHT

I t was 5:15 A.M. by the time I finally left the *Washington Times* newsroom on November 8, 2000. Having written countless versions of an ever-changing story—including one in which I authoritatively reported that George W. Bush had been elected president—I was physically and mentally exhausted. But like so many other journalists who had planned on taking some time off after the grueling, eighteen-month campaign, I was suddenly forced to scrap my vacation. The election was deadlocked and Florida was about to conduct a recount. Unable to remember the Sunshine State's capital, I asked an editor on the way out of the newsroom.

"I dunno," he shrugged. "Tallahassee?"

I stopped at home en route to the airport and stuffed a change of clothes in my briefcase. My wife suggested I pack a proper bag, but I assured her: "It's a two-day story—tops." Then I headed out the door, unaware that I would remain in Florida for the next forty-six days.

Bleary-eyed and suffering from the ravages of sleep deprivation, I found myself reflecting on the long campaign as the plane headed south. Although I had covered Vice President Al Gore almost nonstop for more than a year and a half, I kept coming back to a particular episode from the summer of 1999.

There were only a handful of us on Air Force Two in those early days of the campaign. On that particular trip, there were even fewer reporters than usual because the only public event on Gore's schedule was an environmental photo-op. Those were Gore's "earth tone" days and he wanted to showcase his new, casual wardrobe in a carefully staged canoe ride down the Connecticut River. The vice president's advance staff had even selected a site on the riverbank where news photographers would get the most flattering shot. They pleaded with their boss not to turn and smile at the cameras as he passed by, but instead to gaze purposefully ahead as he knifed his paddle through the pristine waters. The photo would look more candid that way.

At the livery, Gore clambered into a canoe with New Hampshire Governor Jeanne Shaheen and shoved off. The press were instructed to double up and follow.

"If we're short one life jacket, we just won't give one to the *Washington Times* guy," deadpanned Jake Tapper of *Salon*, a liberal online magazine.

"C'mon, Sammon, you're going with me," said *Washington Post* political correspondent Dan Balz.

We grabbed a canoe and pushed off before the other reporters could get in the water. As we began paddling, the bottom of the canoe brushed briefly over pebbles in the riverbed. But once we got into deeper water, we had no trouble whatsoever navigating.

It was a glorious summer day and the scenery was spectacular. At one point we passed under an old-fashioned covered bridge that connected New Hampshire and Vermont. At another point we spotted the gaggle of photographers as they prepared for their preordained photo of the day. But when Gore passed by, he couldn't resist turning to mug for the cameras with a big toothy grin. His aides and even the photographers groaned. So much for a candid shot.

Balz and I kept up a brisk pace in order to stay close to Gore. In addition to the other reporters, who were bringing up the rear, there were state officials from both Vermont and New Hampshire. Toss in the ubiquitous Secret Service and it was quite a little armada.

The four-mile jaunt seemed to end almost before it began. As we disembarked and started walking up the bank to the vice presidential motorcade, a man named John Kassel, director of the Vermont Division of Natural Resources, sidled up alongside me and struck up a conversation.

"They won't release the water for the fish when we ask them to, but somehow they find themselves able to release it for a politician," Kassel groused. "The only reason they did this was to make sure the vice president's canoe didn't get stuck."

When I expressed bewilderment, Kassel explained: The drought that had been plaguing New England all summer had slowed the Connecticut River to a trickle. Gore's advance team and the local environmentalists who organized the photo-op had fretted that there wouldn't be enough water to float the vice presidential canoe. So Pacific Gas & Electric was instructed to open the floodgates of its dam upriver at dawn that morning. By the time Gore got into his canoe, the river was plenty deep enough for the trip downstream.

"There are people on the phone right now telling them to shut it off," Kassel assured me.

As I reached the motorcade and Kassel went on his way, I pulled out my cell phone and began calling officials at PG&E. The other reporters were now milling around and I didn't want them to hear my conversation, so I did my best to remain circumspect. At length I reached a senior PG&E official who confirmed Kassel's account. I even tracked down the dam operator who had pushed the button that morning to open the floodgates.

Their story was nothing short of amazing. The drought was so severe that New Hampshire residents were forbidden from watering their lawns or washing their cars. And yet more than half a billion gallons of water had been released from a dam in order to accommodate Al Gore's environmental photo-op.

The story hit the front page of the *Washington Times* the next morning. As I prepared a follow-up report, I interviewed Sharon Francis, the local environmentalist who had helped plan the entire event. Francis reiterated a point I had made in my first story—that Gore himself had not ordered the raising of the river. But she also explained something I hadn't known. Francis said she informed Gore of the river-raising immediately after the canoe trip, as she and the vice president were walking to a riverbank podium to make brief remarks. How had Gore reacted to this news? According to Francis, he replied that since he was from Tennessee, home of the Tennessee Valley Authority, he was quite familiar with fluctuations in river levels. This bit of detail, while interesting, seemed of no consequence to my follow-up story.

But then at lunch, I had an opportunity to question Gore about the controversy. Careful not to accuse him of ordering the floodgates opened, I instead asked him how he felt about the river being raised "on your behalf."

"I didn't know it was, until I read your story," Gore replied.

As he walked away, I realized he had just contradicted Francis. Now, instead of a routine follow-up story destined for the back pages, I suddenly had another front-page exclusive: What did Gore know and when did he know it?

That afternoon, Gore's press secretary berated me in the driveway of a swank New Hampshire home as the vice president hobnobbed with Democratic donors inside. Chris Lehane was furious that I had written the story about the canoe flap. It was picked up by CNN, MSNBC, the Associated Press, the *Washington Post*, and the *New York Times*, among other hot media barometers. The intended message of the day—that Gore was a better environmentalist than Democratic challenger Bill Bradley—had been utterly obliterated by the new controversy, which was already being dubbed "Floodgate." Suffice it to say that I was the least popular person aboard Air Force Two as we flew back to Washington that night.

Looking back, the whole episode turned out to be inconsequential in the grand scheme of campaign coverage. And yet the canoe flap had taught me something important about Al Gore. When caught in a jam, he reflexively resorted to deception instead of just taking his licks and moving on. He also made it his practice to dispatch staffers to attack the messenger and anyone else who dared question the message of the day. For two weeks after that canoe ride, Gore supporters furiously tried to spin the story. First they disputed the number of gallons released, arguing for days over whether it had been in the tens of millions, hundreds of millions, or even billions, as PG&E originally asserted. When it became apparent that, no matter which number was accurate, it was still an enormous amount of water, Team Gore switched to another argument: The dam routinely released water anyway. But Cleve Kapala, PG&E's director of government affairs, said this particular release was orchestrated specifically for Gore.

"It was a bit artificial, to be honest with you," Kapala said. "The river was pretty dry and no one wanted the canoes to be dragging on the bottom. Vice President Gore's people were concerned that we not raise the level too high, either, because they didn't want it to be dangerous."

He added: "It took a lot of water to get it just right."

Dam operator Dennis Goodwin said raising the river for a VIP was anything but routine.

"It's a first for me, and I've been in this job for sixteen years," Goodwin said. "But if we hadn't done it, they might have hit bottom."

Finally, in desperation, Gore loyalists fell back on the argument first raised by Kassel—that a release would be good for the fish. But even Governor Shaheen's husband, Bill, who was manager of Gore's New Hampshire campaign, threw cold water on that theory.

"When you raise the level for fishing, you have to keep it up or else the fish die," said Shaheen, who acknowledged the river receded to its low level within hours after Gore's departure.

By railing against the story instead of getting it behind him, Gore gave it legs. *The Hotline*, an online compendium of campaign coverage read by virtually everyone in politics, charted each Gore misstep in what was becoming a canoe saga. The Republican National Committee gleefully issued daily news releases, including one headlined "Row vs. Wade." Someone even filed a complaint with the Federal Elections Commission, charging that the release of water had amounted to an illegal campaign contribution. By going to war over a flubbed photo-op, Gore brought this flood of criticism on himself.

Now, fifteen months later, it looked as though Gore was digging in his heels once again. He had conceded the election to Bush, only to call back an hour later and withdraw his concession. He seemed to be hunkering down for a new fight, although no one knew, as my plane touched down in Tallahassee, just how far Gore was willing to go. At that early stage of the standoff, no one could have imagined that Gore would personally direct a smear-and-destroy campaign against Florida's top election official for simply upholding the law. In those innocent days of the automatic statewide recount, no one could have predicted that Gore would resort to disenfranchising GIs serving overseas, not to mention civilians living right there in Florida, even as he publicly pleaded to "count every vote." And not even the craziest of conspiracy theorists would dare posit a scenario in which Gore would privately consult an Electoral College expert to advise him on the possibilities of enlisting "faithless" Bush electors.

Still, as the plane taxied to a stop, I couldn't shake the sense that perhaps we were heading into a profoundly bigger and more important variation of the canoe story, in which Gore would do anything to win, no matter how bad he looked or how ugly it got.

I once spent several years uncovering election fraud in Cleveland for the *Plain Dealer* newspaper. I had seen how messy and imprecise the hallowed exercise of voting really was: disappearing ballots; a rigged vote-counting computer; a cat, I even found, who was registered to vote under the name Morris Feline Stuart, occupation "exterminator." In the end, there were investigations by everyone from the Ohio secretary of state to the FBI. Both Republican and Democratic election officials were forced from office.

Now I wondered if the entire nation was about to get an eyeful of the sausage-making operation known as voting in America.

Thirty-six days after arriving in Florida, most of the reporters finally went home. I remained for ten more days, traveling the state to research just how far Gore had gone to achieve his goal. In the end, when he knew all was lost, he tried to inflict mortal wounds on Bush's fledgling presidency. In the process, he all but obliterated any chance for a political comeback of his own.

In short, Al Gore had tried like, well, Al Gore, to seize the presidency—at any cost.

CHAPTER 1

STIFFING THE PANHANDLERS

Bob Glass was running late. He hustled his little red Geo past Bubba's Bar-B-Q Pit and the 4-H Club and the Lots O' Snacks on his way toward Interstate 10. He was at the westernmost tip of the Florida panhandle and he had to get clear to the other side of Pensacola in less than half an hour. Traffic would be murder, what with all the military personnel streaming out of their installations to vote for a new commander-in-chief. But Glass, fifty, had never failed to cast a ballot in a presidential election—and he wasn't about to now.

Glass sells, well, glass. Don't bother with the wisecracks; he's heard them all. People actually ask him if he legally changed his name as a promotional gimmick for his windshield replacement business, which he runs from the back room of his brother's house six miles from the Alabama border.

"No, I've had this name since 1950," Glass says with a weary chuckle. "For as far back as I can remember."

Glass swung the 1996 Geo onto the highway entrance ramp. The words "WINDSHIELD EXPRESS" fanned across the tinted top of the windshield in white vinyl letters that were slightly askew. The left and right sides of the car were adorned with white magnetic signs that said: "Windshield Express: Keep it local, keep it fast; let us repair your auto glass." Glass had come up with that slogan himself. To anyone who made fun of it, he pointed out that the traveling billboard otherwise known as his car had generated quite a few cold calls from fellow motorists who ended up as paying customers. Oh, and it didn't hurt that the back bumper was affixed with a "Bush-Cheney" sticker.

Out here in Escambia County, people like to say that Florida is the only state in which north is south and south is north. What they mean is that in northern Florida, where the panhandle runs right along the Georgia and Alabama borders, people consider themselves southerners. It's the kind of place where waitresses in even the finest restaurants think nothing of addressing middle-aged businessmen they've never met as "honey," "sugar," "sweetie," and even "baby." This isn't just the South; it's the Deep South. Supporters of Texas Governor George W. Bush outnumbered supporters of Vice President Al Gore by more than 2-to-1 in the panhandle's ten westernmost counties, which collectively form the only region of Florida that falls within the Central Time Zone.

The remaining fifty-seven counties in the state are in the Eastern Time Zone. As far as Glass was concerned, they might as well be in the Twilight Zone. For starters, fully half the people who lived in the eastern fifty-seven counties supported Al Gore. And every time Glass crossed the time line it seemed to get worse. The further he traveled east and then south down the peninsula, the more he ran into liberal Democrats, who continued to invade these warmer climes from up north, particularly from New York and New England.

"I'm a firm believer that everyone from Orlando south is not a native Floridian," harrumphed Glass, who once endured a year in Orlando before retreating to his beloved panhandle.

The problem was even more pronounced further south, especially down around Palm Beach, Broward, and Miami-Dade counties, which collectively form the Gold Coast. Glass found it increasingly rare to encounter people who had a southern accent along the Gold Coast.

"When I was little, my grandparents lived in Palm Beach County," he recalled. "They retired there from Alabama. In fact, everybody that lived on my grandfather's road was from Alabama. Some of my fondest memories are from there.

"'Course, those people have all died off and gone," he added wistfully. "And there's a whole new breed now. Their ideology and ours are not nearly the same."

The little red car chugged east along the northern edge of the city. Glass still had twenty minutes to make it to his polling place, Scenic Heights Baptist Church. He knew that all he had to do was get into line by 7 P.M. Central Time (8 P.M. Eastern) and he couldn't be turned away. Even if the line stretched outside the church and around the block, Glass would be able to vote for president. He might not actually cast his ballot until 7:15 or 7:30 or even 7:45, but he was determined to stand up and be counted for George W. Bush.

Glass was what pollsters called "a highly motivated voter." A rock-ribbed Republican all his life, he had cast ballots for Nixon in 1972; Ford in 1976; Reagan in 1980 and 1984; Bush in 1988 and 1992; and Dole in 1996. Glass considered it a travesty that Bill Clinton and Al Gore had evicted President George H. W. Bush from the White House in 1992. For eight years, Glass watched with growing frustration as the Clinton-Gore team took the nation down what he considered the wrong path. Abandoning his campaign promise to cut taxes on the middle class, Clinton instead raised them—with Gore casting the tie-breaking vote. The new president favored abortion and gun control and bigger government.

He was ruining the military with political correctness. Worst of all, he was constantly mired in scandal. For Glass, a Southern Baptist, the final straw came when Clinton, also a Baptist, had sex with a White House intern young enough to be his daughter and then lied under oath to cover it up. Glass believed the only honorable thing for Clinton to do was resign and spare the nation the wrenching ordeal of impeachment. He was mortified when Clinton insisted on fighting, "tooth and toenail," to the bitter end. Clinton had maintained he was not trying to save his own skin, but merely defending the Constitution. The audacity! But the crowning insult, as far as Glass was concerned, came just hours after Clinton was impeached, when Al Gore stood on the South Lawn of the White House and pronounced his boss one of the greatest presidents in history.

Now Gore himself was running for president, promising to use Clinton's eight years of accomplishments as a foundation on which to erect eight more years of Democratic triumphs. He specifically talked about his presidency as one that would last eight years, not four. The colossal presumptuousness sickened Glass. The idea that the 2000 election might merely be the halfway point in a sixteen-year Clinton-Gore era was simply unthinkable. If anything, Gore was more of a liberal, tax-and-spend Democrat than Clinton.

"I'd had it up to here with Clinton-Gore," Glass said as he flattened his palm and raised it dead level to his blue eyes.

Glass resolved to do everything in his power to help end the Clinton-Gore era. Although he had never been very active in party politics, he began attending meetings of the Escambia County Republican Party. As the election drew near, he agreed to help run a phone bank. Unlike some of the younger volunteers, who used a script in placing their calls, the fifty-year-old Glass spoke from his heart. With a soft southern affability, Glass tried to impart to his fellow Republicans the importance of voter turnout. He even offered to drive them to the polls if necessary, pointing out that as a self-employed business operator, he had plenty of flexibility in his work schedule. The day before the election, Glass and other Republican volunteers stood on street corners, clutching Bush-Cheney signs and waving to motorists on their way to work. It was Glass's way of reminding his fellow conservatives one last time to vote.

"I was—," Glass grasped for words, "—on *fire*," he concluded. "You know, for the *cause*. Oh, I was highly motivated."

Glass found himself spending more and more time on the Internet, visiting conservative chat rooms to share his passion with fellow Republicans. He sensed a unity not just in Florida, but in other states as well.

"It was a feeling Republicans hadn't felt in a long time," he said.

And yet, in the closing days of the campaign, Glass sensed something else, too. He had always known the election was going to be a nail-biter, but now he began to fret that Gore was somehow pulling ahead at the very last moment. He winced when the media went ballistic over an eleventh-hour revelation that Bush had been cited for drunken driving twenty-four years earlier. The story, which had been leaked by a Gore supporter, dominated TV news coverage the weekend before the election.

"I could see it falling away from G. W. Bush—I really could," Glass recalled. "I mean, those last minute tactics like the DUI thing. Oh, it was just horrible. I could just see it slipping away.

"Granted, I think he should have been more upfront with it sooner," added Glass, a teetotaler. "Then they wouldn't have made such a big deal out of it. But the Democrats took it and run with it and beat it till it couldn't be beat any more. And I could see it falling away."

Like anyone else who had paid even passing attention to the campaign in its final hundred hours, Glass was aware that after months of endless speculation about this state or that being a "battleground," the polls and conventional wisdom had coalesced around three as most crucial to the outcome of the election—Pennsylvania, Michigan, and Florida. It was universally believed that Gore, the underdog, could win the election only if he swept the "trifecta," as these states were now being called by conservative and liberal pundits alike. The flip side of this theory was that Bush had to retain at least one of the three—preferably Florida, the largest—in order to become the next president.

Glass had become alarmed by late indications that Gore was firming up his numbers in both Michigan and Pennsylvania. If these warning signs proved true, the entire election might very well come down to the Sunshine State alone. His fears were confirmed when Gore chose Florida as the state in which to end the campaign he had begun eighteen months earlier.

"This is the last official stop of Campaign 2000," Gore announced during a televised rally in Tampa just minutes before polls opened on Election Day. "It's not an accident that it's here, because Florida may very well be the state that decides the outcome of this election."

The vice president's confident optimism troubled Glass.

"Tonight, when the vote comes in, we're going to win Florida and we're going to win the White House," Gore vowed. "It's almost 5:30 A.M., Texas time, and George W. Bush is still asleep. And I'm still speaking to people here in Florida."

Glass couldn't help but worry that Gore was right. The rally was merely the capstone of a furious get-out-the-vote effort by Florida Democrats, who seemed to be gaining momentum with each passing hour. They had deployed an army of union foot soldiers to lobby swing voters up and down the peninsula. It was the kind of ground war that Democrats usually win.

But Glass also knew that Florida Governor Jeb Bush had spent years cultivating a remarkably effective, county-by-county, Republican machine that could fight the Democrats to a draw—or perhaps, with a little luck, a narrow victory. "Jeb, we need to win," George W. Bush had implored his younger brother in the closing weeks of the campaign. Glass knew that if Jeb failed to deliver Florida, the entire election would probably be lost. As one of the innumerable cogs in Jeb's machine, Glass had done his best to kick things into overdrive during those final weeks. Yet he now found himself entertaining serious doubts about whether he and his GOP brethren could pull it off.

Having driven as far east as he could without actually leaving Pensacola, Glass swung onto Scenic Highway and headed south along Pensacola Bay. Expensive, waterfront homes with spectacular views lined the left side of the road. He was now confident he would make it to Scenic Heights Baptist Church by 7:00. Armed with an intimate knowledge of the city's back roads, Glass planned to cut through a nearby sub-development that would get him to the church on time. He was less than half a mile from the turnoff and it was only 6:50. For Glass, that was plenty of time.

On previous Election Days, Glass had voted early in the morning, on his way into work. But on this day he felt compelled to attend a breakfast meeting of the Pensacola Chamber of Commerce. Glass considered such meetings an important forum for "networking" for his fledgling business, which was only two years old. Thanks in part to the contacts Glass developed at such forums, Windshield Express was already grossing nearly half a million dollars a year. Just days earlier, Glass had been thrilled to see new his half-page ad in the Pensacola Yellow Pages.

"It's the only four-process color ad in that section of the phone book," he said, beaming with the satisfaction of a first-time father.

As Glass neared the church, he listened to the radio. Glass was a big fan of talk radio, which he considered the only sector of the American news media not completely overrun by liberal Democrats. Earlier in the day, he had listened to Rush Limbaugh, the most popular and influential talk show host in America. After that he had tuned into a show hosted by a local conservative named Luke McCoy, who happened to live just three townhouses away from Glass on a quiet cul-de-sac just off Scenic Highway. During that afternoon's show, McCoy had received an on-air call from Jeb Bush, who had just arrived in Austin and was heading over to the governor's mansion to monitor election returns with his brother.

"Hey Luke, Jeb Bush," the governor said as if the two were old friends. "I just want to urge you to do everything you can to get the vote out. It's going to be very tight and we need the people of the panhandle."

"I'm honored that you called, Governor," McCoy replied. "This is conservative country. We'll do everything we can."

McCoy's show was over now, so it was no longer possible for Glass to listen to talk radio. As he neared the turnoff that would take him to his polling place, he flitted from station to station in hopes of catching a little Election Night coverage.

"...and so Al Gore has won Florida's 25 electoral votes," crackled a disembodied voice from the radio.

Most people have a kind of heater in their forehead that switches on only in moments of profound anger or perplexity. A mild-mannered person can go years, even decades, without the heater in his or her forehead ever activating. Bob Glass considers himself such a person. Slow to anger and loath to use profanity, Glass nonetheless felt the heater in his forehead switch on at ten minutes before 7:00 on Election Night. Alone in his Geo, he suddenly found himself cursing aloud.

"How can this be?" Glass remembered thinking. "We're not through voting yet!"

Sure, polls had closed in the Eastern Time Zone, where Gore had just as many supporters as Bush, nearly an hour ago. But here in the Central Time Zone, where Bush supporters outnumbered Gore supporters by more than 2-to-1, people were still lined up outside the doors of polling places from Pensacola to Panama City. The election was still very much in progress. Voters could still show up for another ten minutes. And people who were in line by the stroke of 7:00 could vote no matter how long it took. Voters have been known to stand in line for up to two hours in presidential elections. Military personnel were notorious for crowding into polling places on their way home from work. The western panhandle was teeming with military installations. The Naval Air Station was right there on Pensacola Bay. This was the very cradle of naval aviation, the storied home of the legendary Blue Angels. These were not the kind of voters who were going to support Al Gore. They had enlisted to become trained killers in the mightiest fighting machine ever assembled, but instead had spent the last eight years attending sensitivity training sessions and filling potholes in Bosnia. They had been over-deployed to so many far-flung peacekeeping adventures that their divorce rates were soaring and re-enlistment rates were plummeting. Military pay was so abysmal during the Clinton-Gore years that thousands of soldiers and sailors and airmen were reduced to surviving on food stamps. These people would gladly stand in line for an hour or two after poll-closing time for the chance to vote for a new commander-in-chief.

And yet, if Glass had already heard the devastating news, surely so had the military personnel. Would they be willing to continue standing in line now that Gore had already won Florida? Glass's mind was racing. He understood how the Electoral College functioned. He knew all too well that the presidential race would be determined by electoral votes, not popular votes. He grasped the concept that once Florida had gone for Gore, it was pointless to cast a ballot for Bush. The state's 25 electoral votes would not be divvied up to reflect each man's share of the popular vote. It was winner-take-all—and loser-take-nothing. Bush would not get a single electoral vote from Florida. The only thing Glass could accomplish now by continuing his journey to Scenic Heights Baptist Church was to cut Gore's popular vote victory by exactly one measly ballot—out of 6 million cast statewide. It would be an utterly meaningless gesture.

Glass despaired, realizing that his vote had been rendered worthless not just in Florida, which was now a lost cause, but also nationally. It wasn't as though Bush could somehow get "credit" for Glass's vote in some other state, using it to help him squeak out a victory in, say, New Mexico. The Electoral College was nothing more than a series of winner-take-all contests. And each state was its own self-contained contest. Although the presidential election is widely regarded as America's only national political race, no person's vote has the slightest practical impact whatsoever outside of his or her own state.

Flush with anger and a sense of dread that Gore's win in Florida would put him over the top nationally, Glass drove straight past the turnoff. Although there were other Republicans on the ballot that Glass supported, including an acquaintance who was running for sheriff, these candidates suddenly vanished from Glass's radar screen. Crushed by the Gore victory, he kept right on driving down Scenic Highway.

Bob Glass, who had been such a true believer that he manned a phone bank to implore fellow Republicans to vote for Bush, suddenly felt the fire in his belly go out. The windshield salesman who had been inspired to stand on a street corner with a "Bush-Cheney" sign just a day earlier now fatalistically figured that his own ballot wasn't worth casting. For the first time in his adult life, Bob Glass decided not to exercise his sacred right to vote for president of the United States.

"What's the use?" he reasoned. "I mean, if Gore's already won the state, there's no use in voting for Bush.

"I was so infuriated. I was distraught. And I just went home."

Bob Glass was among 187,000 registered voters in the Central Time Zone of Florida who did not cast ballots in the 2000 election. The overwhelming majority of them failed to vote because of good old-fashioned, garden-variety apathy.

But tens of thousands of these would-be voters were dissuaded from casting their ballots by the premature and erroneous declaration of a Gore victory, according to studies conducted by Democrats, Independents, and Republicans. Taken together, these surveys show that the bad call caused Bush a net loss of about 10,000 votes.

"By prematurely declaring Gore the winner shortly before polls had closed in Florida's conservative western panhandle, the media ended up suppressing the Republican vote," concluded John R. Lott, Jr., senior research scholar at Yale University Law School. Lott put Bush's net loss at a "conservative estimate of 10,000 votes."

John McLaughlin & Associates, a Republican polling firm based in Washington, D.C., pegged the loss at 11,500 votes. The company conducted a poll November 15 and 16 that showed that the premature—and as it turned out, wrong—calling of the election for Gore had dissuaded 28,050 people from voting. While 23 percent of them were Gore supporters, 64 percent—or nearly three times as many—would have voted for Bush.

"The premature announcement discouraged many registered voters who, according to our survey's results, would have voted like the rest of their neighbors—overwhelmingly for George W. Bush," said the survey's authors, senior analyst Stuart Polk and data specialist Charlie Banks. "If only a few thousand of these disenfranchised voters had heard that the polls were still open, and the race in Florida was still too close to call—and then voted—George W. Bush would have gained a decisive net positive margin of votes over Al Gore.

"These votes would have helped Bush carry the popular vote statewide," the pollsters concluded, "without uncertainty."

Even the study commissioned by Democratic strategist Bob Beckel concluded that Bush suffered a net loss of up to 8,000 votes in the western panhandle after Florida was called for Gore.

These surveys, like others conducted after previous elections, demonstrated that early projections of victory generally dissuade supporters of the losing candidate more than the winning candidate. When voters hear their candidate has already won, they tend to become energized and often make a point of casting their ballots anyway—if for no other reason than to officially stand up and be counted as part of the winning team. Conversely, voters who learn their candidate has already lost tend to become dispirited, almost bereft. Realizing their vote no longer matters, these citizens see little point in driving out to polling places and waiting in line for the chance to cast ballots in an election that has already been lost. Why bother going through the motions? Who wants to stand up and be counted as an official member of the losing team?

Indeed, Glass would later learn that many of his fellow citizens who had been standing in line at Scenic Heights Baptist Church— and countless other polling places in the western panhandle—got out of line and went home after hearing the news, which spread like wildfire the instant Gore was first declared the winner by NBC

News at 6:49 P.M. News travels fast in the Information Age. In the eleven-minute interval between the network calling Florida for Gore and the polls closing, fully two-thirds of all voters in the western panhandle heard about it, according to the McLaughlin survey.

It is difficult to overstate the political and historical significance of the suppressed turnout in the western panhandle. If the network news had not jumped the gun in projecting Gore to win Florida, Bush would have netted roughly 10,000 additional votes. Those would have carried enormous political weight in an election that ended up being decided by fewer than 1,000 votes. While those 10,000 votes would not have been enough to prevent an automatic recount—which is mandated by Florida law when the statewide margin of victory is less than one-half of 1 percent—they certainly would have presented the Gore team with a much higher mountain to climb in the post-election period. Indeed, one of the crucial calculations that convinced Gore to fight so tenaciously for thirty-six days was that he was only a few hundred votes shy of victory. He was tantalized by the very closeness of the race. His lawyers and spinners constantly laid out scenarios in which they cobbled together enough votes in this county and that county to overcome Bush's razor-thin margin of victory. Such scenarios would have been far less feasible if Bush had been able to pad his victory by another 10,000 votes. A five-digit margin of victory would have been much more daunting to Gore than the three-digit margin he tried so desperately to overcome for more than a month. He might have conceded sooner—perhaps as early as November 10, when the mandatory statewide recount would have affirmed a five-digit Bush lead.

That is, if the media had not convinced Bob Glass and thousands of other Floridians in the western panhandle that voting for Bush was utterly pointless.

NBC's premature and erroneous announcement at 6:49 P.M. that Gore had won Florida set off a stampede among the other networks. While virtually all the network executives later admitted they were wrong, they refused to acknowledge having influenced as much as a single voter in Florida's western panhandle.

"In the case of Florida, it would be extremely difficult to argue any impact on turnout," insisted CBS News President Andrew Heyward. "The polls were closed in all but 5.8 percent of the state's precincts, with the rest closing just ten minutes later."

He didn't mention that those precincts contained half a million registered voters.

ABC News President David Westin was even more dismissive.

"There was no point during the evening when it was likely or even possible that voters would decide not to vote simply because of the erroneous projection of the presidential race in Florida," Westin declared.

Glass called these assertions arrogant.

"These executives are trying to save face," he said. "When you give out information that directly impacts people's behavior, that is just wrong, wrong, wrong. By anybody's standards, it's wrong.

"You know, a lot of people take the news as gospel," he added. "'Course, I realize you have to rely on yourself to discern the truth in what the media says. There's a fine line between the news and what you get out of the news.

"But even then, you depend on news *almost* as gospel. Somebody's got to be responsible for this."

CHAPTER 2

BARKING AT THE MOON

Let's get one thing straight right from the get-go," CBS News anchor Dan Rather lectured viewers at 7:08 P.M. Eastern Time. "We would rather be last in reporting a return than to be wrong. And again, our record demonstrates that to be true. If you hear someplace else that somebody's carried a state—and if you are off, as you shouldn't be, watching them—then come back here. Because if we say somebody's carried a state, you can pretty much take it to the bank. Book it. That's true."

Rather's hubris was nothing short of breathtaking. CBS and the other networks had been blithely awarding states to Bush or Gore for more than an hour without knowing how even a single citizen in those states had voted. They called Indiana and Kentucky at the stroke of 6:00, when hundreds of thousands of voters who lived west of the time line still had another hour in which to cast their ballots. They called Vermont and South Carolina at the stroke of 7:00, before election officials there even had a chance to tally the results.

Rather's implication that the other networks were more likely to make a mistake than CBS was particularly disingenuous. CBS didn't even conduct its own exit polls. The network had joined with NBC, ABC, CNN, Fox News Channel, and the Associated Press to form a single entity, known as Voter News Service, that would do exit polling on the cheap. All the news organizations were getting the exact same data at the exact same time. It was a cost-cutting measure, pure and simple. A dozen years earlier, the networks still employed their own separate firms to conduct exit polls. But such journalistic independence was viewed as an obscenely expensive indulgence by the corporate bean counters at General Electric and the other conglomerates that began gobbling up the networks in the late 1980s. Why should the news agencies hire three or four or five firms to conduct exit polls when it was cheaper to hire just one?

So, like the aging dons of the organized crime families in New York, who occasionally cooperated in controlling the vast resources at their disposal, the TV networks that are normally at each other's throats agreed to collaborate for the twenty-four-hour period known as Election Day. No anchor would dare mention this on the air, but the networks had created a monopoly. They had dumped the awesome responsibility of divining the identity of the next president of the United States into the lap of Voter News Service, a single, faceless entity the networks themselves had created and then allowed to grow hopelessly complacent because it had, after all, no competition.

Indeed, Voter News Service had become sloppy over the years. Its data were riddled with errors. Its statistical models were outdated and unsound. Its computers couldn't even communicate with each other. Yet VNS had been lucky. None of the recent presidential elections had been close enough to expose its flaws.

Professional pollsters, statisticians, or political experts did not conduct VNS election polls—well-meaning but inexperienced

housewives, retirees, college students, odd-jobbers, and other political novices did. Oh, there was the occasional ex-political science
teacher. But for every one of these, there were a dozen other "pollsters" who couldn't name their own member of Congress. Each of
these one-day employees was paid $175 by VNS to stand for
twelve or fourteen hours in the parking lot of a randomly selected
polling place, accost every third or fourth voter who emerged from
the sanctity of the voting booth, and ask intensely personal questions, including: For whom did you vote? How much money do
you make? How old are you?

In some states, these part-time pollsters were forced by local
ordinance to stand at least seventy-five feet away from the polling
places. Voters would emerge from the church or school or senior
center where they had just cast their ballots and step unmolested to
their cars, which were parked directly outside the doorway and
well within the seventy-five-foot poll-free zone. The amateur pollster would be reduced to waiting for that rarest of Americans—
someone who travels to and from neighborhood destinations by
actually walking.

Even pollsters who were allowed to approach voters in the
parking lots were often met with suspicion, rejection, or outright
hostility. Having just exercised their solemn constitutional right to
select the next president, many Americans were not exactly eager
to share their private deliberations with a total stranger who inter-
cepted them en route to their SUV with a lot of nosey inquiries.

VNS placed exit pollsters in just 1 percent of the nation's
precincts. It hired even fewer in Florida, even though the state was
widely viewed as the key to the entire election. VNS exit pollsters
manned just forty-five of the state's 5,845 precincts, or 0.8 percent.
The pollsters managed to coax answers out of 4,356 Floridians—
or 0.07 percent of the 6 million people who cast ballots in the state.

It was an infinitesimal sampling, even if all the respondents had been truthful in revealing their presidential preferences. Worse yet, it did not reflect the will of absentee voters, who for years had been growing as a percentage of the electorate. Florida officials knew in advance that fully 10 percent of the state's voters—or 600,000 people—would cast absentee ballots. Yet VNS was inexplicably blindsided by this massive and important voting bloc.

"We did not correctly anticipate the impact of the absentee vote," VNS editorial director Murray Edelman sheepishly admitted in a confidential memo to clients a week after the election.

Still, the housewives, retirees, students, and odd-jobbers did the best they could, gathering as much information from as many cooperative voters as possible and phoning it in every few hours to their employer for the day. VNS plugged these results into rickety computer models that had been set up, in part, to counterbalance what VNS officials privately called the "Democratic bias" that had been stubbornly pervading their polling process for years. When VNS officials fretted about the "Democratic bias" in their exit polling, they were not using the term in a political, pejorative sense, as in: "The *Washington Post* has a Democratic bias." Rather, they were referring to the statistical, scientific reality that their raw exit polls have, for one reason or another, overstated the strength of Democratic candidates in election after election.

"They've been fairly candid about it in meetings over the years," said a VNS insider. "They are aware there's been a Democratic bias in the survey. They're conscious of that. It's not like they've ignored it.

"And they've spent time and effort over the years trying to determine exactly what it is," the insider continued. "They've just never been able to determine why that pattern has happened. But they know how to weight around it."

Yet efforts by VNS to counterbalance the Democratic bias have never worked. In the 1996 election, VNS exit polling showed Democrat Dick Swett beating Republican Bob Smith in the New Hampshire Senate race by 52 to 47 percent—precisely the opposite of the actual vote.

"For some reason, Democrats in New Hampshire were more willing to talk to us than Republicans," shrugged Edelman after the blown New Hampshire call. "I don't have a good answer why."

VNS was not the only link in the information chain that was tainted by Democratic bias on Election Night 2000. So were most of the networks themselves. Fully 89 percent of Washington journalists voted for the Clinton-Gore ticket in 1992, compared to just 7 percent who voted for President Bush, according to a survey by the Freedom Forum, an independent foundation, and the Roper Center, a respected public opinion firm. Gore remained the heavy favorite in 2000, judging from the chatter among journalists on the campaign trail during the eighteen months leading up to the election. The bias became even more pronounced during the home stretch, when the candidates picked their running mates. The staunchly conservative voting record of Bush's choice—former Defense Secretary Richard B. Cheney—was anathema to most journalists covering the campaign. By contrast, Gore's pick—Connecticut Senator Joseph I. Lieberman—became a media darling whose overt religiosity was championed by the same reporters who had savaged Bush for daring to mention Jesus Christ during a debate. The networks are hypersensitive to the charge of liberal bias and vociferously deny it. But it exists all the same.

In short, the Democratic bias of the VNS exit polling was compounded by the Democratic bias of the networks. Even Fox News Channel—a cable network that has been accused by rivals of hiring and giving air-time to too many conservatives—put three

Democrats and only one Republican on its "decision desk," the team of employees that analyzed the rattletrap VNS data and then projected winners and losers.

That was another subject that Rather and the other anchors avoided mentioning on the air. They weren't the ones actually making the projections. Despite their studied air of authoritativeness, the anchors were being told, through their earpieces, when and how to call each state. The actual projections were made by the "decision-deskers," the handful of obscure number-crunchers and political junkies who were never actually seen by the public.

It is not an exaggeration to say that on Election Night, the decision-deskers were the most influential people on the face of the planet. The raw power wielded by these utterly anonymous backroom kingmakers was nothing short of mind-boggling. No one else on Earth was considered capable of doing what they did. They were the chosen ones, the oracles who supposedly possessed the raw data, analytical skills, and unquestioned authority to anoint the next leader of the world's only remaining superpower. It was an enormous, crushing responsibility. Even the editors of the vaunted *New York Times*, which prided itself on publishing only what its own journalists had actually seen and heard and concluded for themselves, deferred to the decision-deskers on Election Night. For that matter, so did the presidential candidates themselves. And yet the plain fact of the matter was that the public didn't have the slightest inkling that these stupendous power brokers even existed.

Shielded from the glare of cameras and klieg lights, the decision-deskers hunkered over computer screens of deeply flawed data from VNS and essentially made educated guesses about who would win a particular state. They anguished over screenfuls of arcane statistics, obsessively crosschecking and analyzing the ramshackle VNS computer models before giving the whole mess one final, white-knuckled blessing and making a call. Just like that, the decision-deskers divined the collective intentions of millions of voters whose ballots had not yet been counted or, in many cases, even cast. The projections were then murmured into the earpieces of Dan Rather, Tom Brokaw, Peter Jennings, and the other talking heads, who breathlessly repeated what they had just been told to a rapt and waiting world. In most cases, the anchors didn't bother explaining that they were only making flimsy guesstimates. In fact, they gave the distinct impression they were making ironclad assertions of fact.

ABC, NBC, and Fox each had its own decision desk, while CBS and CNN joined forces to share a single desk. The Associated Press, a news cooperative that served the vast majority of American newspapers, also operated a decision desk. Together, these six news organizations comprised the VNS consortium and occupied the seats on its board of directors. VNS also had a decision desk, which was headed by Edelman. The decision-deskers and a few other people were supposed to be the only ones with access to the VNS exit polls, although the data was routinely leaked to politicians, newspaper reporters, and Internet sites.

Up until 6 P.M. on Election Night, exit polls were the only indicators of how the presidential contest might turn out. Physical vote counts were not yet available because election officials usually waited until polling places closed before beginning the tabulation process. Since the election workers themselves had not yet come up with any hard numbers, it was impossible for the decision-deskers to come up with any. Not for one state. Not for one county. Not for one city.

Still, Dan Rather and Peter Jennings and Tom Brokaw were not about to kick off their much-hyped Election Night coverage by advising their prime-time audience, numbering in the tens of millions, to chill out because no actual votes had yet been counted.

These networks had lined up the finest pundits, analysts, field reporters, campaign correspondents, and party hacks for a marathon, wall-to-wall, caffeine-drenched, metaphor-laden, all-nighter of campaign coverage that would provide a fitting finale to the closest presidential race in forty years. No, there was only one way to start off this balls-to-the-wall journalistic extravaganza and that was by immediately declaring Gore or Bush the victor in as many states as possible. Preferably Gore.

Since the networks were all using the same information, the whole business of projecting winners and losers essentially boiled down to one question: Which network would have the guts to pull the trigger first? Despite Rather's insistence that CBS "would rather be last in reporting a return than to be wrong," each network was terrified of being beaten on important calls. To be last on a big projection was nothing short of journalistic death—with the whole world watching. The entire business of determining the next leader of the free world came down to a gigantic game of chicken.

Why, then, did the networks bother waiting for any of the polling places to close before making projections? After all, even with the deeply flawed VNS exit polls and the dearth of hard voting results, plenty of states were virtually certain to go for one candidate or the other. Gore was never going to lose Rhode Island (which he ended up winning by 29 percentage points) or New York (which he took by 25) or the District of Columbia (which he carried by a whopping 77 points). Conversely, there was no doubt Bush would win Texas, (he took the state by 21 points). And no one in his right mind would dare project Bush to lose Utah, Idaho, or Wyoming, the latter being the home of his running mate, Dick Cheney (Bush won each by 41 points).

So why did the networks hesitate to call these states, where one candidate or another was a sure bet by enormous margins? Why wait until midnight to declare Bush the winner of Alaska (which he took by 31 percentage points), when the networks could safely make the same declaration at 6 P.M., as their prime time coverage began? Why not go ahead and project the winners of such states right at the outset, to heighten the drama of the horse race?

Because twenty years earlier, the networks had called states so early for Ronald Reagan that President Jimmy Carter actually conceded while polls were still open in California. Democrats went apoplectic, Congress launched an investigation, and liberals trumpeted a study by the University of Michigan that concluded the early calls dissuaded countless would-be Carter supporters from bothering to cast their ballots. What was the point of going to the polls if you already knew your man had lost?

Under relentless assault by angry Democrats on Capitol Hill, who held indignant public hearings, the networks grudgingly agreed to henceforth withhold projections until the close of most polls in any given state. The key word in the agreement was "most." That one word proved an enormous loophole for the networks because it allowed them to prematurely project winners of about a dozen states that straddle two time zones. If "most" of a state's polling places happened to be located on the eastern side of the time line, the network could project the entire state the moment those eastern polls closed—even if that meant dissuading hundreds of thousands of voters who still had another hour in which to vote west of the time line.

On Election Night 2000, Florida was the only state in which most—but not all—of its polls closed at 7 P.M. Eastern Time. The networks were well aware that up to half a million Floridians would still have another hour in which to cast their ballots. In case they needed reminding, each network had received a news release, dated October 30, from an obscure woman whose name and face no decision-desker or news anchor could have recognized if his or her very soul had depended upon it—someone named Katherine Harris, Florida's secretary of state.

"The last thing we need is to have our citizens in the Central Time Zone think their vote doesn't count—because it certainly does!" Harris exclaimed in the release. She explicitly asked the networks to refrain from predicting a winner until after 8 P.M. Eastern Time, the closing time for polls in the western panhandle.

Surely after all the preelection hype about Florida being the key to the entire election, after all the predictions that this closest presidential contest in forty years would come down to a photo finish in the Sunshine State, after the stern news release from the unfamiliar Florida official, the networks would exercise at least a modicum of self-restraint and withhold their projections until 8 P.M. Eastern Time—when most of the half million registered voters in the western panhandle could no longer cast ballots.

But the desire to be first out of the gate proved overwhelming. The decision-deskers desperately pored over exit polls for hints, however faint, of a winner in Florida. Although Gore seemed to be doing better than expected, the race remained excruciatingly tight. It was impossible to make a projection on the basis of the flimsy exit polls alone. The decision-deskers realized they would not be able to declare a Florida winner at the stroke of 7:00 after all.

Still, the anchors had to give viewers some fresh news at the top of the hour. The beast must be fed. The decision-deskers eyeballed the data from five states in which all polls closed at 7 P.M.—South Carolina, Vermont, Virginia, Georgia, and New Hampshire. The easiest one to call was South Carolina, a conservative state that Bush won by 16 points. The networks dutifully awarded South Carolina to Bush. And they awarded Vermont to the vice president, whose margin of victory there was a comfortable 10 points.

But what about Georgia, a southern stronghold that Bush carried handily by a dozen points? Inexplicably, the networks waited over thirty minutes to project Bush the winner there, just as they waited nearly half an hour to give him another conservative state, Virginia, which Bush won by a solid 7 points. Politically astute viewers were surprised by these delays and began to wonder whether Bush was in trouble. For those less astute, the talking heads practically hit them over the head with a two-by-four.

"Look at this! Look at the war in Georgia!" marveled CNN's Bernard Shaw. "Too close too call!"

"This has got to be a shocker in Austin," replied Jeff Greenfield in the gravest of tones. "They had this one put away in their pocket for weeks, if not months."

"What's happening in Virginia?" Shaw added. "Again, the race too close to call."

"Bernie, Virginia has not voted for a Democrat for president since Lyndon Johnson in 1964," Greenfield said in an ominous voice. "It is the heart of the Republican base in the south. They should have won this one goin' away!"

At 7:30 P.M., polls closed in three more states—North Carolina, Ohio, and West Virginia. Although Bush won North Carolina by a hefty 13 points, the networks delayed the call for about thirty-five minutes.

"The idea that North Carolina is still too close to call does come as a surprise this evening," intoned Tom Brokaw on NBC.

Ohio, which Bush won by 4 points, was not called for an hour and forty-five minutes. And while Bush's margin of victory in West Virginia turned out to be a respectable 6 points, the call was held up for a bewildering two hours and forty minutes. These delays sent an unmistakable message to even casual observers—Bush was crashing and burning.

By now, the double standard was coming into focus. The networks wouldn't give Bush a trio of states in which all polls had closed and his margins of victory were 13, 4, and 6 points. Yet these same networks couldn't wait to give Gore Florida, where hundreds of polling places were still open and the margin of victory, regardless of who won, would surely be a tiny fraction of a single percentage point.

John Ellis was the lone Republican who headed up Fox News Channel's decision desk. Astonishingly, he was also the first cousin of George W. Bush. In fact, he had already held several phone conversations with Bush that afternoon to discuss Gore's stronger-than-expected showing in Florida. Ellis didn't mention to Bush what he had already confided to colleagues at Fox that afternoon—that he felt his cousin was going to lose the election.

"Although Gore was 'ahead' in the Florida exit polling, his margin was not substantial enough to allow us to call it without more and better information," Ellis wrote later in *Inside*, an online magazine. "We waited for actual vote tabulations from sample precincts to confirm what the poll was telling us. In the interim, between 7 and 7:30, we twice characterized the race as 'too close to call.'"

There was nothing scientific about the selection of these "sample" precincts. Rather, they were chosen for just one reason—they were the rare polling places where results were actually tabulated on site before the totals were forwarded to county election headquarters. The vast majority of Florida's 5,845 precincts simply shipped all ballots, uncounted, directly to county headquarters for tabulation. But there were a few hundred self-tabulating precincts that would have hard numbers before the tabulation of countywide vote totals. VNS selected 120 of these precincts and staffed them with another batch of temporary, one-day workers known as "stringers." Like the VNS exit pollsters, the stringers were not exactly political pros.

"Basically we're using volunteer groups," said the VNS insider. "We sponsor this as an activity for them."

This source acknowledged that VNS was "very light" on stringers in Florida, even though the state was universally considered the most important in the election. And while Edelman took great pride in the scientifically random placement of exit pollsters (he once insisted on staffing an Indian reservation even after tribal elders voted not to cooperate with the hapless pollster) there was no such careful methodology in the placement of stringers to gather hard vote counts from sample precincts. Nor was there much precision in the stringers' data collection methods. They simply grabbed whatever numbers they could and hurriedly telephoned them into VNS's temporary headquarters on the ninety-third floor of the World Trade Center in New York. Calls from stringers in the Sunshine State were routed to the VNS "Florida desk," which consisted of two people sitting on folding chairs at a pair of computer terminals on a folding table in a utilitarian room that also housed "desks" for several other states. The numbers, usually incomplete, were hurriedly typed into the computers and sent to the networks.

Results from the stringers began trickling into newsrooms shortly after 7:30 P.M. As unscientific and paltry as these numbers were (98 percent of Florida's precincts were not manned by VNS stringers), at least the decision-deskers were now getting a look at some actual vote tallies. They tried to determine whether the sample precinct numbers reinforced—or contradicted—the exit poll numbers. Of course, they were looking only at sample precincts east of the time line. No hard vote tallies from sample precincts in the western panhandle were available yet because polls there had not yet closed. Since the eastern precincts were decidedly more Democratic than the western, this created a third tier of Democratic bias that reinforced the tiers that already existed in the exit polls and the networks themselves.

At 7:45 P.M., the VNS exit polls were showing Gore ahead of Bush by 6.6 percent. When adjusted by the results from the sample precincts, the Gore lead dropped to 5.4 percent. But both sets of data were fatally flawed. In reality, Bush was slightly ahead, according to early hard numbers gathered by the AP.

Although the AP was a member of the VNS consortium, it also maintained its own apparatus for gathering vote totals. That's because the AP's newspaper customers needed the results of local races, not just the state and national contests that were tracked by VNS. So the cooperative put its own reporters at election head-quarters in each of the sixty-seven counties. The AP's apparatus, which was faster and more accurate than VNS, began tabulating hard vote totals as soon as the first polls closed at 7 P.M. These num-bers were updated every few minutes as returns streamed in from across the state. This AP data showed Bush ahead of Gore at the stroke of 7:00 and at every interval for the next full hour. Although the networks all subscribed to the AP, they ignored its hard numbers showing Bush ahead and focused instead on the tainted VNS esti-mates showing Gore ahead. If anything, the conflicting data should have been an enormous red flag to the decision desks.

But the networks were so desperate to give Florida to Gore that they threw caution to the wind. Ignoring the warning from Katherine Harris, NBC pulled the trigger at 7:49 P.M. Eastern Time.

"We're going to now project an important win for Vice President Al Gore," Brokaw declared. "NBC News projects that he wins the 25 electoral votes in the state of Florida."

Republicans were stupefied. Gore had just been awarded the most important state in the election, even though fully 96 percent of Florida's votes remained uncounted. In the western panhandle, a Bush stronghold, not a single ballot had been tallied.

Despite claims by the networks that they are not influenced by each other's calls, all of them rushed to match NBC's projection. CBS waited less than a minute before giving Florida to Gore, even though Rather had just finished assuring viewers that Florida was "so close that it may be a long while before anybody is able to call it."

Even the AP, whose own hard numbers showed Bush ahead, declared Gore the winner at 7:53 P.M. The desire to join the stampede was so intense that this normally cautious news cooperative was willing to contradict its own reporting in order to make an utterly irrational projection on the most important state in the election.

Similarly, CNN coughed up Florida for Gore at 7:52, even though senior political analyst Bill Schneider had warned viewers that the state might not be decided until after midnight.

"This is a roadblock the size of a boulder to George W. Bush's path to the White House," said Greenfield, as if he were describing a terminally ill patient. "They have counted these 25 electoral votes from the moment George Bush entered the campaign, before he was even nominated."

Even Fox News, whose decision desk was headed by Bush's first cousin, felt the pressure to join the herd. Fox News vice president John Moody informed John Ellis that the other networks had called Florida for Gore.

"The only TV decision desk team that hadn't called Florida for Gore was ours," Ellis recalled.

He insisted it wasn't family loyalty that made him hesitate. Rather, he said that two other members of the Fox decision desk team doubted that Gore had indeed locked up Florida. Pollster John Gorman and consultant Arnon Mishkin, both Democrats, were not ready to make the call.

"Mishkin was still dubious and so too was Gorman," Ellis wrote. "'Let's wait for a couple more precincts,' they said, and so we hung back."

Still, Ellis was painfully aware that Moody was waiting for a decision that the executive could relay to the control room, which in turn would pass it along to Brit Hume. The highly respected anchor was already twisting in the wind while his competitors at the other networks merrily pontificated on the significance of Gore's stunning victory in Florida. Ellis scoured the data for anything that would purge the doubts that were still plaguing his team. He and his teammates, including Democratic statistician Cynthia Talkov, even searched other states for signs that might somehow reinforce the notion that Gore had won Florida.

"By now, we could see that Bush was not making his numbers in the southeast, at least in the VNS exit polls," Ellis wrote. "Gorman noticed it. Mishkin noticed it. Talkov noticed it. And it influenced our thinking about Florida, although no one ever said so. But the logic was simple. If Bush was running below his target numbers in southeastern states long ago abandoned by Gore, he was probably running below his target in Florida, where Gore had waged a serious, multimillion-dollar campaign."

Try as he may to base his decision strictly on the numbers that filled his computer screen, Ellis now found his mind wandering back to Gore's multimillion-dollar campaign in Florida. And he couldn't help but notice that Moody was still waiting for an answer. After perusing a few more creaky numbers that trickled in from sample precincts, Ellis jettisoned his reservations and called Florida for Gore for at 7:52. Although it was only three minutes after the NBC call, in the news business that was an eternity.

"We'd been beaten," Ellis lamented, "by a mile."

Within moments, Ellis received another phone call from Austin. Only this time it wasn't George W. It was Jeb, who had just watched the networks essentially announce that he had failed to deliver Florida to his brother.

"Are you sure?" Jeb asked Ellis, according to the latter's account in *Inside* magazine.

"Jeb, I'm sorry," Ellis answered. "I'm looking at a screenful of Gore."

"But the polls haven't closed in the panhandle," Jeb protested.

"It's not going to help," Ellis replied. "I'm sorry."

Ellis later wrote: "I felt terribly for him. There was nothing more to say."

Actually, there was plenty more to say about Florida. But the only talking head who dared to question the call on the air was CNN's Mary Matalin. A conservative Republican who once worked for the elder President Bush and later married Democratic strategist James Carville, Matalin pointed out that Gore's supposed lead could easily be reversed by "half a million absentee ballots out there." Her concerns were tut-tutted by CNN's Schneider.

"Well, when we do call the state, we've taken the absentee ballot count into account," he told Matalin. "When we call the state, we're pretty sure that the state is going to go for the winner."

Over at CBS, Dan Rather was up to his eyeballs in, well, Ratherisms.

"Now remember, Florida is the state where Jeb Bush, the brother of George Bush, is the governor," Rather said at 8:15. "And you can bet that Governor Bush will be madder than a rained-on rooster that his brother the governor wasn't able to carry this state for him."

Fifteen minutes later, he added that Bush's "lead is now shakier than cafeteria Jell-O."

Karl Rove, Bush's top political strategist, was unconvinced. At 9:30 P.M., he appeared on NBC to admonish the network for jumping the gun on Florida.

"Florida has been prematurely called," he declared. "It was a little bit irresponsible for the networks to call it before the polls closed in the western part of Florida. Florida is split among two time zones—Eastern and Central. You all called it before the polls had closed in the Central part."

Ten minutes later, Bush himself blasted the networks.

"I don't believe some of these states that they've called," he told reporters in the governor's mansion in Austin. "Like Florida."

When the networks erroneously called Florida for Gore, three out of four registered voters in America still had time to cast their ballots. Up to 100 million people in thirty-nine states and the District of Columbia might have been influenced by the knowledge that Gore had already locked up Florida, the state that everyone knew held the key to the White House.

Just minutes after the Florida call, both CNN and CBS pronounced Gore the winner of Michigan, the second component of the all-important trifecta. The projection came at 8 P.M., the closing time for most—but not all—of the polls in Michigan.

"We were stunned," wrote Ellis. "The margin was close, there was very little sample precinct data in the models—and yet they had Dan Rather pull the trigger without hesitation. I turned to Gorman and Mishkin and said: 'Wow, that's an aggressive call.'"

When the NBC decision desk passed word to Tom Brokaw to call Michigan for Gore, the anchor was in the midst of recapping the states Gore had won so far—including Florida—and slipped into the first person plural voice, as if he were openly rooting for Gore.

"But the critical states that we still have to win—," Brokaw began just before someone murmured new instructions into his earpiece. "We have just made a projection in the state of Michigan."

Brokaw later defended his Freudian slip in an angry letter to the editor of the *Wall Street Journal*, in which he denied being "a spokesman for liberal causes."

The vice president's margin of victory in Michigan was a slim 4 points, the same spread by which Bush had won Ohio thirty minutes earlier. Yet the networks were still mum about the Bush win. The tiers of Democratic bias were now working unmistakably in Gore's favor.

"The fact that we projected Florida and Michigan before we projected Ohio for Bush is very telling," Tim Russert told NBC viewers, hinting that Bush was lagging in states that should have been his and losing close states far too easily.

Michigan and Ohio were both important battleground states that held large numbers of electoral votes. Both were won by four percentage points. Although all polls closed in Ohio at 7:30 P.M., the networks waited an hour and forty-five minutes to declare Bush the winner. Yet they raced to call Michigan for Gore the instant the first polls there closed—even though voters west of the time line had another hour in which to cast their ballots.

The lopsided calls in Gore's favor continued all night. The clarity of the double standard is downright jarring when one examines the calls made by CNN, which was typical of the networks:

Gore won Illinois by 12 points and CNN crowned him the winner in one minute. Bush won Georgia by 12 points and CNN waited thirty-three minutes.

Gore won New Jersey by 15 points and CNN announced it in one minute. Bush won Alabama by 15 points and CNN waited twenty-six minutes.

Gore won Delaware by 13 points and CNN waited just three minutes. Bush won North Carolina by 13 points and CNN waited thirty-four minutes.

Gore won Minnesota by 2 points and CNN waited thirty-seven minutes. Bush won Tennessee by 3 points and CNN waited twice as long—an hour and sixteen minutes.

Withholding Tennessee from Bush was especially mendacious because news of the vice president's failure to carry his home state would have sent a powerful political message to the rest of the nation. If Gore couldn't carry Tennessee, how could he be expected to win the presidency? Even Walter Mondale managed to carry his home state of Minnesota in 1984, when Ronald Reagan won the other forty-nine states in a landslide.

Similarly, the networks were reluctant to call President Clinton's home state of Arkansas for Bush, which would have sent another potent message. Arkansas was one of the few states in which Gore had given Clinton permission to campaign for him. Timely news of Gore's failure to carry the state would have shocked Democrats and heartened Republicans nationwide. Instead, CNN waited three hours and thirty-three minutes before awarding Arkansas to Bush, who had won the state by six points. This inexplicable delay was even longer than the two hours and forty-one minutes CNN waited before giving Bush West Virginia, which he had also won by six points. By contrast, CNN waited only thirty-six minutes to give Maine to Gore, who had carried the state by only five points.

The pervasiveness of the double standard was shocking. Whenever Gore won a state by double-digit margin, the networks projected him the winner in three minutes or less. But in state after state, Bush posted double-digit victories that the networks refused to acknowledge for at least thirty minutes.

When Bush won Missouri by 4 points, CBS waited two hours and six minutes to hand it over. When Gore won Pennsylvania by the same margin, CBS shortened the lag time to forty-eight minutes. This was an enormously important call because it told America at 8:48 P.M. Eastern Time that Gore had already pulled off the trifecta, which was tantamount to winning the White House.

"Pennsylvania drops for Gore—23 electoral votes," crowed Rather on CBS. "And for the first time tonight, mark it—if you're in the kitchen, Mabel, come back in the front room—145 for Gore, 130 for Bush, 270 needed to win."

At this point, Mabel might have been deciding not to bother voting. After all, more than a third of all registered voters in America still had time to cast their ballots. From Atlantic to Pacific, in all six time zones of the United States, polls remained open—in some cases for more than three additional hours. In all cases, they remained open longer than the tiny sliver of time in which Gore padded his lead by 10,000 votes in Florida's western panhandle.

When ABC's Peter Jennings gave Pennsylvania to Gore, ex-Clinton aide George Stephanopoulus let out a little involuntary whoop on the air. Over at CNN, the talking heads all but held a Bush funeral.

"This is a major disappointment for Bush," Judy Woodruff said. "Makes it all the harder for him to put together a winning combination."

"It absolutely does," Jeff Greenfield replied. "It means that of the states that are now undecided, we can begin to say that George Bush more or less has to run the tables on them."

Over at NBC, Tom Brokaw made the same point.

"That makes it, fair to say, all the more difficult for Governor Bush to put together a winning coalition here tonight," Brokaw said. "With Florida, Pennsylvania, and Michigan in his column, Vice President Al Gore begins to build the foundation that could get him to 270 electoral votes. And it begins to look like, well, the missile defense shield. That in fact, the governor has to hit every state with a laser beam—and not miss any of them."

Greenfield upped the rhetorical ante, practically declaring that Bush had a better chance of winning the lottery than being elected president.

"The states begin to close around the hopes of George W. Bush," he warned viewers. "There are simply fewer and fewer places where he can pick up enough votes to get to 270, unless an amazing upset happens out West."

Such dire pronouncements had a profound impact on voter turnout in the West and elsewhere in America. At 5:48 P.M. Pacific Time, tens of millions of would-be voters suddenly learned that it was essentially impossible for Bush to win the presidency. After all, Gore had already swept the trifecta. The news hit just as huge numbers of citizens on the West Coast were leaving work and heading for the polls. California Republicans who had been expecting record numbers of voters reported precipitous drop-offs in turnout shortly after news of the Gore juggernaut. Voters were seen getting out of line and going home. GOP volunteers at polling places followed in disgust. Several Republicans running for Congress blamed their defeats solely on the networks' premature and erroneous calls, which dramatically depressed turnout.

As the talking heads chattered incessantly about the significance of Gore's sweep of the three most important states, they neglected to mention one important fact. Bush was ahead in Florida. Now that all the polls in the state had closed, election officials were finally tabulating hard results. The numbers showed Bush, not Gore, in the lead.

Even VNS noticed it. Having finished collecting data from its 45 exit pollsters and one 120 stringers at the sample precincts, VNS now turned to its third and final batch of temporary employees for the day. The company called these employees "reporters" and dispatched them to election headquarters in each of Florida's 67 counties. The reporters were now phoning in results not from mere precincts, but from entire counties—or at least significant chunks of those counties. These hard numbers superseded the skewed data from the exit pollsters and sample precinct stringers. It quickly became obvious that the earlier data had been wrong.

The change was even more obvious to the Associated Press, whose hard numbers showed Bush ahead by 30,000 votes at 8:45 P.M. By 9:00 the lead shot up to 80,000. At 9:15 Bush was winning Florida by a whopping 120,000 votes. By 9:45 it had ballooned to more than 130,000.

And yet the networks maintained a disciplined silence about Bush piling up this increasingly impressive lead for more than two solid hours. Bush's lead was nearing 150,000, but the talking heads didn't utter a peep about this remarkable development that would rock the Sunshine State and, indeed, the entire nation. Instead, they kept chattering about the significance of Gore's trifecta and rushing to add more narrow victories to the Gore column while inexplicably withholding states that Bush had won by landslides. Those two hours, between 8:00 and 10:00 P.M., were the very heart of prime time, the period of greatest influence over the tens of millions of viewers who still had time to cast their ballots in the West and elsewhere.

Finally, just before 10:00, the networks could no longer ignore the obvious. They took Florida out of the Gore column. But instead of awarding it to Bush, who was ahead by nearly 150,000 votes, the networks pronounced the state "too close to call." The same decision-deskers who had so eagerly given Florida to Gore when the vice president supposedly led in the ramshackle VNS models now refused to give the state to Bush, who had been indisputably ahead for more than two hours and whose hard-number lead was rising toward 150,000. While the Democratic bias of the VNS exit polls had been superseded by unbiased hard numbers, the Democratic bias of the networks lived on.

"What the networks giveth, the networks taketh away," said a grim-faced Brokaw.

"Bulletin!" Rather blurted. "Florida pulled back into the undecided column. Computer and data problem."

The man who had bragged that viewers could take his projections "to the bank" was now blaming a computer for this blunder of historic proportions. It was the oldest and lamest excuse in the book.

At least Jeff Greenfield, to his everlasting credit, instantly owned up to his presumptuousness.

"Oh, waiter," he deadpanned. "One order of crow."

Incredibly, the networks waited four more hours before giving Florida to Bush. By that time, his lead had dwindled to fewer than 50,000 votes—barely a third of what it had been when the networks insisted Florida was too close too call. But the networks could no longer continue the charade. Bush had been in the lead for six solid hours—yet never declared the winner. The networks simply could no longer deny reality.

Still, the shell-shocked decision-deskers were terrified about making another blunder. They had already subjected the networks to unprecedented humiliation and universal scorn by erroneously giving Florida to Gore and then taking it back. The last thing they wanted was to give it to Bush and then be forced to pull it back yet again.

By this point in the evening, Florida had lived up to its advance billing as the state that would hold the key to the White House. With most other states tallied, both candidates remained short of the 270 electoral votes needed for victory. So it was now official: Whoever won Florida's 25 electoral votes would have enough to win the presidency.

While each of the decision-deskers had wanted to be first in awarding Florida to Gore, none of them wanted to be first in awarding it to Bush. In fact, if Bush's own cousin hadn't been heading up one of the decision desks, Bush might never have been declared the winner of Florida that night.

"I called George W. and asked him what he thought," Ellis wrote. "What do *you* think?" he quoted Bush as saying.

"I think you've got it," Ellis replied.

Ellis hung up and decided it was time to pronounce his cousin president. He passed the word to the anchor desk.

"Fox News now projects George W. Bush the winner in Florida and thus, it appears, the winner of the presidency of the United States," Brit Hume announced at 2:16 A.M.

The other networks followed like lemmings. NBC and CBS waited all of one minute.

"Bush wins," rang out Rather's staccato voice. "Florida goes Bush. The presidency is Bush. That's it. Sip it. Savor it. Cup it. Photostat it. Underline it in red. Press it in a book. Put it in an album. Hang it on a wall. George Bush is the next president of the United States."

Precisely one minute later, CNN jumped off the cliff. ABC sweated it out for two additional minutes before joining the herd at 2:20 A.M. The networks flashed pre-packaged "President Bush" graphics on the screen, prompting a tremendous cheer from Bush supporters who had gathered in a cold, miserable rain in Austin.

Gore telephoned Bush at 2:30 A.M. to offer his concession and congratulations. He did not realize that his call to Bush had indirectly been prompted by Ellis's call to Bush just minutes earlier. Gore then left his hotel, boarded his limousine, and began the short ride over to the Nashville War Memorial, where his own crowd of supporters was waiting in a slightly warmer but infinitely more miserable downpour. The crowd was told to expect a concession speech.

Frazzled newspaper reporters across the nation began rewriting their stories for the umpteenth time. It had been an ulcer-inducing night for these ink-stained wretches. Since no newspaper had ponied up the money to conduct its own nationwide exit polls or independently gather hard returns from coast to coast, they all relied on the networks to tell them who the next president would be. Even the mighty *New York Times* was reduced to trusting TV news, a form of journalism it regarded as infinitely inferior, for the biggest story of the year. The headline "BUSH APPEARS TO DEFEAT GORE" was hastily plastered across the newspaper's front page in the wee hours of the morning. Countless other newspapers, including the *Washington Times*, made the same blunder.

Yet there was one news organization that held back. The AP's own vote-counting operation showed Bush's lead in Florida had dwindled to just 30,000 votes at 2:16 A.M. The difference was now nearly small enough to trigger an automatic recount, which was mandated by state law whenever a candidate wins by half a percentage point or less. By 2:30, it had fallen to 19,000, which was well within the realm of an automatic recount. At 2:37 A.M., twenty-one minutes after Bush had been pronounced president by his cousin at Fox, the AP alerted newspaper editors that the two candidates were separated by only "the narrowest of margins."

Unfazed, the network talking heads continued to dissect the Bush presidency as if it were a *fait accompli*. They were still relying on the VNS data, which lagged far behind the AP and showed Bush's lead nearly twice as large. Incredibly, the networks could have had access to the more up-to-date AP numbers. In fact, they all subscribed to the AP. But instead of paying a nominal fee for access to a special, election-night database that updated vote totals a dozen times an hour, the networks had opted for the cheaper, run-of-the-mill database that updated results only three times an hour.

Still, the networks should have been getting the updated AP numbers through VNS, which was routinely given free access to this database as a way of double-checking its own vote totals.

"We normally use the AP as a backup, but this was the first election where we didn't have their system in-house to look at," explained the VNS insider. "It was supposed to be built into our system in a very sophisticated way so that you could actually call it up and look at it in a direct comparison to VNS numbers. But it wasn't there. Our systems department never got it completed on time."

The failure severely hampered VNS's ability to make authoritative projections, the source acknowledged. Worse yet, it left the networks with hopelessly outdated numbers. At 3:11 A.M., after the talking heads had discussed the Bush presidency for nearly an hour, the AP cautioned all customers that Bush's lead had dropped to 6,000 votes—or one-tenth of 1 percent of the 6 million ballots cast in Florida.

"Good grief," Brokaw muttered on NBC. "That would be something if the networks managed to blow it twice in one night."

Over at CBS, Rather was coming unglued.

"Hello, 911? Cardiac arrest unit please," he said.

"Let's not joke about it folks," Rather added. "You have known all night long and we have said to you all night long that these estimates of who wins and who loses are based on the best available information that we have. CBS News has the best track record in the business—over a half century plus—for accuracy on Election Night. But nobody's perfect."

Alas, it had come to this. The anchor who just eight hours earlier had bragged that "if we say somebody's carried a state, you can pretty much take it to the bank," was now sheepishly shrugging "nobody's perfect."

At 3:27 A.M., VNS sent the networks a disturbing bulletin. The company advised its customers that the Florida secretary of state's web page was showing a much slimmer margin of victory for Bush than the data VNS had been distributing. The subtext of the message was clear: VNS no longer trusted its own data.

In Nashville, Gore's motorcade had almost reached the War Memorial. Chris Lehane, the vice president's press secretary, received an urgent call from AP political correspondent Ron Fournier. "We don't think you guys have lost this thing," the reporter said. At campaign headquarters in Nashville, Gore's field director, Michael Whouley, was getting the same feeling as he viewed numbers from Secretary of State Katherine Harris's office, which were much more up to date than the VNS figures. Whouley paged chief of staff Michael Feldman, who was riding in the motorcade. Whouley instructed Feldman to stop Gore from publicly conceding the race. Feldman relayed this bombshell to campaign chairman William Daley, who reached Gore in his limousine about a block from the War Memorial.

"Whatever you do," Daley told his boss, "do not go out on the stage."

Gore and Daley met backstage at the War Memorial. Daley called several TV networks to find out what they knew. Even after all their colossal blunders, the mighty decision-deskers still held sway over the candidates themselves. Daley also conferred with Fournier, the AP reporter, who opined that it would be "ridiculous" for Gore to throw in the towel. Bush's lead was now just above 1,000 votes, with ballots still being counted. Even if the lead held, there would be a mandatory, statewide recount—a process that could take days. Daley agreed and told his boss so. Someone called Gore's Florida campaign manager, Attorney General Bob Butterworth, to tell him the vice president was mulling whether to concede. "Don't do it!" Butterworth begged from his home north of Miami.

Gore considered his options. His concession speech was already loaded into the teleprompter. He had spent his time on the ride over preparing to explain to his drenched and disappointed supporters that "democracy may not always give us the outcome we want." Besides, he had already called Bush and conceded the presidency. How could he possibly justify withdrawing his concession?

On the other hand, the race had become breathtakingly close. Perhaps he would slip into the lead after all. And even if he didn't, Florida election officials would proceed with a statewide recount, regardless of whether Gore requested one. In fact, he was powerless to stop it. Gore pondered the possibilities. It could be argued that the mandatory recount, which was out of his hands, justified a withdrawal of his concession. After all, how could he possibly give up the fight before the votes were counted and then recounted? It would be nothing short of irresponsible to his followers and, indeed, to the very nation.

As he stood backstage at the Nashville War Memorial, Gore mulled the speech that was waiting in the teleprompter. What if he gave that speech and then the election were reversed after all? Once he publicly threw in the towel, it would be difficult, if not impossible, to stake a claim to the presidency. But if he withheld a public concession until after the recount, at least his political viability would be preserved. He could always concede later. And while it might be awkward to retract his private concession from Bush right then and there, it would be infinitely more awkward to retract a public concession two or three days from then. It might even cripple his ability to govern. Gore knew that recounts rarely reversed the outcome of elections, but there was always a chance. He had been up nearly forty-eight hours straight. He was exhausted. The prospect of walking onstage and effectively ending his twenty-four-year political career was not pleasant. Perhaps the most prudent option would be to let the recount work its course. In the meantime, maybe he would think of another way to keep his presidential hopes alive.

At about 3:30 A.M., Gore telephoned Bush again.

"Circumstances have changed dramatically since I first called you," the vice president said. "The state of Florida is too close to call."

"Are you saying what I think you're saying?" Bush asked incredulously. "Let me make sure I understand: You're calling me back to retract your concession?"

"You don't have to get snippy about this," Gore retorted. "I don't think we should be going out and making statements with the state of Florida still in the balance."

Bush explained that his brother, Jeb, was standing right there in the room with him. Jeb had just assured him that Florida was in the bag.

"Let me explain something," Gore condescended. "Your younger brother is not the ultimate authority on this."

"Do what you have to do," Bush said icily.

He hung up and called his cousin at Fox News Channel.

"Gore unconceded," he told Ellis.

"You've got to be kidding," the decision-desker said.

"Nope, I'm not," Bush said. "I hope you're taking all this down, Ellis. This is good stuff for a book."

Dick Cheney would later look back on this moment as the darkest in the entire, thirty-six-day standoff. It was as though he had been on a harrowing roller coaster that suddenly careened off the tracks.

"We went through this long count in Florida," Cheney recounted to the author. "It was called for Gore and then called for us. Then Gore called to concede and we were waiting for his announcement and then he didn't make it. And then he called back and said he withdrew his concession. That was the most frustrating part."

Ten minutes later, the humiliated networks began pulling Florida back from Bush and reclassifying it as "too close to call." The same decision-deskers who had been unwilling to pull Florida back from Gore until the vice president was trailing by 150,000 were now yanking the state from Bush, even though he had not fallen behind by a single vote.

"Frankly, we don't know whether to wind a watch or bark at the moon," sputtered Rather, who was in the midst of drinking twenty-one cups of black coffee. "We just don't know what to do here under these circumstances."

At 4 A.M., Daley took the stage at the Nashville War Memorial.

"I've been in politics a very long time, but I don't think there's ever been a night like this one," said the son of the late Chicago Mayor Richard Daley, infamous for collecting the votes of dead residents in a previous election.

"The TV networks called this race for Governor Bush," Daley said. "It now appears that their call was premature."

Daley confirmed what had been true for nearly two hours— the narrowness of Bush's lead would trigger an automatic recount. "Without being certain of the results in Florida, we simply cannot be certain of the results of this national election," he said.

"Vice President Gore and Senator Lieberman are fully prepared to concede and to support Governor Bush if and when he is officially elected president," Daley promised. "But this race is simply too close to call, and until the... recount is concluded and the results in Florida become official, our campaign continues!"

Half an hour later, Bush campaign chairman Don Evans addressed Bush supporters in Austin.

"We hope and we believe we have elected the next president of the United States," Evans said. "They're still counting. And I'm confident that when it's all said and done, we will prevail."

NBC, which had been the first to give Florida to Gore and the last to take it away, seemed to realize all too late the spectacular chaos the network had unleashed.

"We don't just have egg on our face," anchor Tom Brokaw confessed to viewers at 4:45 A.M., nearly nine hours after first toppling the network dominoes. "We've got omelette all over our suits."

A bleary-eyed Rather was similarly contrite, telling CBS viewers: "If you're disgusted with us, frankly, I don't blame you."

Around 5 A.M., Florida election officials finished counting ballots and declared Bush had won by 1,784 votes—out of 6 million cast. His margin of victory was just 0.03 percent, far smaller than the 0.5 percent margin that triggers an automatic recount under state law. This factoid was repeated incessantly by the talking heads as dawn broke along the Florida peninsula Wednesday morning.

Gore's forces had already begun to mobilize. Daley called former Secretary of State Warren Christopher in Los Angeles, who stumbled out of bed and hurried to Tallahassee to front the public relations effort taking shape on the ground. At 4 A.M., the Democratic National Committee placed a call to a Mark Herron, a Tallahassee lawyer who had been an adviser to the Florida Democratic Party. Herron jumped at the chance to join Gore's post-election legal team, even though the move would get him fired by his law partners.

In Nashville, seventy-two Gore loyalists giddily commandeered Lieberman's campaign plane and took off for Tallahassee. Other true believers openly wept because there was no room for them on the plane. They already saw themselves as embarking on a political holy war, a cause much bigger and purer than anything they had ever experienced. Like Gore himself, these loyalists resolved to do anything to wrest the presidency from Bush. The jihad had begun!

It is impossible to say with certainty how many Americans were dissuaded from voting by the networks' premature and erroneous calls on Election Night. But if Bush suffered a net loss of 10,000 votes in the ten counties of Florida's western panhandle—where the projection of a Gore victory was only eleven minutes premature—it is not unreasonable to surmise that Bush was deprived of 2 million or more votes in the rest of the nation—where many state's polls were open for hours after the "trifecta" had been called for Gore.

After all, the 10,000 votes in the panhandle amounted to about 2 percent of the registered voters in that region of Florida. By this formula, Bush would have suffered a net loss of more than 2 million votes in other states—twenty-two of which kept their polls open not just eleven more minutes, but an additional one, two, or three hours. His losses likely mounted further after Gore cinched the trifecta. Indeed, tens of millions of voters still had more than an hour to contemplate the futility of casting a Bush vote after the election was declared pretty much over.

To be sure, no one believes Bush would have actually carried California and its 54 electoral votes. But if the networks had refrained from calling states early—or at least called them accurately—Bush might have netted hundreds of thousands of additional votes in California and other states across the nation.

In short, if not for the networks' early and erroneous projections, Bush might easily have won the popular vote, and carried a few congressional seats with him. Gore, who ended up winning the popular vote by roughly 500,000 of 100 million votes cast, would have been deprived of a potent political weapon in the post-election struggle—the argument that more Americans had voted for him. Indeed, a Gore loss in both the Electoral College and the popular vote would have significantly limited his political ability to wage a protracted battle to overturn the election. Thus, it is entirely arguable that the bad calls by the networks led directly to the standoff that paralyzed the nation for thirty-six days.

CHAPTER 3

"THE DADBURN BALLOTS ARE
STILL IN THE CAR!"

The underwear was what did it. When Deanie Lowe saw the dirty laundry, including the underwear, laid out there in the driveway of the Volusia County Elections Office, she knew things had finally spiraled out of control. The sheriff's deputies were actually photographing the underwear for evidentiary purposes. The mortified owner of the clothing, Debbie Allen, sat sobbing on the bench. Allen's mentally handicapped brother, Mark Bornmann, traumatized by the flashing lights, kept saying, "Did I do something wrong? Did I do something wrong?"

It was still dark in the parking lot as the gawkers surged forward for a glimpse of Allen's dirty laundry. Democrats, Republicans, cops, election workers—they were all rubbernecking. The only people missing were the journalists, who had departed a couple of hours earlier, disgusted by the county's wildly inaccurate election returns. But they would be back soon for the mandatory recount. The place would once again be crawling with newspaper reporters, photographers, TV cameramen—all ravenous for scandal and innuendo. And oh, would they love to get an eyeful of this suspicious little drama being played out in the parking lot. An election worker being searched for stolen ballots would provide a suitably sinister backdrop for the otherwise dry coverage of the recount. The search, complete with dirty laundry, would probably be captured on grainy videotape, à la *Cops*, the gritty TV show about real-life arrests. The whole sordid spectacle would no doubt be replayed with the frequency of the Rodney King beating. As supervisor of elections, Lowe cringed at the thought of her dedicated employee's underwear being flashed on CNN.

It had been that kind of night. The election board's vaunted computer system had been brought to its knees by a faulty "memory card" that caused incalculable confusion both here and—unbeknownst to the Volusia election officials—at the decision desks up North. At one point, 16,000 votes were mysteriously subtracted from Gore's tally. Another 8,642 votes appeared out of nowhere for Bush. And eight votes that had been cast for an obscure Socialist candidate named James Harris were suddenly inflated into 9,888 votes. Harris had barely garnered that many votes in the entire nation. So much for the election board's decision to go high-tech by trading in its old punch-card machines for fancy new optical scanners.

All these mishaps were like blood in the water to the lawyers and "observers" who were pouring into Florida for the mandatory recount. There was already a gaggle of them there in the parking lot of the Volusia County Elections Office, arguing as if it were a courtroom. Lowe could hear them as she stepped out the back door at 3:45 A.M. to finish locking up the building. She had been up for twenty-four hours straight and wanted nothing more than to go home and collapse into bed. It had been a disastrous night and she knew she would have to return soon to oversee the mandatory recount. But as she activated the alarm system and turned toward her car in the reserved parking space a few steps away, Lowe was suddenly accosted by a Democratic observer who had been hanging around all night. The observer said she had just seen a woman and a man slip out of the building with a pair of dark bags that looked suspiciously like the blue canvas satchels used for transporting ballots. Who were these people? Were they stealing ballots? The Democrat was full of accusatory questions. A Republican lawyer, smelling voter fraud, joined in the interrogation. Soon someone was insisting the mystery woman and her shadowy accomplice, both of whom had departed in a vehicle of vague description, be stopped and searched.

At first Lowe didn't realize who they were talking about. She racked her brain as the scrum of lawyers and political observers jabbered on about stolen ballots and the integrity of the entire election being in jeopardy and the need to send sheriff's deputies after the thieves posthaste. And then it dawned on her. They must mean Debbie Allen, the election board's outreach coordinator, the woman who ran the phone bank for election complaints. Having known she would be working all day and then pulling an all-nighter, Debbie had packed a change of clothes in a blue bag. The other bag must have been her brown leather briefcase. The man with Debbie was undoubtedly her disabled brother, Mark Bornmann, who volunteered for the day to courier messages between phone bank operators and the "mappers" who tracked complaints by precinct. Lowe tried explaining all this to the Democrats and Republicans in the parking lot. She told them it was impossible for Debbie or Mark to have stolen any ballots, which were all locked up in the vault inside the elections office. But the people in the parking lot insisted that Allen be hauled in.

Lowe lived a couple of blocks from Allen in a neighborhood that was thirty-two miles from election headquarters. The two women drove the same route home and sometimes traveled in tandem after working late at the office. Lowe reluctantly turned to Deputy Sheriff Mary Pascale and told her the route Allen would be taking. She described the woman's Jeep Wagoneer, right down to the wood-grain side panels. She emphasized Allen's innocence and Bornmann's handicap.

"Please don't scare her," Lowe remembered saying. "Don't give her a heart attack."

Pascale called her supervisor, who put out an alert for Allen's Wagoneer. The officers used a special radio frequency that could not be monitored by the press. The last thing Lowe needed was a media circus.

By this time the lawyers and observers had become frenzied by the power of their own accusations. One of the Republicans demanded to use the phone inside election headquarters so that he could alert his superiors of the apparent ballot heist. Lowe deactivated the alarm system and reopened the building so that everyone could come back inside.

As the arguing intensified, so did Lowe's sense of dread. This was turning into 1996 all over again. That was when Volusia switched to the new optical scan voting system, which was supposed to eliminate all the problems of the old punch card system. Instead of pushing a stylus through chads on a punch card, voters darkened circles on a ballot. They used a No. 2 pencil or one of several very specific brands of black, felt-tipped markers that could be read by the ballot-counting machines. This worked fine at polling places, but was a little trickier for absentee voters, who might not have the specified markers or No. 2 pencils lying around the house. Thousands of voters in the 1996 election marked their absentee ballots with ballpoint pens or the wrong types of felt-tipped markers. Some even used crayons. The machine refused to read them. Lowe could think of only one way to avoid disenfranchising a sizeable chunk of the electorate.

"We took a felt tip pen that could be read and we put a mark on top of the voters' mark and fed it through," she said.

The solution worked perfectly. But the Volusia County sheriff's election turned out to be extremely close. When the loser learned that ballots had been remarked, he took the election officials to court. Volusia County Circuit Judge John Doyle stopped short of overturning the election, but found "gross negligence" on the part of the elections supervisor and the canvassing board. At that time, Lowe was both the elections supervisor and one of the three members of the canvassing board. "We have a sordid history of voting fraud in this county," Doyle lamented in his ruling. Lowe, a Republican, essentially got the blame for perpetuating that sordid history.

Now, four years later, it was happening all over again. Only this time the stakes were exponentially higher. Instead of getting blamed for screwing up the local county sheriff's race, Deanie Lowe began to fear that she would take the fall for the deadlocked presidency. She was already bracing for the morning newspapers, which would surely be filled with withering assessments of last night's fiasco in Volusia County. And now she had sent the sheriff's department after one of her own employees to search for stolen ballots. The press would go crazy. She looked at the Republican lawyer pacing in her office. He had the phone pressed to his ear and was excitedly telling someone about the electoral disaster unfolding in Volusia County. Lowe waited until the Republican hung up before placing a call of her own. She knew of only one person who could restore order to the burgeoning chaos.

Michael McDermott, chairman of the Volusia County Canvassing Board, had left the office a couple of hours earlier, exhausted. When the phone rang, he was in bed. When Lowe told him what was happening, he asked to speak to the Republican lawyer. Lowe stood by and watched the lawyer's animated half of the conversation. Then the phone was thrust back into her hand and she heard McDermott's voice. He told her to call 911 and get some more police down there. He would be right over.

McDermott, a county judge, lived just a few blocks away. Lowe was shocked to see the usually dapper McDermott wearing rumpled clothes and loafers with no socks. But his disheveled appearance didn't stop him from taking charge of the situation. He ordered deputy sheriffs and police officers to surround the building and block entry to anyone who was not an elections employee. He set up a checkpoint and instructed officers to search everyone going in or out of the elections office. He even ordered the perimeter sealed off with black-and-yellow crime scene tape. Then he drove back home.

Meanwhile, out on LPGA Boulevard, Deputy Sheriff Paul Thomas spotted a dark Jeep Wagoneer with wood-grain side panels. Debbie Allen had almost made it home when Thomas turned on his flashing lights and pulled her over. Allen and her brother were bewildered when Thomas ordered them to return to election headquarters. The deputy insisted on escorting them because he wanted to make sure they didn't throw any evidence out the windows.

In the darkened parking lot, Allen and Bornmann were questioned by investigators. The Jeep was thoroughly searched. The bags were emptied of their contents—underwear and all—and extensively photographed. Only then did the Democrats and Republicans concede that no ballots had been stolen.

"They huffed and puffed and walked off," Lowe recalled. "I don't think any of them ever apologized to her for the trauma they put her through."

By this point, Lowe figured she might as well stick around. She thought she should warn her staff, as they started arriving shortly before 8 A.M., that they would be frisked before they entered the office.

"Women sometimes carry personal things and I have an almost total female staff," she explained. "I wanted to make sure that if they had anything they did not want to be pulled out, that they go back and put it in their cars."

At 8:15, Lowe began the long drive home. When she arrived an hour later, she fell into bed without bothering to change clothes. She set the alarm to awaken her in two hours so that she could get back to the office in time for the recount. But five minutes after her head hit the pillow, the phone rang. She dared not ignore it because it might be some new calamity. It turned out to be Clay Roberts, statewide director of elections under Secretary of State Katherine Harris. He was calling from Tallahassee, 250 miles away. Roberts had received a complaint that members of the public were being barred from the Volusia County Elections Office. He reminded her that a public building could not be sealed off to taxpayers. Lowe said she wasn't about to countermand McDermott's orders. If Roberts wanted the building opened, he should talk directly to McDermott.

Lowe had barely hung up when the phone rang again. This time it was Channel 13 News, which had heard a rumor that one of Lowe's employees had stolen two bags of ballots and was chased down by sheriff's deputies and arrested.

"I told them that's a bunch of bull, that's the furthest thing from the truth that ever was," recalled Lowe, who added that she didn't want to explain the whole story until she was back in the office. "I said, 'You'll know later, I'm going back to the office right now.' So I got up and took a shower and changed clothes and came on back."

By the time Lowe arrived, that old sinking feeling had returned. The place looked like an armed camp. Police and sheriff's deputies were everywhere. Employees were still being searched at the door. Canvassing board member Ann McFall, exhausted by the previous night and groggy from a couple of cold tablets, took one look at the crime tape and figured someone had been shot. The press and public, barred from entry, were milling around outside. The portion of the parking lot that wasn't taped off as part of the crime scene was packed with cars. Lowe had to park across the street. Spotting a county employee being interviewed by a TV crew, Lowe ducked around to the back entrance, stopping every few feet to gather snatches of information from the deputies.

By now the press was manic over the rumors of stolen ballots. Their suspicions were further heightened by the crime scene tape and the fact that they weren't allowed in the building. When McDermott finally relented and the tape was removed, the press and public crowded into the lobby to witness the canvassing board's mandatory recount.

Lowe told the skeptical reporters that no ballots had been stolen. It was all a misunderstanding. Every ballot in the county was safely locked in the election headquarters vault. The journalists, unconvinced, jammed their cameras, microphones, tape recorders, and notebooks at Lowe. She began directing the recount, determined to redeem the integrity of the Volusia County Elections Office. Just then, the front door opened and a seventy-nine-year-old man walked in. The crowd parted as he approached the big curved counter that separated Lowe and the election officials from the public. The old man hesitated a moment until everyone stopped talking and gave him their undivided attention. Then he plopped a big blue canvas satchel on the counter.

"Deanie!" he exclaimed. "Look at what they left in my car last night!"

It was as if all their heads were mounted on swivels. The press and the public and even Lowe's staff all stared at the old man for a full two beats and then swiveled over, in unison, to gape at Lowe.

"I could have crawled through the floor," she recalled. "Why couldn't he have called me ahead of time and quietly met me at the back door? One of the canvassing board members turned to me and says, 'Is that a bag of ballots?' and I says yes.

"The press and the whole place went into an uproar. Everybody was talking at the same time. And I let it go for about thirty seconds and I'm sitting there thinking this is going to be the biggest mess. And I've got to get their attention and so I just shouted out above everybody: 'Hold on just a minute! Before you go into a frenzy here, let me explain to you what we have!'"

Lowe recognized the old man as Gene Tracy, who had been in charge of one of the precincts the night before. She quickly surmised what had happened. When Tracy had taken the ballots and other voting materials to one of the county's four drop sites that had been set up for collection on Election Night, the workers who were responsible for unloading his backseat must have overlooked the bag of ballots in the darkness. Lowe tried to explain this to the crowd. She told them that the ballots had already been counted because Volusia was one of the few counties in Florida that actually tabulates its ballots at the individual polling sites, not at election headquarters. So even though these ballots had remained in Tracy's car all this time, they had already been tallied. She pointed to the seal on the blue satchel and emphasized that it had not been broken. She said Tracy had done the right thing by bringing the ballots in as soon as he discovered them in his car. In fact, poll workers had explicit instructions not to get out of their cars and unload the ballots on Election Night. That task was to be handled by the workers at the drop sites.

But no one was really paying much attention. They were still in an uproar over this sensational new development. McDermott summoned Tracy to the other side of the counter and ordered police to begin taking a statement from the old man. Lowe, realizing that Tracy never went anywhere without his wife, suggested he be allowed to go back to the parking lot and tell his wife that he would be delayed. But McDermott refused to let Tracy go. Someone else was sent to retrieve Mrs. Tracy, while Tracy himself was taken aside to complete police paperwork. When the police had Tracy's statement, every journalist in the place followed him outside.

"Oh, they couldn't wait," Lowe recalled. "The minute he walked outside, the whole lobby emptied out. We continued what we were doing. But it was just breaking my heart that I couldn't be there by his side. He's one of my best poll workers. He's been a poll worker for as long as I've been in office."

Surrounded by the press, the old man did his best to explain what happened.

"I about had a cotton-pickin' stroke," Tracy exclaimed to a reporter. "I hollered for my wife and I said, 'The dadburn ballots are still in the car!'"

The press went ballistic. They were finding it all too easy to caricature Volusia County as a corrupt backwater. Someone discovered there had only been one bag of ballots in Tracy's car from the start, which made the oversight even more inexplicable. Then it was revealed that the poll worker who was responsible for unloading the car had mysteriously marked a log sheet to show that the bag of ballots had indeed been removed. And yet here was the bag, up on the counter, big as life. The press no longer placed the slightest credence in Deanie Lowe's explanations. They had all the delicious details they needed for their stories. Deputies searching for stolen votes. Election headquarters sealed off like a crime scene. An entire bag of ballots discovered in the back seat of an ancient poll worker's car. It was all too rich.

Bush lawyer James Clayton told the *Washington Post*: "No wonder people in the North think we're a bunch of bumbling idiots—

because we are." He singled out Lowe, in particular, as a "bumbling idiot. How do you lose a bag of ballots?" Gore lawyer Douglas Daniels predicted there would be "television movies about how the election was stolen in Volusia County." Conspiracy theorists, he said, would come to view Volusia as the new "grassy knoll gunman."

Lowe feared an unmitigated fiasco.

"You feel like you're on a freight train that is headed toward a ten-foot thick concrete wall and you have no way of stopping it," she said. "And you know, you talk a blue streak, you talk until you just can't talk any more. My tongue was sticking to the roof of my mouth. I couldn't take time to get a drink of water. You're talking to everybody and trying to get them to understand what is going on. And you can just see it in their eyes: They're not paying any more attention to you than the man in the moon."

Volusia County was not the only scene of chaos in Florida that day. From one end of the state to the other, armies of litigious lawyers, argumentative observers, and impertinent journalists were descending like locusts into the offices of county canvassing boards. Election officials, having just survived the most harrowing all-nighter of their careers, now realized they would have to begin the mind-numbing process of retabulating the very ballots that had just caused them so much grief. Having barely completed the first count, they grimly embarked upon the second.

Technically, county canvassing boards had until Tuesday, November 14, to turn in their mandatory recounts to state headquarters in Tallahassee. But Florida Secretary of State Katherine Harris made it clear she wanted all the recounts done by 5 P.M. Thursday—the very next day. In any case, county election officials needed little prodding. With so many contentious out-of-towners in their midst, the locals had no appetite for dragging out the process any longer than necessary. Although many were exhausted, they all resolved to finish the recount on time.

The enduring myth of Florida's first recount is that all sixty-seven counties tallied their ballots by machine, employing a uniform, statewide standard. In reality, some ballots were counted by machine, while others were tallied by hand. Some counties didn't bother counting the ballots in any fashion. Instead, election officials simply ran tests on the computer software that had been used to tabulate the votes on Election Night. Or they examined tally sheets to double-check that all the precincts had added up properly.

Even among the counties that used machines to recount the votes, standards varied significantly from one county to the next. The disparities were at least as dramatic as the shifting chad standards that would vex hand recounts in the coming weeks. But in the dizzying seventy-two hours immediately after Florida's first vote count, few noticed the inconsistencies of the second.

Volusia County was one of the counties that didn't actually recount ballots in the election's immediate aftermath. Although Harris explicitly instructed all counties to physically run the ballots through the machines, Lowe and the other Volusia officials merely compared results from the various precincts to totals on a printout generated by the main computer at election headquarters. When the numbers matched, the canvassing board concluded a physical tally was unnecessary. Lowe, who had recused herself from the canvassing board because she was on the ballot that year, told the three board members that Clay Roberts had mentioned just hours earlier that ballots should be run through the machine. But the board members held firm, saying their position was backed by a Florida law that requires a physical recount only when there is a tabulation discrepancy.

Thus, by the end of the day, Volusia County had completed its mandatory "recount," which showed Bush and Gore getting precisely the same number of votes they had garnered on Election Night. Deanie Lowe was relieved because she could now claim Volusia County had gotten it right the first time after all. Her nightmare finally seemed to be ending.

Volusia wasn't the only place where vote totals barely budged. The mandatory recount produced little or no change in the overwhelming majority of Florida's sixty-seven counties. In fact, after receiving recount results from fifty-three counties, state officials confirmed on Friday evening that Bush's lead remained exactly the same as it had been after the initial statewide count—1,784 votes. It was a striking coincidence, but it pointed up the historical reality of recounts—they tend to reaffirm the original winner and loser. This was certainly proving true in Florida. While Gore picked up handfuls of votes in dozens of counties all over the state, they were invariably negated by comparable Bush gains in dozens of other counties. The law of averages was functioning with amazing exactitude.

Even when another ten counties were added into the mix, the resulting sixty-three counties, when taken together, produced a net change of fewer than 100 votes—not for Gore, but for *Bush*. Collectively, these sixty-three counties found roughly 1,000 new votes for Gore and 1,100 for Bush—votes that essentially canceled each other out.

However, the remaining four counties broke big for Gore. Pinellas, Duval, Gadsden, and Palm Beach allowed the vice president to slash Bush's margin of victory from 1,784 votes to just 388. Although these counties contained only 18 percent of all Floridians who cast ballots for president, they accounted for 58 percent of the newly discovered Gore votes statewide. They pushed the vice president's new vote tally to over 2,500—or more than double that of

Bush, who ended up with fewer than 1,200 new votes by the time the statewide mandatory recount was completed.

One of Gore's largest gains came in Pinellas County, which encompasses St. Petersburg and Clearwater on the Gulf Coast. On Wednesday, the day after the election, officials in Pinellas said they found 404 new votes for Gore. They explained to livid Bush lawyers that county workers had failed to run 1,326 punch cards through a ballot counting machine on Election Night. Another 570 cards were run through a machine not once, but twice. When these errors were detected and corrected on Wednesday, Gore posted a huge gain.

Republicans were not satisfied with this explanation and demanded that all ballots be run through the machines a third time. But this new count, conducted on Thursday, was even worse for the Republicans, awarding Gore a net gain of 478 votes, his second largest pickup in the state.

Gore also benefited from the mandatory recount in Duval County, which voted overwhelmingly for Bush. Encompassing Jacksonville on the Atlantic Coast, Duval County residents favored Bush over Gore by a margin of 3-to-2. Yet the new tally, which was completed by 5 P.M. the day after the election, turned up 184 new votes for Gore and just 16 for Bush—producing a net gain of 168 votes for the vice president. Election officials could not explain how Gore ended up with nearly twelve times as many new votes as Bush.

The margin was nearly as lopsided in Gadsden, one of the state's most overwhelmingly Democratic counties—and the only one where blacks outnumber whites. Nestled along the Georgia border just west of Tallahassee, Gadsden was the first county in which election workers examined individual ballots by hand, trying to divine the intent of the voters. Although neither Gore nor Bush had asked for a hand recount, the Democrat-controlled

Gadsden County Canvassing Board unilaterally decided to manually scrutinize 2,124 ballots—or roughly 15 percent of the county's total vote—that had been rejected by vote-counting machines the night before.

Gadsden County had not used the old-fashioned machines that count punch cards. Rather, Gadsden had used optical scanners—relatively modern machines that read pencil marks made on paper ballots. Voters chose candidates by darkening a particular circle, or "bubble," much like students darken bubbles on standardized tests.

But 2,124 Gadsden voters had not made a choice for president—or at least not one that could be detected by the optical scanners. Instead, some of these voters left bubbles both for Bush and Gore blank, although they put an asterisk, star, circle, or some other mark by one of the candidates' names. Other voters filled in both bubbles and tried to erase at least one of them—with varying degrees of success.

The Gadsden County Canvassing Board got together the day after the election—Bush lawyers later said the meeting was private and illegal—and picked through these ballots, one by one. Their interpretation of the questionable ballots produced 170 new votes for Gore. Bush had picked up only a tenth as much, or 17 votes. The 10-to-1 margin mirrored the county's ratio of registered Democrats to Republicans. This overwhelmingly Democratic county had just handed the vice president a whopping net gain of 153 votes—which was equal to 1 percent of all votes cast in the county.

Republicans were not the only ones who smelled a rat. The region's top prosecutor, a Democrat, said the board should not have hand counted these ballots. State Attorney Willie Meggs told the St. Petersburg Times that "what went on was kind of bizarre." In fact, he was so troubled by the hand count that he personally delivered to Katherine Harris an affidavit on the episode from

Assistant State Attorney John Leace. Leace had met with the canvassing board's lone Republican, Judge Richard Hood, who told
him the board members had "interpreted" a number of ballots that
"were not properly completed," according to the affidavit.

But the biggest bonanza for Gore came from Palm Beach
County. This subtropical swath of ritzy real estate hugging the
Atlantic coast conducted its mandatory recount on Wednesday,
discovering 751 new votes for the vice president. Bush, by contrast,
picked up just 108 new votes, leaving Gore with a net gain of 643.

Elections supervisor Theresa LePore explained that more than
half that gain came from a single precinct just west of Lake Worth.
LePore, a Democrat who had worked at the elections office for
nearly thirty years, said none of the votes from Precinct 29E were
counted in the original tally on Election Night. She explained that
a county worker loaded the precinct's punch cards into a vote-
counting machine and mistakenly pushed the "clear" button,
which wiped out the entire count.

After discovering the error on Wednesday, election workers
counted the precinct's votes and came up with an overwhelming victory for Gore. It seemed that 368 voters in Precinct 29E had cast their
ballots for the vice president, while only 23 had chosen Bush. It was
an astonishing margin of victory, even by Palm Beach standards. Gore
had won more than 94 percent of the vote in Precinct 29E, while gar-
nering just 58 percent in the rest of the county. This one, mysteriously
overlooked precinct had suddenly surfaced to hand Gore 345 votes—
nearly as many as the combined total from all 530 precincts in the rest
of the county. In fact, Precinct 29E single-handedly delivered more
votes to Gore in the mandatory recount than any other precinct and
every other county (except for Duval, which boosted Gore's vote total
by 478) in the entire state. When Republicans learned of Gore's dramatic gains in Palm Beach County, they were furious.

"This is a disturbing difference," Bush campaign manager Karl Rove told reporters in Austin on Thursday. "In fact, we have sent a letter to the Palm Beach authorities raising a question."

Bush officials did more than just raise a question. They demanded another machine recount. Later that day, Palm Beach County announced it would conduct this new recount on Saturday. But when Saturday came, this third tally of Palm Beach ballots netted Gore even more votes. In fact, when county workers completed this final machine count, they announced that the vice president had gained 36 more votes and Bush had actually lost 3 votes. Taken together, the two machine recounts had handed 787 votes to Gore and 105 to Bush, leaving the vice president with a net gain of 682. In short, the mandatory recount in Palm Beach County alone netted nearly as many votes for Gore as all of Florida's sixty-six other counties combined.

All counties completed their mandatory recount within seventy-two hours of the conclusion of the original count on Election Night. But there was lag time between the completion of these new tallies and their reflection in new numbers at the secretary of state's office in Tallahassee. By Wednesday evening, numbers were available from only fourteen counties, which collectively reduced Bush's lead by only 8 votes. Early the next afternoon, with thirty-nine counties reporting, Bush's lead had dropped by another 3 votes. By Thursday evening, with fifty-three counties reporting, Bush was back to the 1,784-vote lead he had secured at the completion of the first count.

But the Associated Press had more up-to-date numbers. The news cooperative had stationed reporters at canvassing board offices in all sixty-seven counties in order to obtain recount results as soon as they were completed. All day Wednesday and all day Thursday, these constantly updated numbers were aired on the twenty-four-hour cable news networks as a running tally of Bush's shrinking margin of victory. It was like Election Night all over again, only in slow motion. By Wednesday evening, according to the AP, Gore had slashed more than a thousand votes from Bush's lead, which now stood at 782. By Thursday evening, when state officials had compiled official results from fifty-three counties, the AP had unofficial results from sixty-six. At that point, the wire service reported that Bush's lead had dwindled to just 229 votes. The last county, Seminole, finished its recount at 3:29 P.M., handing Bush a net gain of 98 new votes and boosting his statewide lead to 327. Although the statewide estimates proved to be slightly off, AP's efforts over those two days provided the best real-time, running tally that was available to a rapt and waiting world.

By Friday evening, the numbers coming out of Harris's office had largely caught up with the AP—although she was still missing Palm Beach County. That's because a circuit judge, responding to complaints about confusion over the Palm Beach ballot design, had issued a preliminary injunction Thursday that barred the county canvassing board from certifying its results until the judge had a chance to hold a hearing on Tuesday. Tallying up the other sixty-six counties, Harris announced that Bush was still ahead by 961 votes. But everyone knew that Palm Beach County had already found enough Gore votes to slash that Bush lead by two-thirds.

Still, by Thursday evening, it had become clear that Bush's lead, however diminished, would hold. Despite Gore's big gains in Palm Beach, Pinellas, Gadsden, and Duval counties, he had fallen just short of victory.

But the standoff had only begun.

CHAPTER 4

A BUTTERFLY FLUTTERS BY

From Gore's perspective, the beauty of the first recount was that he didn't have to ask for it. It was mandated by law because the race had been so close. Gore might have appeared petty and disagreeable if he had been reduced to actually demanding a new tally. Instead, he was able to position himself as merely waiting, statesmanlike, for Florida to discharge its lawful duty to double-check the ballots. It was, after all, out of Gore's hands. Come to think of it, he was powerless to stop it. But his journey on the high road would not last long.

Gore had known even before the first ballot was recounted that his odds for success were slim. Having been a professional politician for twenty-four years, he realized that recounts rarely reverse elections. Oh, there was some genuine hope in the Gore camp, especially during those first heady hours, that a new tally would produce a new winner. But there was also a more realistic assessment of the situation. The cold-eyed pros on Team Gore immediately viewed the recount in purely pragmatic terms: It bought them time. No more than a couple of days, to be sure, but enough time to come up with a Plan B. One thing was certain: They couldn't wait until the conclusion of the recount, which would probably confirm Bush's win, to disabuse the press and public of the expectation for quick closure. If the Gore team didn't come up with a secondary strategy almost immediately, there would be tremendous pressure on the vice president to concede at the conclusion of the mandatory recount.

Surveying the Floridian landscape for opportunities that would keep their hopes alive, Gore officials seized on a controversy that had been simmering since Election Day in Palm Beach County. In fact, the Democrats had begun stoking this brouhaha even before the polls closed. Alarmed by the excruciating closeness of the race, Gore loyalists noticed the proximity of Gore's name to that of Patrick J. Buchanan, the Reform Party candidate, on the Palm Beach County ballot. The names appeared on opposite pages and each was accompanied by a bold, black arrow that pointed directly to a corresponding hole that could be punched in a strip between the two pages. The design, known as a "butterfly" ballot because of its facing pages on a common spine, posed absolutely no confusion to the overwhelming majority of voters.

However, Gore officials latched onto an angle that could be exploited. They began asserting that voters who had intended to vote for Gore had been confused into voting for Buchanan. The claim was impossible to prove, since there was no way to trace a ballot to the individual who had cast it. But the Democrats didn't let that stand in their way. Gore had lost and it was time to seize upon something, anything, that would raise the political noise level. So the Gore backers pounced on the butterfly ballot and made their best case. It went like this:

Above and below each name on the ballot was a thin, horizontal line demarcating one candidate from the next. The line above Gore's name terminated directly opposite the hole for Buchanan. The line didn't have an arrowhead at its terminus, like the bold black arrow on the opposite page that actually pointed to the hole for Buchanan. Still, Gore insisted that tens of thousands of his supporters looked at the line above his name, traced it over to the end and punched the hole for Buchanan.

The theory doesn't end there. According to Gore, most of these voters immediately realized they had mistakenly voted for Buchanan. But instead of following the instructions they had been handed (which advised: "If you make a mistake, return your ballot card and obtain another"), these citizens did something that can only be described as stupendously irrational. Having already voted for Buchanan, they simply voted for Gore as well. On the same ballot. Fully cognizant that they had now voted for two presidential candidates, which rendered their ballots utterly void and meaningless, these tens of thousands of people still did not ask for the fresh ballots to which they were perfectly entitled. Instead, they turned in their ruined and worthless punch cards and silently departed the polling places. Only afterward, according to Gore, did the terrible truth dawn on them.

At least that was the theory being peddled by Democrats in Palm Beach County by the middle of Election Day, when it was increasingly evident that Gore was going to need Florida if he wanted to win the White House.

Gore officials knew the only way to exploit this theory was to round up as many voters as possible who would swear out affidavits claiming they had been confused by the butterfly ballot. Shortly before 6 P.M., or roughly an hour before polls closed in Palm Beach, the Democratic National Committee called TeleQuest, a Texas-based telemarketing firm, and instructed the company to phone thousands of Palm Beach voters. The idea was to compile a list of Democrats who would agree to testify that they had been confused. TeleQuest officials hastily mobilized every telemarketer they could lay their hands on and began burning up the phone lines. In a single, forty-five-minute flurry of calls, the company reached 5,000 voters in Palm Beach, 98 percent of whom had already voted.

There is no way to know how many of these voters were consciously aware of the butterfly ballot's supposedly confusing design before they received the call from TeleQuest. But for those blissfully ignorant citizens who were under the impression that they had voted without a hitch, the ominous phone call they received surely planted the seeds of doubt.

"Some voters have encountered a problem today with punch card ballots in Palm Beach County," the script for the call intoned. "These voters have said that they believe that they accidentally punched the wrong hole for the incorrect candidate."

The script added: "If you have already voted and think you may have punched the wrong hole for the incorrect candidate, you should return to the polls and request that the election officials write down your name so that this problem can be fixed."

The company was able to collect the names of some 2,400 voters—nearly half of those called—on a list that was turned over to the Democratic Party. The survey, known in the industry as a "push poll" because of its leading questions, accomplished its desired result. Hundreds of Palm Beach voters complained to election officials.

But these behind-the-scenes machinations and the resulting list of "confused" voters were not made public on Election Night. After all, it was not yet clear that these people would be needed. But on Wednesday morning, when final results revealed that Bush had squeaked to victory, the butterfly ballot took on new significance in the Gore camp. The vice president's men had found their Plan B.

And so, as canvassing boards all over the state began recounting ballots for the first time, Gore lawyers began tracking down the voters on the TeleQuest list and urging them to swear out affidavits that the butterfly ballot was confusing. Democrats characterized these "victims" as elderly retirees who were understandably confused by the butterfly ballot. But the very first lawsuit against the butterfly ballot (and the first suit of any kind in the post-election debacle) was filed by a savvy and ruthless Democratic operative named Andre Fladell. His political philosophy was summed up in the opening sentence of a newspaper article that he proudly displayed on his office wall: "Palm Beach county political consultant Andre Fladell follows just one rule: Win at any cost." The 1999 profile by the *New Times* of Palm Beach was headlined "Politics as Blood Sport."

Fladell was a chiropractor who in 1988 was fined and placed on probation for Medicare fraud. Now a fifty-three-year-old bachelor, he carefully cultivated the image of a wealthy beach bum who delighted in crushing opponents half his age at volleyball. He also relished hardball politics. "It's where the best and worst in people comes out," he said. "You get the adrenaline of war without having to physically hurt anyone."

Despite his decades of political expertise, Fladell claimed he was confused into voting for Buchanan instead of Gore. But during numerous media interviews after filing suit in Palm Beach County Circuit Court, Fladell gave conflicting answers about when he realized he had voted incorrectly. Shortly after filing the suit at 4:01 P.M. Wednesday, he told the *Sun-Sentinel* newspaper in Florida: "I punched the second hole, then I realized what I had done. I came out of the voting booth thinking I was stupid, that I had just made a dumb mistake. Then I realized other people were making the same mistake."

But that evening, during an appearance on CNN's *Larry King Live*, Fladell said he realized his error much later in the day, after hearing about the ballot confusion from friends in a restaurant. A week later, the story shifted yet again when Fladell told the *New Times* that his epiphany had occurred as he was chatting with a fellow volleyball player on the beach just before a game.

Fladell, who was joined by two other Democratic activists in his lawsuit, asked the court to declare the butterfly ballot "deceptive, confusing and/or misleading." He also demanded that the presidential election in Palm Beach County be nullified and a new election be held.

Fladell had called his lawyer, Henry Handler of Boca Raton, shortly after 10 A.M. on Wednesday, setting into motion the first of half a dozen lawsuits that would be filed over the butterfly ballot in the next few days. While Democratic plaintiffs and lawyers took the battle to the courts, Democratic ground troops mobilized in the streets.

The Reverend Jesse Jackson led hundreds of angry protesters in a march on the Palm Beach County government office building on Thursday. The demonstrators shouted "We want justice!" and "Bush is goin' down!" As reporters and protesters pressed in from all sides, Jackson declared: "Every vote must count! And to this point, we do not know who won the election, because all the votes have not been counted."

As TV cameras rolled, Jackson was handed one of the infamous butterfly ballots. It had been festooned with a blue-and-white "Gore-Lieberman" bumper sticker.

"This ballot is fuzzy," Jackson said, clutching the offending document aloft. "It is deceptive. But, my friends, if we remain disciplined and focused, then we win. Because we voted!"

Various Democrats were encouraged to come to the microphone and share stories about their confusion. One man named Gustav Sallas made no secret of his contempt for Theresa LePore, the Palm Beach County elections supervisor who had designed the butterfly ballot. "She's a Democrat, I know, but let's face it: In this case, she screwed the pooch."

Some Democrats asserted that Gore supporters who mistakenly voted for Buchanan included Jewish survivors of the Holocaust. They expressed horror that Jews had been tricked into voting for a man they suspected was anti-Semitic. On Thursday evening, ten frail Jews were positioned in the front pews of a black Baptist church. Jackson took the pulpit and thundered: "We have an historic alliance, the blacks and the Jews." There was no mention of Jackson's 1984 reference to Jews as "Hymies" and New York City, the hometown of many Palm Beach retirees, as "Hymietown."

Even the alleged anti-Semite himself, Patrick J. Buchanan, who had won disproportionate support from Palm Beach County voters in previous presidential efforts, went on national television to say that he thought some citizens who had voted for him had meant to cast their ballots for Gore.

Gore let the controversy roil all day Wednesday and past noon on Thursday before coming out and publicly siding with Fladell and the other plaintiffs in the butterfly lawsuits. At that point Bush was ahead by fewer than 800 votes and it seemed likely, judging from the AP tally of county-by-county results, that the lead would hold. With the counting expected to be wrapped up as early as that evening, it was time for Team Gore to openly embrace the butterfly lawsuits.

The task was assigned to two men who would become the public face of the vice president's post-election struggle for weeks to come—Gore campaign chairman William Daley and Warren Christopher, who had once been Clinton's Secretary of State. They stepped before reporters in a conference room on the first floor of the statehouse building in Tallahassee that had become ground zero in the fight for the White House.

"Secretary Christopher and I have been in Florida now for over twenty hours and I'm here to report that what we have learned has left us deeply troubled," Daley intoned to a packed house. "Most notably, it appears that more than 20,000 voters in Palm Beach County, who in all likelihood thought they were voting for Al Gore, had their votes counted for Pat Buchanan or not counted at all.

"Because this disenfranchisement of these Floridians is so much larger than the reported gap between Governor Bush and Vice President Gore, we believe this requires the full attention of the courts in Florida and concerned citizens all around our country. More than 100 million Americans voted on Tuesday and more voted for Al Gore than Governor Bush."

The Gore strategists had agreed early on that one way to stave off the public's impatience with the lack of closure was to emphasize that Gore had won the nationwide popular vote. Ironically, before the election, there had been widespread speculation that Bush would win the popular vote and lose the Electoral College. Gore supporters had prepared for this scenario by preemptively reminding Republicans that the presidency is decided by the Electoral College, not the popular vote. But now that the shoe was on the other foot, Gore supporters reversed their argument. At every opportunity, Democrats reminded the public that Gore had won the popular vote. They resorted to the precise tactic they had warned Bush not to wield. By trumpeting the fact that Gore had won the popular vote, the vice president's supporters sought to play on America's basic sense of fairness. Why shouldn't the man who received the most votes win? The Electoral College was suddenly under attack as a quaint anachronism devised by the nation's well-meaning but hopelessly short-sighted founders.

"I love the founding fathers. I love their wigs; I love their hearts; I love their brains," allowed presidential historian Doris Kearns Goodwin on NBC News Wednesday morning. But the Electoral College "is one part of their institution that, I think, we've got to change."

This sentiment was echoed by First Lady Hillary Rodham Clinton, who had just been elected to the U.S. Senate, although she had not yet been sworn in.

"We are a very different country than we were two hundred years ago," Clinton said. "I believe strongly that in a democracy, we should respect the will of the people. And to me, that means it's time to do away with the Electoral College and move to the popular election of our president."

But Daley was not content to play the popular vote card nationally. He went ahead and pronounced Gore the winner of Florida as well. He insisted it was only a matter of time before the votes were properly tallied and the presidency would rightfully be awarded to his boss.

"Here in Florida, it also seems likely that more voters went to the polls believing that they were voting for Al Gore than for George Bush," Daley said. "If the will of the people is to prevail, Al Gore should be awarded a victory in Florida and be our next president."

That statement rankled the editorial board at the *Washington Post*, which had been watching Daley's press conference on TV. The board immediately fired off a blistering editorial that branded the statement "reckless" and "poisonous." The *Post*, which had endorsed Gore in October, was now denouncing Daley and others in the campaign for continuing "to imply that Mr. Gore's narrow lead in the popular vote somehow gives him superior status—if not quite a partial claim to the office, then a greater right to contest the electoral outcome in Florida. But that's false, and they know it. The electoral vote is what matters."

But Daley was way beyond kowtowing to the *Post* by this stage of the game. He plunged into the specifics of the Palm Beach controversy. He said it "seems implausible" that Buchanan had garnered 3,407 votes in Palm Beach, more than triple the amount he had won in any other Florida county.

"Based on the totals from other counties, there seems every reason to believe that well over 2,000 of these votes were votes for Vice President Al Gore—more than enough to make him the winner here in Florida," Daley extrapolated. "In addition, there were more than 19,000 ballots cast in Palm Beach County that were not tabulated at all because voters, faced with this confusing ballot, apparently punched two holes instead of one. These logical conclusions are reinforced by the phone calls, faxes, and other reports from over 1,000 residents of Palm Beach County that have poured into us, saying that they believe they were the victims of this ballot confusion."

Daley made no mention of the DNC hiring TeleQuest, the telemarketing firm, to prod many of these people into actually making the complaints. Instead, he made it look as though the Gore campaign was merely responding to a bona fide, grass-roots uprising. "Today, I'm announcing that we will be working with voters from Florida in support of legal actions to demand some redress for the disenfranchisement of more than 20,000 voters in Palm Beach County," he said.

Not content to demand 2,000 of the Buchanan-only votes, Daley also laid claim to more than 12,000 of the double-punched ballots. He reached this conclusion by further extrapolation: Since Gore received 63 percent of the valid votes in Palm Beach, he should also receive 63 percent of the 19,000 "overvotes."

"Take a percent that Al Gore got on the votes that were counted, and put that into the 19,000 that were punched [with] two holes," Daley suggested. "He would clearly have the votes [to overcome] the spread between the two at this point in the recount."

Although Daley denounced the butterfly ballot as "deliberately confusing," it had been designed by none other than Theresa LePore, the loyal Democrat who was supervisor of the Palm Beach Elections Office. Not only had LePore designed the ballot, she had published it in the local newspaper before the election and invited Democrats and Republicans alike to complain if they objected to the design. No one had uttered so much as a syllable of complaint.

When a reporter pointed this out, Daley coolly threw LePore to the wolves. "A party official of either party doesn't have the right to disenfranchise thousands and thousands of voters in a county in Florida." Down in Palm Beach, LePore was devastated.

Asked by another reporter why these supposedly confused voters didn't simply ask for assistance from election judges and other poll workers at the precincts, Daley said: "Election workers are well taxed and strained on Election Day, especially with the tremendous turnout that was going on." He offered no further explanation.

Warren Christopher, who let Daley do most of the talking at that first press conference, used even stronger language in denouncing LePore's design. "That ballot was confusing and illegal," he declared.

Christopher was not the first ex-secretary of state to stand behind the podium that day. So had James A. Baker III, who once served the elder President Bush and was now in Tallahassee to safeguard the interests of the younger Bush.

"When I put Jim Baker in there, there wasn't much more I could do," Bush told the author. "I had great confidence in Jim Baker. I talked to him every day."

After talking with Bush on Thursday morning, Baker preemptively pooh-poohed Democratic concerns about the butterfly ballot.

"The ballot in Palm Beach County that has been alleged to be confusing is a ballot that has been used before in Florida elections," Baker told reporters. "It is a ballot that was approved by an elected Democratic official. It is a ballot that was published in newspapers in that county and provided to the candidates, to the respective political parties, in advance of the election in order that complaints, if any, could be registered.

"And hey: Guess what?" Baker said. "There were no complaints until after the election."

Besides, Baker added, there wasn't much anyone could do about ballots that had been double-punched.

"There's not a jurisdiction in this democracy of ours that does not discard ballots where a voter votes twice for two different candidates for the same office," he said. "That's what happens in our democracy. If that's what happened here, I don't see how you can count those ballots."

In his heart of hearts, Gore knew Baker was right. It was hard to imagine how he was ever going to prove conclusively that the double-punched ballots were rightfully his. It was also a stretch to believe he would ever get credit for ballots that had been punched for Buchanan and not for himself. Gore's complaints about the butterfly ballot may have been convincing to the press and a sizable chunk of the public, but the remedy to those complaints was another matter altogether. Fladell and the other Democrats were demanding a new election. But such a remedy was unprecedented in U.S. history. Even the Gore lawyers acknowledged they knew of no case in Florida or anywhere else in which a judge had ordered a partial revote in a presidential election. The Constitution grants Congress the final say in determining when federal elections are held. And Congress had long ago mandated that the presidential election shall be held once every four years—on the first Tuesday after the first Monday in November. Even if Democrats somehow succeeded in convincing a county judge in Florida to order a new election, Bush lawyers would have ample constitutional grounds on which to appeal such a ruling all the way up to the U.S. Supreme Court. And even if Gore still managed to prevail in the courts, how would the public react? Would the rest of America give its blessing to a brand new, unprecedented election in which the next president of the United States would be determined by Palm Beach County alone? Would the 50 million Americans who had voted against Gore sit still while a single, hand-picked Democratic stronghold in Florida was anointed the final arbiter? The fury that would accompany such a revote would surely make most Third World elections seem tame.

No, even the Gore team quietly acknowledged the reality of the situation. The butterfly ballot was, at best, an issue that helped Democrats create a vague sense that Gore had been wronged. It was Plan B, the best the Democrats had been able to come up with in the immediate aftermath of the most chaotic Election Night in modern history. It had served its purpose by buying them a little more time.

The question now was whether to come up with a Plan C. Or should Gore simply prepare to concede the election to Bush? After all, it was now obvious that the mandatory, statewide recount would not give Gore the votes he needed to defeat Bush. And Gore had signaled that he would step down if he didn't win the recount.

"Vice President Gore and Senator Lieberman are fully prepared to concede and to support Governor Bush if and when he is officially elected president," Daley had promised just a day earlier. "But this race is simply too close to call, and until the... recount is concluded and the results in Florida become official, our campaign continues!"

Well, the recount was now nearly concluded and it looked as though Florida election officials were about to call Bush the winner for the second time in a row. The Texas governor was considered the *de facto* winner anyway, thanks in part to the networks having spent two hours calling him President Bush. Those two hours had left a powerful impression on the minds of Americans, many of whom went to bed before Bush was stripped of his new title. When they awoke the next morning to learn that Gore had retracted his concession, they came to view the vice president as the pretender to the throne and Bush as the defender. After all, Gore had never been declared president, even temporarily. In fact, he had never been ahead in the official Florida vote count, not by a single ballot, not for a single moment. Pollsters were already taking surveys that would show that the majority of Americans, regardless of whom they had supported, now believed Bush had the more legitimate claim to the presidency. Oh, the hardcore Democratic base still insisted Gore would somehow prevail. But to Middle America, Al Gore was increasingly viewed as the interloper who was holding up the Bush presidency.

The whole nation, including most Democrats, wanted closure. Americans were deeply troubled by the unprecedented deadlock. They were accustomed to learning the identity of their new president on Election Night, not at some indiscernible point in the future, when lawyers and political operatives had finished tying the nation into knots with their ugly and contentious quarrels. The fiasco was already becoming something of a national embarrassment. Foreigners were having a field day poking fun at the United States, the once-mighty bastion of democracy that couldn't even pick a new president. The financial markets, already in decline, were further roiled by the historic indecision over a new leader. Foreign policy experts began to worry that enemies might view America as vulnerable for mischief, perhaps even a terrorist strike. Political analysts warned of a constitutional crisis.

All these considerations were obvious on Thursday, November 9, a true day of reckoning for Al Gore. But there were other considerations as well. For one thing, he had come so agonizingly close to victory. About an hour after Gore had withdrawn his concession, Bush's lead shrank from over 1,000 votes to just 224. To be 224 votes short of the presidency, even temporarily, in an election in which 100 million people had cast ballots, was an exquisite form of political torture. Gore had come close enough to victory to catch its intoxicating scent.

He had also come close enough to defeat to taste its bitterness. Gore knew the political ignominy that awaited him if he gave up now. Oh, there were pundits in those early days who insisted that if Gore did the right thing and walked away, he would instantly elevate himself to front runner status for the Democratic nomination in 2004. They cited Richard Nixon, who had declined to push for a recount in 1960, even though it was widely believed that John F. Kennedy's narrow victory had been aided by voter fraud (courtesy of the legendary political machine of Chicago Mayor Richard J. Daley, whose son now ran Gore's campaign). Nixon had come back eight years later to win the White House. Perhaps Gore could do the same thing in 2004 or 2008.

But Gore knew better. The new generation of political parties had little use for losers. The ash heap of history was littered with the carcasses of candidates who had failed to win the White House on the first try. Gore was loath to follow in the footsteps of Bob Dole, Michael Dukakis, and Walter Mondale. As vice president to a popular, two-term president, Gore had been the automatic front-runner for the Democratic nomination this time around. Talented, ambitious Democrats like House Minority Leader Richard Gephardt had put their presidential aspirations on hold in deference to Clinton's presumptive successor. But no such deference would be granted the next time. There would be recriminations for Gore's failure to hold the White House in an era of unprecedented peace and prosperity. With the wind at his back and the powers of incumbency at his command, Gore had failed to carry even his home state of Tennessee. Besides, there would be a whole new field of ambitious Democrats in 2004. By then, sixteen years would have passed since the Democratic ticket hadn't featured the name of Al Gore. It would be time for a fresh face, perhaps someone like Evan Bayh, the handsome and telegenic senator from Indiana. Gore would be lucky to get a prime speaking role at the Democratic National Convention. And who could blame the party for not wanting to showcase the man who had been beaten by George W. Bush, whom Democrats had once dismissed as a political and intellectual lightweight?

No, Gore had stepped to the brink of the abyss and peered inside. He recoiled at the fate that awaited him if he quit now. He might as well go for broke. National turmoil be damned. Something much more important was on the line—his political career.

Gore was so upfront about putting his own skin above the national interest that, according to the *Washington Post*, he sat his senior aides down and drew them a picture. Literally. On an easel of butcher paper in the dining room of his residence at the Naval Observatory in Washington, Gore drew four concentric circles to represent his priorities. He and Lieberman occupied the innermost circle. The next circle was reserved for big supporters like AFL-CIO president John Sweeney, civil rights leader Jesse Jackson, and abortion advocate Kate Michelman. The Democratic Party was third in Gore's circle of priorities. Finally, in the very last circle, Gore placed the country. The man who was seeking to lead the United States of America into the new millennium placed the national interest not first, not second, not even third. In Al Gore's hierarchy of priorities, the nation came dead last.

Americans, alas, are a corny lot. They still like to think their presidents place the national interest above their own. They would find it difficult to imagine men like George Washington, Thomas Jefferson, Abraham Lincoln, Franklin D. Roosevelt, or Ronald Reagan drawing four concentric circles and explaining that their own hides were more important than the national interest. But Al Gore wasn't like those other leaders. He was looking out for Number One, plain and simple.

While Gore realized the nation had no stomach for a protracted legal and political war, he had learned from President Clinton that the public's patience could be stretched to remarkable lengths. There had been moments during the Monica Lewinsky scandal when even congressional Democrats came close to asking Clinton to resign in order to spare the nation the ordeal of impeachment. But Clinton had held firm against a seemingly endless torrent of sordid revelations that would have shamed any ordinary politician into full-fledged retreat. And when it was all over, he was still in the White House.

Now it was Gore's turn. The man who had commemorated his boss's impeachment by pronouncing him one of the greatest presidents in history now contemplated whether to unilaterally take the nation through another protracted period of unprecedented political turmoil. While Gore did not possess the sheer charisma that had helped Clinton pull it off, he certainly had the raw political ambition. He had long ago acknowledged his ruthlessness when it came to seeking the presidency.

"You make the decision to run first and then you run with all your heart and soul," Gore told reporters in 1991 as he mulled a campaign for the White House. "You're going to rip the lungs out of anybody else who's in the race. And you're going to do it right."

Gore reaffirmed his scorched-earth philosophy during the 2000 campaign.

"I'm not like George Bush," he told aides. "If he wins or loses, life goes on. I'll do anything to win."

And so, on Thursday, November 9, Gore made the most momentous decision of the post-election struggle. He would fight on. There was no turning back. He would seize the presidency at any cost. In the chaos of the moment, Gore's decision did not seem nearly as important as the call he had made a day earlier to retract his concession. But that call had been relatively easy. The mandatory recount had been out of Gore's hands. Besides, it would only delay the selection of the president by two or three days. By contrast, Gore was now embarking on a strategy in which he would single-handedly prolong the outcome of the presidential election indefinitely.

The only way for Gore to win was to find new votes. Since Florida had already counted all 6 million ballots not once, but twice, Gore decided to seek a third count, this one strictly by hand. Unlike the mandatory recount, which was statewide by Florida law, the new tallies would have to be requested on a county-by-county basis. Gore did not have the time or the manpower to request recounts in all sixty-seven counties. Besides, even Gore realized the public's patience had its limits.

So he settled on two counties that had experienced the most problems on Election Night—Palm Beach and Volusia. Both had more registered Democrats than Republicans. And Palm Beach, home of the infamous butterfly ballot, was especially promising because it contained thousands of disqualified presidential punch cards that perhaps could be resurrected in a recount.

On the advice of one of his new Florida lawyers, Kendall Coffey, Gore also asked for recounts in Miami-Dade and Broward counties, two Democratic strongholds where vote-counting machines had failed to read large numbers of "undervotes," or ballots on which the voter had not made a clear choice for president. These two counties, together with Palm Beach, collectively formed the Gold Coast, the glittering expanse of real estate along southern Florida's Atlantic shore. The Gold Coast contained large pockets of liberal Jewish retirees from the North, particularly New York City, who had enthusiastically supported Lieberman, the first Orthodox Jew on a major party ticket.

Democrats had prepared in advance for a post-election fight. DNC general counsel Joseph Sandler had even put together a battle plan that included state-by-state explanations of election laws and deadlines for requesting hand recounts. Under Florida law, losing candidates had seventy-two hours after Election Day in which to ask for recounts from individual canvassing boards. That meant the deadline was midnight on Friday. But with many government offices taking Friday off in observance of Veteran's Day, which was actually Saturday, Gore decided to play it safe and request the hand recounts by the close of business on Thursday.

Gore knew that although he was entitled to request the new counts, the canvassing boards were under no obligation to actually grant his requests. The vice president needed to leverage every ounce of political influence at his disposal. He felt he had enough loyalists on the Gold Coast to make sure the new tallies would go forward. For starters, Coffey himself was a major force in southern Florida's Democratic circles. Acting on the recommendation of Attorney General Janet Reno, President Clinton had appointed

Coffey U.S. attorney for the Southern District of Florida in 1993. The tall, rawboned prosecutor had been the most powerful law enforcement official on the Gold Coast until 1996, when he lost a big case and decided to drown his sorrows at Lipstick, a Miami strip joint on South Dixie Highway. The forty-three-year-old married man used his American Express card to buy a $900 magnum of Dom Perignon and $200 in "Lipstick money," which can purchase just one thing—nude "lap dances." After retiring to the notorious "champagne room" with a thin, blonde dancer named Tiffany, Coffey got a little carried away and, according to Tiffany, bit her, drawing blood. The most powerful law enforcement official on the Gold Coast was unceremoniously slammed into a cab by a Lipstick bouncer. After an inquiry by the Justice Department, Coffey was summoned to Washington, where Reno told him to resign. And yet Coffey's influence in the region lingered. In fact, Coffey had been one of the lawyers who represented the Miami relatives of Elian Gonzalez, the little Cuban refugee who had touched off a national furor. Although that made him unpopular with many Democrats, Coffey had now redeemed himself by throwing his considerable clout behind Gore's quest to seize the presidency.

But Coffey's influence did not extend to Volusia County, which was 120 miles north of the Gold Coast. Besides, the Volusia canvassing board, unlike those on the Gold Coast, was controlled by Republicans. Gore would have to find another ally, someone with even more political muscle. He turned to the chairman of his Florida campaign, Bob Butterworth, who was also Florida's attorney general. The silver-haired, fifty-eight-year-old lawyer had once been regarded as a potential candidate for governor or perhaps even the U.S. Senate. But such speculation had died after a family tragedy in 1986. Butterworth's wife, Saundra, whom police described as mentally ill, shot their teenage son to death before killing herself on a street in northeast Miami. Saundra had used the gun Butterworth had given her for protection before their divorce in 1976. The slain Robert A. Butterworth III—who inherited his father's passion for politics and was running for president of his high school class—had just finished passing out leftover "Bob Butterworth" buttons from his dad's campaign for attorney general. The tragedy was said to have left lasting scars on Butterworth, making him reluctant to take his successful political career to that next, infinitely more public level. And yet here he was, fourteen years later, stepping into a media spotlight unlike anything he had ever witnessed in his years as prosecutor, sheriff, county judge, and head of the Florida Department of Highway Safety and Motor Vehicles. He was awestruck to be ushered into a meeting with former Secretary of State Warren Christopher, Gore's point man in Florida. This was heady stuff for Butterworth. Oh sure, back in the early 1970s, he and another young prosecutor had been dubbed "Batman and Robin" for fighting corruption in the Broward County Courthouse. And in 1998, Butterworth had played a crucial role in wresting $13 billion out of tobacco companies. But none of that even remotely prepared Bob Butterworth for the maelstrom he was entering.

Gore put Butterworth in charge of the recount request in Volusia County. The vice president knew it would be difficult for the local canvassing board to refuse a request from the state's top law enforcement officer. Still, the request might be tricky. The board was chaired by a no-nonsense Republican judge named Michael McDermott.

Butterworth accepted his assignment with gusto. After all, he had been begging Gore to stay in the fight since Election Night. Butterworth telephoned McDermott's boss, a man named Robert Rouse, chief judge of Florida's Seventh Judicial Circuit. He instructed Rouse to call McDermott and insist on a manual recount.

Evidently not satisfied that he had gotten his message across, Butterworth called Rouse a second time that same Thursday and directed him to ring up McDermott again so the three of them could converse on a conference call. Having received two phone calls in the same day from the state's chief law enforcement officer, Judge Rouse hopped to it. He again called McDermott, this time going so far as to summon the Republican out of a meeting of the canvassing board. As soon as McDermott picked up the phone, Butterworth began arguing for a hand recount. McDermott immediately demanded to know whether he was calling in his capacity as the state's chief law enforcement officer, or as manager of Gore's Florida campaign. Butterworth replied that he was wearing his attorney general's hat.

"I said, 'Mr. Butterworth, with all due respect, I believe you should disqualify yourself from any involvement in this matter,'" McDermott recalled. "He got huffy. He said, 'Well, I guess I'll leave the room.' I heard the door slam, even."

McDermott stood his ground, at least for the moment.

"I just thought it looked bad," he said later. "This is the only time I ever spoke to the attorney general, and it will probably be the last."

But even after Butterworth had stormed out of the room, his assistants remained on the conference call and tried to convince McDermott to manually recount the votes. The prosecutors reminded McDermott that Volusia County had not actually tabulated its ballots during the mandatory recount, as the secretary of state had directed. Rather, Volusia had merely double-checked computer tallies. Perhaps now it was time to go beyond that cursory review—even beyond a machine recount—and tally the ballots by hand. McDermott listened, although he still thought any contact from the attorney general's office—even from Butterworth's assistants—was highly improper. Besides, he and the other members of the Volusia County Canvassing Board had already decided against a manual recount.

However, shortly after the phone call from Butterworth on Thursday, the board reversed its decision. McDermott insisted the reversal was not related to the Butterworth call. But there was no denying that Volusia election officials were still embarrassed by their wildly fluctuating vote tallies on Election Night. They were also still smarting from the Keystone Cops episodes that plagued Wednesday's mandatory recount—from Debbie Allen's underwear to Gene Tracy's backseat ballots. Now the state's top legal officer—who also happened to be Gore's campaign chief—was demanding a hand recount. To refuse such a request might somehow result in yet another black eye for the local election officials, who were already being portrayed as the hicks who threw the election.

Butterworth's call to McDermott was kept quiet for five days. When it finally leaked out and he was confronted by reporters, Butterworth claimed to have resigned his chairmanship of Gore's Florida campaign just before placing the call to McDermott. But Butterworth never publicly disclosed this resignation until the press got wind of the phone call. Only then did he retroactively announce his resignation as Gore's go-to guy in Florida.

Regardless of which hat he was wearing, Butterworth effectively kicked off the first phase of Gore's Plan C for wresting the presidency from Bush. Plan A, the mandatory recount, had never really been expected to reverse the outcome of the election. Plan B, the butterfly ballot brouhaha, had merely served to buy the vice president a couple of days of patience from the public. Plan C, the request for hand recounts in counties most likely to discover new votes, was Al Gore's best hope for seizing the presidency.

CHAPTER 5

IT'S A CHAD, CHAD, CHAD, CHAD WORLD

B ob Nichols never signed on for this. No, when he agreed to become the spokesman for the Palm Beach County Canvassing Board, starting on Saturday, November 11, he was never warned that the board might change its vote-counting rules in the middle of the game. Several times. Right there in front of two hundred reporters.

Now Nichols was expected to go out in front of those jackals and explain that the three board members, all Democrats, couldn't make up their minds when it came to counting the ballots that might very well decide the next leader of the free world. Well, Nichols had no intention of diving on that particular grenade. He had already been harangued by this rowdy, unkempt, arrogant scrum of reporters earlier in the day. He had tried to remain pleasant during that first briefing, but they turned on him in an instant. The insolence of those bastards! They hadn't even let him finish a sentence. The least they could do was show him a little respect. Thirty-one years as a TV newsman right there in the heart of south Florida ought to count for something.

In fact, that was the whole point of him being brought on board. Theresa LePore, the supervisor of elections, was hopelessly out of her league when it came to dealing with the press on a story this huge. The woman looked as though she would fall over every time a reporter glanced at her sideways. She was shell-shocked. Her own party had publicly turned on her for having designed the infamous butterfly ballot. Now reporters from all over the globe wanted a piece of LePore. There was no way she could even begin to satisfy the voracious media beast. No, that was Nichol's job. He was the big gun who could swim with the sharks of the Fourth Estate. He could relate to these people. After all, he had been one of them until April, when he finally got out of the racket and started flacking for the New England Institute of Technology, Palm Beach campus.

He made a point of mentioning his journalistic pedigree two or three times during that first briefing, but these sons of bitches seemed supremely unimpressed. Seven months out of the business and already he was being treated like an outsider. He even looked like one. Nichols was nattily dressed in a taupe, double-breasted suit with pointed lapels. He wore lots of big, flashy jewelry on his hands and wrists, which he waved in the air as he tried to calm the unruly gaggle of reporters. *They* were dressed like slobs. Rumpled, wash-and-wear shirts over shapeless, Dockers slacks or blue jeans. One newspaper reporter was actually wearing shorts. The man's shirt-tails were untucked as if he were out mowing his backyard on a Saturday afternoon. Sure, the TV people in front of him wore suits, but even they were subversively shod in running shoes. The whole lot of them screamed disrespect.

Nichols had been around a few media feeding frenzies in his day, but none compared to this one. These reporters had spent the last eighteen months covering the presidential campaign, including the sleepless finale leading up to Election Day. They had been planning vacations for months, only to cancel them in order to cover this disaster. Suffering from lack of sleep and jacked up on caffeine and junk food, these journalists were in an ugly mood. Of all the hand recounts that had been requested by Gore, this was the very first day of the very first tally. The vice president had made requests in three other counties, but Palm Beach was the first to actually begin the process. The board had agreed to conduct a sample count of 1 percent of the precincts to determine whether a countywide tally was warranted.

The count had begun four hours ago and quickly degenerated into a circus. Board members were holding ballots up to the light to see whether voters had successfully punched out "chads"— those tiny rectangles of paper that denote one candidate or another. One by one, the ballots were picked up and passed around by the members of the canvassing board, who gaped at the tiny, imperfectly punched chads as if they were trying to decipher the Dead Sea Scrolls. The whole time, Democratic and Republican observers were straining to get a look at these arcane documents. They pressed in so closely to the board members that they were practically in their laps. The entire spectacle was being broadcast live on the twenty-four-hour cable news channels, thanks to the army of cameramen who kept clattering their lenses against the windows of the counting room as if it were an aquarium and the ballot counters were some rare species of marine life.

Only one "pool" reporter at a time was allowed inside the counting room and these reporters weren't allowed to broadcast live. So the crush of journalists pressed up against the glass outside had to rely on an utterly worthless audio feed from the Palm Beach County government television station. They could barely make out what the board members and ballot counters were saying. The press could see these people holding ballots up to the fluorescent lights, but they couldn't hear the actual proceedings.

That was why Nichols was sent out to inform the media of what had just happened. The board had changed its counting standards for the third time in four hours. The original guideline was the board's decade-old definition, in writing, of what constituted a valid vote. According to that guideline, a vote counted only if the voter had at least partially dislodged the chad.

"A chad that is hanging or partially punched may be counted as a vote, since it is possible to punch through the card and still not totally dislodge the chad," the guidelines stated. "But a chad that is fully attached, bearing only an indentation, should not be counted as a vote."

These standards, set forth by the canvassing board of 1990, seemed reasonable to the canvassing board of 2000. So the new board voted to adopt the old guidelines at its public meeting before starting the hand recount on Saturday, November 11.

And yet, almost as soon as they began actually eyeballing ballots, the standard slipped. The board began holding ballots above their heads in order to see whether any fluorescent light shone through the scored edges of the chad. Whenever a shaft of light clearly shone through, the board counted it as a vote—even if all four corners of the chad were still attached to the ballot. This was clearly a more liberal standard than the one the board had just voted to adopt.

As the hours crawled by, the standard became even more liberal. Now, instead of counting ballots where a ray of light shone clearly through the scored edge of the chad, the board began to count even a micron of light. In fact, when board members had difficulty discerning any light at all, they were advised by a Democratic lawyer to turn the card over to get a better angle. Over the strenuous objections of a Republican lawyer, the board members followed the suggestion of their fellow Democrat. Lo and behold, he was right. They could see a tiny speck of light if they flipped the card over from side to side and held it at various angles above their heads. The votes for Al Gore began to multiply.

But then, four hours into the mind-numbing tedium of individually scrutinizing ballots, the board members changed the rules yet again. Circuit Judge Charles Burton began feeling pangs of guilt that the board's standards had slipped so far since its meeting that morning. He read aloud the 1990 guidelines that said "a chad that is fully attached, bearing only an indentation, should not be counted as a vote."

"Clearly, we've counted as votes chads that were attached," Burton confessed. "I want to do this right."

So the board members reverted to the 1990 standards once again. And now it was time for Nichols to break the news to the media. Knowing the press would jump on the shifting standards, Nichols brought along Leon St. John, a county lawyer who was representing the canvassing board. The way Nichols saw it, St. John was better equipped to explain the legal nuances of the bombshell that had just detonated inside the aquarium.

"I'm going to call on Leon St. John from the county attorney's office to come up here," Nichols told the muttering media mob. "Leon is going to explain to you exactly what happened there now. And this is Leon St. John with the county attorney's office: Leon."

The two men were a study in contrasts. While Nichols was a tan, well-fed schmoozer who dressed a little on the sharp side, St. John was a pale, spare, tight-lipped man with a bald head and a bow tie. He looked as though he could have posed with a pitchfork for *American Gothic*. He also looked as if he would rather be somewhere else, and was eager to get this over with.

"The Florida statutes, in chapter 102, state that a purpose—," he began.

"Louder, please!"

"Pardon me?"

"Louder!"

"Florida statutes, in chapter 102, state the responsibility of the canvassing board when there's a manual count," St. John began again. "If there's a discrepancy or a question on a ballot, the canvassing [board] will look at the ballot to the best of their knowledge to discern the intent of the voter. That's all it says.

"So the question is, what do you do? Does the chad have to be punched all the way out? Do you look at a dimple? Is that enough? It's within the discretion of the canvassing board.

"In 1990 the canvassing board at that time adopted a procedure which was adopted by this canvassing board this morning at the meeting at 9:00, and copies of this were given to all of you that wanted it. That policy, in pertinent part, said as follows: 'A chad that is fully attached, bearing only an indentation, should not be counted as a vote.'"

Nichols seemed relieved that St. John was doing all the talking. He wouldn't have to explain this mess after all. The lawyer was already explaining the part about board members having lapsed into the ray-of-light standard.

"Now, when they did that, they were looking for—to see if you could see sunshine or light through where the chad is," St. John was saying. "After the first batch went through, the chairperson of the canvassing board, the judge, indicated that he had a concern that the light test—if you can use the term 'light test,' that's my term—was possibly not consistent with the guidelines that were adopted this morning."

Possibly not consistent. It was like poking a stick in a nest of vipers. Nichols could see the reporters coil.

"The canvassing board discussed that and—just moments ago—they had decided to not go with the light test, but to go with the test that's reflected on the procedures where, if one of the four corners of the chad is detached, then that will be a vote."

Just moments ago. The press antennae went on high alert. Something new had just happened. They would have fresh information to report. St. John plowed on.

"They are proceeding with the second batch now," he said. "When they are through, they are going to go back and go through the stack of the questioned ballots from the first batch."

"How long is this going to take?" demanded a reporter. The scrum could no longer restrain itself.

"How long is it going to take?" St. John stalled. "If I knew that question, you know, I could sell the answer. We don't have an answer."

"Sir, that sounds like a lesser standard," said another journalist. "Is that a lesser standard for the vote?"

"That's your term," said St. John, who was not about to go down that road. "You can term it that way."

"Well, I was wondering what your interpretation of it is," the reporter persisted.

"I don't have an interpretation on it," the lawyer held firm.

Another reporter demanded to know the fate of ballots that been the subject of legal objections.

"The canvassing board is going to deal with that before the night is over," St. John ventured. "I'm not sure of that yet."

Nichols was feeling comfortable enough by now to add his own two cents to the mix. Besides, he didn't want St. John getting so far ahead of himself that he said something Nichols would have to explain away later.

"Ladies and gentlemen, be careful now," Nichols said. "Remember, you have your pool reporters and you're going to have the opportunity to get information from those pool reporters and, in situations like the one you're talking about, please depend on that area. We caution you."

But these reporters were in no mood to be cautioned. They began directing their pointed queries at Nichols.

"Can you tell us how many ballots ended up in the question mark pile?" somebody said.

"No, I can't," said Nichols, now straining to hear multiple questions shouted at once. "One at a time. What is it?"

"How late do they plan on going tonight?"

"Until they stop," Nichols replied. "I wish I could tell you, ladies and gentlemen, that we're all going to be able to go home and have a nice dinner in the next hour or so. I'm sorry, that's not going to happen."

Amazingly, the reporters were not focusing on the shifting vote-counting standards. The magnitude of what St. John had told them must not have sunk in. Instead, Nichols was peppered with boilerplate, logistical questions about times and numbers of ballots. This wasn't so bad after all. Nichols wasn't even cracking a sweat. In fact, he didn't seem to notice when Leon St. John, who had been standing at his side, slipped away while Nichols was in the middle of an answer.

"So you say at 4:00, 5:00 in the morning, they could be here, still looking at ballots?" a reporter said.

"I wish I didn't have to say that, but I think, yes, it's possible," Nichols said before turning to another reporter. "Yes, ma'am?"

"Did the party representatives object to the one-out-of-four-corners test?" she said.

Nichols knew it had been too good to be true. Sure enough, the reporters were starting to ask about the shifting standards. St. John's explanation must have finally sunk in. All of a sudden, Nichols realized the lawyer was no longer at his side. Nichols was flying solo in front of these irritable reporters and, for that matter, the entire nation.

"I don't know," Nichols said. "I was not privy to that part of it. But all of you can see and hear what's going on in there, so—"

"Actually, we can't," a reporter piped up. "Is there any way to move the microphones closer to them?"

"Is there somebody saying you can't hear?" said Nichols, who himself had trouble hearing the questions.

"We can't hear all the stuff," someone complained.

"The microphone isn't close enough," groused another.

"We're doing the best we can," Nichols said. "Make sure you touch base with your pool people. They can help you."

"Sir, earlier in the day—," began a woman.

"Speak up, ma'am," said Nichols, cupping his hand behind his ear.

"Earlier in the day, we were told that if only one corner of the chad was detached, it would not be counted as a vote," the woman said. "Are you now saying that it is going to be counted as a vote?"

"That's what's Leon said, right?" Nichols asked no one in particular.

It was unbelievable. St. John had high-tailed it out of the press conference just before the reporters started hurling questions about the shifting standards. Where in hell had the lawyer disappeared to? It wasn't like Nichols could just wander off and haul him back here before this tremendous tangle of microphones. After all, this was a live press conference on the most hotly disputed American election in more than a century. Nichols would just have to stand there and answer the questions as best he could.

"The original policy of the canvassing board is what they're going to go by, without the light test," Nichols ventured. "That's best way I can answer it. The original, that's what they're doing."

"Sir, the original policy," began another inquisitor, "was that if it was only attached by one corner, it would not be counted as a vote."

Now the reporters themselves were confused. The questioner had evidently meant to say "detached," not "attached." But Nichols didn't catch the reporter's mistake.

"If that's what was in the policy, that's what they're going by," he replied matter-of-factly. Nichols had just unilaterally set yet another standard.

"But that's different from what he just said," protested a journalist.

Nichols punted: "I can't respond to you directly on it."

"Tell us what the policy is with the chad," demanded a reporter, smelling uncertainty. "Restate the policy."

"Restate the policy?" Nichols stalled. "The policy that was done this morning is that there was, and I believe, and I—where is Leon? Did you—get the attorneys, because I'm not an attorney. Want to make sure they're here before I give you—I can only tell you what they tell me, that the policy would be that if you don't—they were using the light test. Now if there is one corner, or three corners attached still, it won't be counted as a vote. That's the way I understand it."

Nichols was in a free fall.

"He said it would be counted as a vote," persisted a female reporter.

"That's why I'm asking you to come back," said Nichols, craning his head around in a desperate search for St. John. "We'll clear it up before we leave here. Don't worry. We're not going to leave you hanging, I promise you."

Nichols was the one who had been left hanging. The reporters seemed to be all shouting at the same time.

"No matter what happens, does this change your strategy in future elections, to go to a different approach, a different way of equal vote, so you don't get into this situation again?" someone scolded.

"I wish I could tell you what's going to happen in the future," Nichols said. "I'm quite certain that this is going to be debated over and over again and that there are going to be all kinds of procedural things that are going to be debated for possible change in the future. I wish I could read the future. I'd tell you when we'd be out of here tonight."

"How would you characterize the level of bickering that's going on inside the recount room?"

"I can't answer that," Nichols said. "I haven't been witness to any of it."

"Do you have to essentially begin over again?"

"I can't answer that one either," Nichols acknowledged. "That will be up to the canvassing board. But I can find out."

A woman shouted something.

"I can't hear you, ma'am."

"If you change the standard, it makes sense you have to start over again."

"Well, they're going to continue from where they are now and then go back to that batch," he explained.

"Could you recap what is exactly left for the board to do?" said a reporter, evidently sensing Nichols was due a procedural softball.

"A little bit louder," Nichols said.

"Can you recap what is exactly left, in terms of the counting for you all to do?"

"I cannot," he said, missing the softball by a mile. "I don't know exactly how many they have gone through."

"What's the total number?"

"Tell us the policy on the chads!"

"I'm waiting for Leon to come back," Nichols pleaded. "He's on his way back. Be calm."

Be calm. Lecturing reporters to be calm was practically a confession that the press conference was careening out of control.

"Are you concerned at all, as the night goes on, about fatigue among those working on ballots?"

"Am I concerned about their fatigue?" said Nichols, now openly stalling for the return of Leon. "I think we're all concerned about fatigue."

While Nichols was talking, someone thrust a copy of the 1990 guidelines on counting ballots into his hand. He promptly launched into a doctoral dissertation on a subject that was utterly foreign to the millions of TV viewers who had been watching him flounder—"chads."

"All right, this is the page and we'll try to make it so that it is easy to understand," began Nichols, relieved to have something in black-and-white that he could wield against these assassins. "These are the guidelines on ballots with chads not completely removed.

"The instructions in the voting machines are as follows," said Nichols, plunging into the mundane how-to guide as if it were a newly discovered document of historic import. "To vote, hold the punch straight up and punch down through the card next to the preferred candidate's name or issue position.

"The guidelines assume that these directions have been understood and followed. Therefore, a chad that is hanging or partially punched may be counted as a vote, since it is possible to punch through the card and still not totally dislodge the chad. But a chad that is fully attached, bearing only an indentation, should not be counted as a vote.

"An indentation may result from a voter placing the stylus in the position but not punching through. Thus, an indentation is not evidence of intent to cast a valid vote. That is the procedure approved by the November 6, 1990, canvassing board," Nichols said. "That is the policy they're going back to."

It was the longest stretch in which a reporter had not been able to ask a question. But as soon as Nichols came up for air, the frenzy resumed. Some of the questions were downright incomprehensible.

"That doesn't explain the discrepancy between what was told this morning to us and what was just said here, versus the one grade point," a reporter said.

"They're going back to go by this policy. They're will continue—I didn't say that. I said they're going to continue what they have not done under this policy. They will go back to the other batches and go according to this policy."

"So what the judge said—," a journalist began.

"That's the explanation," Nichols snapped.

"So what the judge said this morning no longer holds?"

"I wasn't privy to what the judge said this morning. I'm telling you what I know now. Obviously, he's not—he's back in the canvassing board now, but he sent this out so that we can clear it up. We'll discuss this individually with you if you want, if this doesn't clear it up.

"I reiterate to you: this policy they adopted this morning, they are now going to continue to adhere to it. There was a change in the middle. They are going to adhere to this policy. Anything that was counted after they changed was going to be back and retraced. They will redo those batches."

A change in the middle. The journalists had extracted an incriminating sound bite.

"Now that doesn't mean they're going to go and start all over again. What they're going to do is: Those that they have not done yet, will go back to the original policy. They're going to do it this way. And those that were done in any other way, they will go back and redo them. That's as clear as I can make it."

Clear? The explanation had been utterly confusing. And the reporters were far from placated. In fact, they were just getting started.

"The policy you just read doesn't say anything about one corner being detached," said an accusatory voice. "Where did you get that from?"

"I didn't," Nichols said, gesturing to a female reporter. "She brought that up."

"You brought that up," charged a male voice.

"No, I was just answering her question," Nichols insisted.

"If all of us are this confused, how do we know that they understand the rules?" said a journalist, referring to the board members and other ballot counters.

"I can't answer that," Nichols said.

For some reason, the reporters wouldn't let go of this business about one corner of the chad being detached.

"When was it decided that the one corner detached was going to be the standard?" someone demanded. "Because that's not what it—"

"I can't answer the when," said Nichols, now parsing the questions. "I cannot answer when."

"But you said you're adhering to the standards and that's what the standard says," came the rejoinder.

"Excuse me. Listen to me," said Nichols, his nerves obviously fraying. "I can only tell you that this is what they have decided to follow from this point on. There's no point to belabor it."

But belaboring it was precisely what these reporters had in mind. Having been slow to digest the significance of the board's breathtaking fickleness on a matter this important, the press hounds were now in full cry. They had poor Bob Nichols treed.

"Based on what we've heard today, they could again change the standard in a next few hours," a reporter bayed. "There's no written guideline that says—"

"I'm sure you're all watching," Nichols said. "If they do that, you'll know."

"Do they have the right to change it again if they desire?"

"The canvassing board, as you can tell by the statute, they make the rules," Nichols said. "I don't think that will happen. I don't know. But keep watching."

Incredibly, Nichols was hinting at yet another change of standards.

"Will there ever be an end to this with all these controversies?" someone said.

"Trust me, everything has an end," Nichols said with the look of a man who truly wants to believe his own words. "This might not be in a hurry, but it will have an end at some point. Anybody else?"

He was trying to wrap it up, but the reporters were far from finished. They were having a merry old time!

"How are they going to evaluate these ballots?" one of them demanded. "And if Leon is the person who can answer that, why can't he walk out again to answer it?"

"I'm going to tell you one more time," said Nichols, clearly at the end of his rope. "This is it. I will let you read it yourself if you don't like the way I did it."

Still the questions came in great waves.

"One at a time please," Nichols said. "One at a time."

"Let me try to clarify this," began a reporter. "Because Leon did say something about one corner attached and yet it is not in—"

They simply refused to let go of this business about the one corner.

"We'll clear it up," Nichols said.

"Could you clear it up for us now?"

"Who's right, you or Leon?"

Now they were pitting him against his own lawyer, who had deserted Nichols in his hour of need.

"There's no difference," Nichols said. "I am not right or wrong. I'm a conduit of information. And this is the information that I'm telling you."

I am not right or wrong. Another incriminating sound bite! The credibility of Nichols and, by extension, the entire recount was disintegrating before the nation's very eyes. And still the questions kept coming. Another jangle of them filled the air.

"Excuse me," said Nichols, brandishing the 1990 guidelines. "This is the policy that's being followed. The canvassing board made the decision and they're following this policy."

"Why did Leon say something different, then?"

"When will be the next briefing?"

"We're going to do another one for you at 9:00 to give you an opportunity to make sure you know what's going on," Nichols said. "And I will make every effort to get Leon here, too."

"Leon said that if one corner of the chad—," began yet another reporter.

"I'm not going to debate it with you anymore," Nichols snapped. "Write your questions down and get them to me. That's the procedure we set."

By now even the press was beginning to feel sorry for Bob Nichols. CNN, which had been broadcasting live coverage of the news conference, mercifully cut away.

"You've just finished listening to Bob Nichols, Palm Beach County spokesman," said CNN anchor Andria Hall. "And if you did, you might be a little confused as to what they are doing now. How will they judge the invalid ballots there in West Palm Beach?"

Even CNN, which conservatives derisively referred to as the "Clinton News Network," was appalled by the chaos that had overwhelmed the recount. Unable to resist the spectacle of the wheels coming off in Palm Beach County, CNN soon went back to live coverage of Bob Nichols discussing the new American sensation—chad.

"The hanging chad—that is a description of a chad which has been punched, but it is hanging from the top," he said. "They call it the hanging door chad. That is counted.

"The second type is the swinging door, which is counted. It's attached at the top and swings out. A hanging chad will be hanging by one corner. And that's counted.

"The other one that's counted is what they call a tri. And the tri chad also is counted.

"The ones that are not counted are those that are called the pregnant chad. That's where the indentation is there, and it bulges. But the chad doesn't go through in any way.

"The other one that is not counted is the dimple. So those are the descriptions of the kinds of chads."

Nichols then had a brainstorm. He decided to pass out sample ballots to all the reporters and have them take paper clips and try to create the dizzying array of chads he had just described.

"I want you to give it a shot and see what you can do," he said, hoisting a batch of ballots in his beefy, sparkling hand. "You're going to find, I think, that it is very difficult to make a pregnant indention. It's very difficult to make the dimple indention without the chad actually falling through."

Bush operatives monitoring the press conference could scarcely believe their good fortune. Not only had the hand recount gone into unmitigated meltdown in front of the entire nation, but now the spokesman for the Democratic canvassing board was publicly pooh-poohing the very foundation of Gore's hopes for victory—chads that had not been fully dislodged.

"The tri hangs from basically one corner there," Nichols plowed on. "It's hanging on three. Only one corner has been opened up. And it's extremely difficult to do. You try to punch this out and only get one. As hard as you try, it's difficult to do. You'll see when you get a chance at these."

"Is there any way that you all can do that for us?" a reporter whined.

"Well, I've got to tell you the truth—and I'll be totally honest with you: I have a hard time getting them to do that," Nichols confessed. "I can't do it. But the idea is that if it's hanging by one corner, by two corners, or by three corners—but it is punched out like the tri—it counts as a vote. If it's a pregnant and it's attached at the four corners, it's a pregnant one.

"But it's not out, it's not counted. And nor is a dimple. Those are not counted under this procedure. All right, now listen up..."

But CNN had once again had enough. They cut away, this time for good.

"Bob Nichols, Palm Beach County spokesman, adding a new phrase to the political lexicon: a pregnant chad," said CNN host Howard Kurtz. The punch line to a thousand late-night jokes had been born, right there at the Palm Beach County Elections Office.

Other stations, like Fox News Channel, continued to air Nichols's death by a thousand cuts. Again and again, he was asked to explain the shifting standards. No longer attempting to mask his exasperation, Nichols flatly declared: "The standard was not changed. It wasn't changed." Never mind that he had just admitted to two hundred angry reporters and millions of mortified TV viewers that "there was a change in the middle."

Again and again, the exasperated ex-anchorman launched into painfully detailed descriptions of chads in all their bewildering incarnations—pregnant, dimpled, tri, hanging, swinging. When he explained the swinging door chad, he wagged his finger back and forth in an exaggerated impression of a portal hinged not on the side, but at the top, like a pet door.

The cameras kept zooming in on his beefy, tan hands, laden with gold and diamonds. The man must have been wearing half a pound of jewelry. He gesticulated with a batch of ballots, dropping one—but never stopping. He kept emphasizing how it was next to impossible to impregnate a chad.

"If you see the difficulty of doing this, my friends, you're going to understand, you know, exactly what's going on here," he said. "And of course, we certainly hope that you're going to show the world community the same thing."

Oh, the world community had just gotten an eyeful of the vaunted hand recounts that Al Gore insisted were the only fair and accurate way of determining the next president of the United States.

And George W. Bush thanked his lucky stars.

CHAPTER 6

"THE FIRST FAINT WHISPER
OF THE AX"

When the Palm Beach County Canvassing Board finally got around to voting on whether to proceed with a countywide recount, it was 2:15 A.M. on Sunday, November 13. Chairman Charles Burton urged caution, saying the board should ask for an advisory opinion from Florida's Division of Elections, which was part of the secretary of state's office. A lawyer from that office, who happened to be in attendance, said the countywide recount was unwarranted. But board member Carol Roberts pooh-poohed this verbal advice, insisting board members could do whatever they wanted.

What Roberts wanted was a fourth tally—there had already been three machine tallies—of the county's 462,657 ballots. Roberts was a Democratic partisan who openly supported Gore. Although Florida law required canvassing board members to remain neutral in political campaigns, Roberts had attended a rally by Gore's running mate, Joe Lieberman, and festooned her car with a "Gore-Lieberman 2000" bumper sticker. She was encouraged that Gore had netted 19 votes in the chaotic sample recount of 1 percent of the county's precincts. She extrapolated that Gore could net 1,900 votes if 100 percent were recounted. That would be more than enough to reverse the outcome of the election. After all, Bush's statewide lead had dwindled to just over 300 votes.

But Gore, who had the legal right to select the precincts for the sample hand count, had chosen the most overwhelmingly Democratic precincts in the county. Statistically, it would be nearly impossible for him to maintain such a high rate of success in the remaining 99 percent of the precincts. Still, Roberts insisted on pressing forward. At the end of an acrimonious public meeting, she voted for a countywide hand tally. Board member Theresa LePore, who was so dazed that her lawyer had to prop her up as she cast the deciding vote, sided with Roberts.

The chaos of Florida's hand recounts had only just begun.

Later that day, the Volusia County Canvassing Board, which didn't bother with a sample hand recount, plunged ahead with a recount of all 184,000 ballots in the county. As soon as they began the countywide tally, workers discovered hundreds of previously uncounted ballots that had been cast at a place called the DeBary Civic Center in Precinct 305. It turned out that a vote-counting machine there had malfunctioned at around 8:30 A.M. on Election Day. When voters tried to insert their ballots, the machine's computer screen flashed: "Ballot not accepted." The precinct clerk, Rosemary Obenland, unplugged the power cord several times and finally got the machine to work. But it started counting from zero, as if no votes had been cast until that point. Obenland called election headquarters and summoned a workman to replace the defective machine. She explained the whole problem on her ballot accounting form, which she turned in to election headquarters at the end of the day. She also said she verbally told election workers about the snafu.

And yet 320 ballots remained undiscovered until Sunday, a full five days after the election. Red-faced Volusia election officials insisted they would have discovered the ballots even without the hand count. They said the missing votes would have turned up during a review of paperwork before the deadline for certifying final election results, which was November 14. But a review of the paperwork had already been completed. After all, Volusia's response to the original call for a statewide recount had been to merely review the paperwork, not count ballots.

As the recount dragged into Monday and then Tuesday, Gore's gains in Volusia mounted. Republicans complained that the canvassing board, having failed to set standards at the outset, was making up the rules as it went along. Since Volusia County didn't use a punch-card system, there were no arguments over chads. But election officials routinely counted ballots on which voters had clearly failed to follow the instructions.

At 2:30 P.M. on Tuesday, someone phoned in a bomb threat to the Volusia County canvassing board. The caller said: "My vote had better count or the building is going to blow up." But McDermott decided to keep it quiet. The final results were due in less than three hours and the deadline would surely be missed if counters had to evacuate the building for what would probably turn out to be a hoax anyway.

By the time the tally was finished at 4:55 P.M., Gore had a net gain of 98 new votes. The results were immediately handed to a courier sent by Florida Secretary of State Katherine Harris. Volusia County had met the deadline with five minutes to spare. The gang that couldn't shoot straight had redeemed itself, proving once and for all that a countywide recount could be completed by Florida's legally mandated deadline. Suddenly Volusia looked like the only county on Gore's recount list that had its act together. And no bomb had exploded.

Meanwhile, on the Gold Coast, Gore lawyers had been unable to convince the other three counties to even begin full recounts of their 1.7 million ballots. In fact, to the vice president's dismay, the Broward County Canvassing Board voted 2-to-1 on Monday not to proceed with a countywide recount at all. The vote followed a sample recount of 1 percent of Broward's precincts, which netted Gore a paltry four votes. A change that small did not justify a full count, according to the Broward County officials.

The Miami-Dade Canvassing Board came to a similar conclusion. The board didn't even begin its sample count until 4 P.M. on Tuesday—an hour before final results had to be submitted to the Florida Secretary of State. Finishing at 8 P.M., or three hours past the deadline set by state law, the Miami-Dade board voted 2-1 against conducting a countywide tally. Their review of 5,871 ballots had turned up no new votes for Bush and just six for Gore.

The entire Gore strategy was going down in flames. Even Palm Beach, which had voted at 2:15 A.M. on Sunday to proceed with a countywide recount, had not even started the new tally. The board had taken the rest of Sunday off and figured it would have to spend Monday training workers and otherwise preparing for the recount. So it didn't schedule the actual counting of ballots to begin until 7 A.M. on Tuesday—the very day the results were due. Having spent nearly ten hours counting just 1 percent of the precincts, the board now left itself a grand total of ten more hours to tally the remaining 99 percent. (The job would actually take ten days.)

But even those ten hours would elapse without a single ballot being counted. That's because on Monday morning, Republican lawyer J. Reeve Bright of nearby Delray Beach came to the Palm Beach County Canvassing Board meeting and pulled a maneuver that effectively paralyzed the recount for days. When board chairman Charles Burton resumed his public anguishing over whether the board had the legal authority to go ahead with the recount, Bright saw his opening. He knew that if he could get the board to request a written advisory opinion from the secretary of state's office on the legality of hand recounts, that opinion would become legally binding. Florida law specifically states that a county board must abide by any advisory opinion it requests from a state agency. However, if the same advisory opinion is issued verbally, or in the absence of such a request, it has no legally binding authority whatsoever.

Mustering his most angelic demeanor, Bright suggested that perhaps Burton could put everyone's mind at ease by asking the state's division of elections for an opinion. "I'm not saying not to proceed with the recount," Bright added innocently.

The suggestion sounded so reasonable, so reassuring, that Burton immediately agreed. Astonishingly, so did Roberts. The woman who just a day earlier had openly rejected a verbal opinion from the elections division was now seconding Burton's motion to seek a written opinion from the same division. She was oblivious to the danger. Having prevailed in her demand for a full recount at the previous meeting, she felt invincible.

Moving with split-second timing, Reeves buried the hook.

"The request to be made in writing?" he asked innocuously.

"Yes, absolutely, absolutely," Burton replied.

The third member of the canvassing board, Therese LePore, was still too shell-shocked to realize what was happening. She voted with the other two, making the ruling unanimous. Palm Beach County faxed its request to the Division of Elections at 6:03 P.M. Monday.

Clay Roberts, director of the elections division, had been primed for the request. On Sunday, he had received a call from Frank Jimenez, Jeb Bush's acting general counsel. Jimenez wanted to know why the elections division hadn't issued an advisory opinion questioning the legality of hand recounts. Clay Roberts explained that he had already drafted such an opinion, but had not yet received a written request for it.

Thus, when the request from Palm Beach arrived late Monday, Clay Roberts was loaded for bear. He rushed out his advisory opinion that same evening. The opinion said hand recounts were illegal unless there had been a failure in the machinery that counts the votes.

By the time Carol Roberts realized her mistake, it was too late. She tried to proceed with the count anyway, but was reminded by the board's attorney of the law that requires agencies to abide by advisory opinions they have sought. The ruling from the elections division was officially binding unless the board could get a judge to say otherwise.

Gore was livid. He once again turned to Bob Butterworth, manager of his Florida campaign. But Butterworth had already missed his chance. He, like Bright, knew in advance that the board would be bound by any advisory opinion it requested from a state office—including his own. So on Monday, he had personally instructed his staff to call the Palm Beach Board and prod them into requesting an advisory opinion from Butterworth. The board acquiesced on Monday evening, sending a written request for the opinion. But Butterworth's opinion did not arrive until Tuesday, after the board had already locked itself into the opinion from the Division of Elections, which arrived Monday evening.

Thus, the board's plans to commence the countywide tally at 7 A.M. on Tuesday were scrapped. Palm Beach officials would have to go to the Florida Supreme Court before even beginning the countywide recount.

Butterworth was furious. Palm Beach was ignoring his opinion. His office argued that the earlier ruling by Clay Roberts was "clearly at variance" with the law. It was the first time in decades the Florida attorney general's office had issued an advisory opinion on an election issue. In fact, Butterworth's own web page said he had neither the jurisdiction nor the authority to provide advisory opinions on election issues. It said he does not issue opinions "on a question falling within statutory jurisdiction of some other state agency." It added: "Questions arising under the Florida Election Code should be directed to the Division of Elections in the Department of State."

Having now violated his own policy, Butterworth declared that he was "appalled" by Harris's handling of the recounts. It was a startling turnabout for a man who less than a week earlier had gone out of his way to vouch for Harris's integrity. Standing next to Florida Governor Jeb Bush at a news conference the day after the election, Butterworth took pains to "assure the rest of the nation that there is no way that... Secretary of State Harris would certify election results [if she] had any doubt at all they may not be in perfect order." Coming from the chairman of Gore's Florida campaign, the statement had been a powerful and unsolicited testimonial to Harris's honesty. The vice president's go-to guy in Florida was telling the world that Harris was a straight shooter, even though she also happened to be honorary chairman of Bush's Florida campaign.

But now it was time to take a different approach toward Harris. On Monday, November 13, Gore personally instructed his team to smear Florida's chief elections officer. The vice president of the United States, micromanaging the Florida war from the dining room of his residence at the Naval Observatory in Washington, was now directly engaged in the politics of personal destruction. Privately referring to Harris as Cruella De Vil, the puppy-stealing villainess of Dodie Smith's book and Disney's film *101 Dalmatians*, Gore told Deputy Campaign Manager Mark Fabiani and Press Secretary Chris

Lehane to plant damaging press stories that would discredit Harris as a Bush partisan.

Team Gore went after Harris with chilling efficiency. Lehane publicly derided her as a "Soviet commissar." Fabiani denounced her as a Bush "crony." Alan Dershowitz, a Harvard law professor who was helping Gore by representing Palm Beach residents in the butterfly ballot controversy, openly slandered Harris on CNN. "She's a crook," declared the defender of O. J. Simpson. "She's corrupt."

Gore aides had no trouble convincing the press to pursue the story line. Unable to criticize Harris over her enforcement of Florida law, the press resorted to hurling personal invective. Liberal female journalists were especially cruel. On Thursday, November 16, *New York Times* columnist Maureen Dowd told radio shock jock Don Imus that Harris was "obviously trying to steal this election for Jeb." The next day, *Boston Globe* columnist Joan Vennochi called Harris "Florida's ghoulishly made-up secretary of state. Her mask of mascara and eye shadow cannot hide the obvious. Ambition empowers her to hide behind the letter of the law and thwart the spirit of the Constitution."

Warming to this theme, *Washington Post* columnist Robin Givhan delivered an even more vicious personal attack the next day.

"Her lips were overdrawn with berry-red lipstick—the creamy sort that smears all over a coffee cup and leaves smudges on shirt collars. Her skin had been plastered and powdered to the texture of pre-war walls in need of a skim coat. And her eyes, rimmed in liner and frosted with blue shadow, bore the telltale homogenous spikes of false eyelashes. Caterpillars seemed to rise and fall with every bat of her eyelid."

"Her mouth is set in a jagged edge," Givhan noted gravely. "One of the reasons Harris is so easy to mock is because she, to be honest, seems to have applied her makeup with a trowel. At this moment that so desperately needs diplomacy, understatement and calm, one wonders how this Republican woman, who can't even use restraint when she's wielding a mascara wand, will manage to use it and make sound legal decisions in this game of partisan one-upsmanship."

Inexplicably, Givhan continued to obsess over Harris's personal appearance, as if it had some bearing on the post-election struggle in Florida.

"Harris looks harsh," she wrote. "She looks bad."

In one particularly vituperative passage savaging Harris's wardrobe, Givhan came right out and summed up the feelings of the Fourth Estate: "Hate the suit. Hate the buttons. Hate you."

Gore aides were horrified. The press had gone too far. Bouquets of flowers began to pour into Harris's office in Tallahassee. She received 400,000 e-mails of support and prayers from ordinary Americans who were appalled by the smear job.

Harris did her best to ignore the personal attacks. She tried to focus on her duty under Florida law, which was abundantly clear when it came to enforcing deadlines.

"If the county returns are not received by the Department of State by 5 P.M. of the seventh day following an election, all missing counties shall be ignored, and the results shown by the returns on file shall be certified," said Chapter 102.111 of the Florida Statutes.

The statute, enacted in 1978, was still the law of the land. But so was a slightly more flexible law, enacted in 1989, that provided Democrats a glimmer of hope.

"If the returns are not received by the department by the time specified, such returns may be ignored and the results on file at that time may be certified by the department," said Chapter 102.112.

Gore's lawyers pounced on the difference, which they characterized as crucial. While the older law said late returns "shall be ignored," the newer law said they "may be ignored."

Still, the discretion was vested in the secretary of state alone. Harris said she might have been willing to stretch the deadline for "a natural disaster, such as Hurricane Andrew, where compliance with the law would be impossible. But a close election, regardless of the identity of the candidates, is not such a circumstance." On Monday, November 13, Harris preemptively announced that she would stick to the deadline set by Florida law. The public, after all, had a right to closure.

"The law unambiguously states when the process of counting and recounting the votes cast on Election Day must end," Harris said in a written statement. "For this reason, that time is 5 P.M., November 14."

Gore went to court to force Harris to extend the deadline. But Leon County Circuit Judge Terry Lewis, a Democrat, ruled essentially that it was Harris's call to make. Individual judgment is the very definition of discretion.

Still, Harris refrained from certifying the results on Tuesday evening. She invited the Gold Coast counties to tell her, in writing, why she should accept tardy recounts. She gave them until 2 P.M. Wednesday to submit their excuses. When Harris issued this invitation on Tuesday, Palm Beach was the only Gold Coast county that had even voted to proceed with a countywide hand tally. Broward and Miami-Dade had voted against countywide recounts, although Gore's lawyers were already in court trying to force the hands of these canvassing boards.

Meanwhile, the Broward County Canvassing Board, like its counterpart in Palm Beach, had asked the Division of Elections late Monday for an advisory opinion on the legality of hand recounts. In fact, the Broward request was submitted at 4:46 P.M., more than an hour before the Palm Beach request. The Broward request was issued in the midst of the board's sample hand count, which had begun at 3:30 P.M. By the time the sample tally was completed several hours later, the board had received an answer from Clay Roberts of the Division of Elections—a countywide hand tally was illegal unless the machinery had malfunctioned. That opinion is what convinced board chairman Robert W. Lee, a Democrat and the first openly gay judge in Broward County's history, to join the board's lone Republican in opposing the countywide tally.

But Lee's position began to soften the next morning, when the Democratic Party filed a lawsuit in Broward Circuit Court seeking to force his hand. His position softened even further in the afternoon, when Broward Circuit Judge John A. Miller ruled that the board could go ahead with a full count—although Miller could not force Harris to accept the results. Later that afternoon, the board met and decided that it might conduct a full recount after all—but only if the Florida Supreme Court cleared the way. Harris had asked the high court to block all tardy recounts and a decision was expected soon.

To no one's surprise, the Florida Supreme Court rejected Harris's request on Wednesday morning. The court's seven justices, all appointed by Democrats, were unanimous in their ruling.

That was enough for Lee, who switched his vote before noon on Wednesday. The board voted 2-to-1 to conduct a countywide hand recount. A letter requesting an extension of the deadline was sent to Harris before 2 P.M. Almost immediately, election workers began sifting through the county's 587,928 ballots.

Gore was encouraged to see the first of the Gold Coast hand counts finally begin in earnest. But he was growing increasingly worried about Palm Beach, which had still not begun its countywide tally, and Miami-Dade, which was still refusing to conduct a new count. The vice president knew that Broward County alone would probably not give him enough new votes to reverse Bush's victory. He also fretted that the certification by Harris, which was expected at any moment, would have the effect of legitimizing Bush's win. From that point on, Gore would be in the unenviable position of railing against official, state-sanctioned election results that reaffirmed Bush's Election Night triumph. With polls already showing most Americans considered Bush the rightful president, Gore could not afford to lose any more ground in the public relations war. He had to do something—fast.

Gore decided to give a televised address that would preempt Harris. Ever mindful of the media's power, he timed it to coincide with the evening news broadcasts. With his running mate, Joe Lieberman, at his side, Gore stepped before the cameras in his residence at the Naval Observatory.

"What is at stake here is not who wins and who loses in a contest for the presidency, but how we honor our Constitution," Gore intoned. Even his own aides later acknowledged they winced at that line—of course it was about Gore winning or losing. And Republicans couldn't help but be reminded of President Clinton's audacious insistence that the entire Monica Lewinsky scandal had been about defending the Constitution.

"This is a time to respect every voter and every vote," Gore said. "I propose this evening a way to settle this matter with finality and justice, in a period of days, not weeks. First, we should complete hand counts already begun in Palm Beach County, Dade County and Broward County."

Gore promised that if these tallies were included in statewide results, "I will abide by the result, I will take no legal action to challenge the result, and I will not support any legal action to challenge the result. I am also prepared, if Governor Bush prefers, to include in this recount all the counties in the entire state of Florida."

Gore knew his proposal had no chance of being accepted. After all, Bush had gone to a variety of courts in an effort to stop the Gold Coast recounts. Bush's entire post-election philosophy was based on the notion that the votes had been counted once, twice, in some cases three or four times, and he had always come out the winner. He wanted the hand counts to stop.

As for Gore's proposal for a statewide recount, that was an equally empty gesture. A day earlier, Bush spokesman James Baker had said: "The idea that you're going to have a manual recount of all the state of Florida is crazy." Moreover, everyone knew the deadline for requesting hand recounts had expired five days before. And they could be requested only by the loser, not the winner. Besides, there was no provision in Florida law for a statewide hand recount. Such tallies could only be requested on a county-by-county basis. In sum, Gore had no authority at this late date to secure a recount in even a single new county, never mind the entire state.

But Gore was playing strictly for public relations. And he was by no means finished.

"Now, second, I propose that Governor Bush and I meet personally, one-on-one, as soon as possible, before the vote count is finished—not to negotiate, but to improve the tone of our dialogue in America."

The man who had personally instructed his surrogates to unleash a vicious verbal assault on Katherine Harris thought no one would notice the hypocrisy when he called for an improvement in "the tone of our dialogue."

Gore's proposal for a meeting with Bush was telling. It was essentially an acknowledgment that the Texas governor had the upper hand. Gore needed to level the playing field. After all, Bush was the *de facto* winner of the election and had public opinion on his side. Gore figured a joint appearance would suggest to the public that both men, standing side by side for the inevitable photo-op, had an equal claim to the presidency. A meeting would allow some of Bush's legitimacy to rub off on Gore. In fact, the very act of agreeing to such a meeting would be interpreted as a subtle sign of weakness on Bush's part, a tacit admission that perhaps he did not have a lock on the presidency after all.

It was a skillful political ploy, given Gore's dire circumstances. But it also carried the faint whiff of desperation. Gore believed that he was setting a trap that Bush could not possibly escape. He felt that Bush would appear unsportsmanlike if he refused a meeting. Gore would later privately express bewilderment and anger that Bush had not been pilloried for snubbing the vice president's offer.

Three hours after Gore made his speech in Washington, Katherine Harris took her turn before the cameras in Tallahassee. She explained that she had spent the last six hours mulling requests from the Gold Coast counties for deadline extensions.

"As a result of these deliberations, I have decided it is my duty under Florida law to exercise my discretion in denying these requested amendments," Harris said. "The reasons given in their requests are insufficient to warrant waiver of the unambiguous filing deadline imposed by the Florida legislature."

With that, Harris announced that she and the two other members of the state Election Canvassing Commission had conditionally certified the results of the election. George W. Bush was officially ahead by 300 votes. The only ballots remaining to be counted were the absentee votes from overseas, which by law could still be received until midnight Friday.

"I expect that after the receipt, tabulation and certification of the overseas ballots by the counties, the state Elections Canvassing Commission will finally certify the presidential election in Florida on Saturday," Harris said. "The schedule, of course, is subject to judicial intervention."

Although Harris's conditional certification of Florida's statewide results had been expected, Gore's speech had caught Bush by surprise. Unlike the vice president, who was consumed with managing every detail of the all-out legal and political war raging across Florida, Bush had largely gone into seclusion at his ranch in Crawford, Texas. The place was a two-hour drive from Austin and wasn't even wired for cable TV, so Bush was blissfully undistracted by the wall-to-wall coverage of the twenty-four-hour cable news channels. He spent most of his time lying low, planning his transition, and reading a biography of baseball player Joe DiMaggio.

"I was serene," Bush told the author. "I was never dark. My mood was never dark, because I felt like I had given it my all. We had run the best race we could conceivably have run."

By the time Bush got to Austin and stepped before the cameras to respond to Gore's proposal, it was around 10 P.M. Eastern Time. He looked slightly ill at ease, but he got his point across.

"I was encouraged tonight that Vice President Gore called for a conclusion to this process," Bush said. "Unfortunately, what the vice president proposed is exactly what he's been proposing all along: Continuing with selective hand recounts that are neither fair nor accurate, or compounding the error by extending a flawed process statewide.

"This means every vote in Florida would be evaluated differently, by different individuals using different judgment, and perhaps different local standards—or perhaps no standards at all. That would be neither fair, nor accurate. It would be arbitrary and chaotic."

Then Bush slipped the knife in.

"We have a responsibility to conduct ourselves with dignity and honor. We have a responsibility to make sure that those who speak for us do not poison our politics. And we have a responsibility to respect the law, and not seek to undermine it when we do not like its outcome."

The rebuke was extraordinary. Bush had practically come right out and said it: Gore lacked dignity and honor.

"The outcome of this election will not be the result of deals or efforts to mold public opinion. The outcome of this election will be determined by the votes and by the law. Once this election is over, I would be glad to meet with Vice President Gore."

It had been a long time since anyone had so publicly snubbed the sitting vice president of the United States. Worse yet, Bush had dismissed Gore's proposals as sleazy, back room deals and public relations ploys. It was a flashback to the primaries, when Democratic challenger Bill Bradley had pointedly refused to shake Gore's outstretched hand.

By Thursday, however, Democrats were doing some snubbing of their own. In Broward County, Judge Lee pressed on with the countywide recount, despite Harris's rejection of the county's request for a deadline extension. "Of course we're going to continue," said Lee. "Her case was thrown out of the [Florida] Supreme Court. Ours was not. If we get an order from the Supreme Court, we will stop."

Indeed, the Florida Supreme Court was just getting warmed up. One day after rejecting Harris's request to shut down hand recounts, the court on Thursday announced that the tallies could proceed. "There is no legal impediment to the recounts continuing," the court said in its one-paragraph ruling, issued at 4:30 P.M.

That was enough to release Palm Beach County from its self-inflicted paralysis. The canvassing board finally began its countywide hand tally at 7:14 P.M. By this time, there was no guarantee such a count would ever be included in the county's certified results. The deadline for recounts had passed two days earlier and Harris had already announced she would not accept tardy hand counts. She was pressing forward with plans to definitively certify

Florida's statewide results on Saturday, the day after absentee ballots were due from overseas. Thursday's ruling by the Florida
Supreme Court did not force Harris to accept tardy hand counts.
But the Gore lawyers insisted the high court would not have let the
tallies proceed if it didn't want the results to count.

Gore was pinning his hopes on yet another lawsuit, this one
attempting to force Harris to accept the tardy counts. But on Friday
morning, Judge Lewis ruled that Harris had not abused her discretion. The vice president was devastated. In just over twenty-four
hours, Bush would be certified the winner of Florida's twenty-five
electoral votes. Although Gore planned to challenge the certification with another lawsuit, he feared he would take a shellacking in
the court of public opinion by posthumously railing against a bona
fide, certified, official winner. Already his Gore-Lieberman campaign signs had been morphed into "Sore Loserman" signs that
seemed to be multiplying like mushrooms. Republicans, never much
at protesting, had set up camp across the street from the Naval
Observatory. Day and night, they shouted "Get out of Cheney's
house!" so loudly that it could be heard inside Gore's high command. At one point Gore became so rattled that he ordered his aides
to have AFL-CIO President John Sweeney round up some union
members as counter-demonstrators. But Sweeney was nowhere to
be found.

Now the sand seemed to be slipping through the hourglass at
an alarming rate. Although Democrats on Capitol Hill were publicly united in their support of Gore, they privately acknowledged
their patience was wearing thin. Cracks were beginning to develop
in the Democratic front. Even the talking heads began speculating
about a Gore concession. Dan Rather of CBS called the ruling by
Judge Lewis "a bullet through the heart" of Al Gore. Reaching
even deeper into his bottomless bag of Ratherisms, the quirky

anchor remarked that the vice president could now hear "the first faint whisper of the ax."

CHAPTER 7

DISENFRANCHISING GIS

As the sun came up, the hole got more pronounced. When a wave came by, water would go right inside. I mean, it was horrifying."

Navy Lieutenant John Russell was struck by the sheer size of the blackened crater that had been ripped from the hull of the USS *Cole*—it must have been forty feet in diameter. He stood on the fueling pier right next to the stricken destroyer and peered inside the cavity where seventeen fellow sailors had been blown to bits by a terrorist bomb seventeen days earlier.

Russell, forty, was one of those rare navy officers who had come up through the ranks of enlisted men. Ten years and three months it had taken him to earn his commission. Now he was in charge of the technicians who fixed the radar systems, tactical computers, and communications gadgetry aboard the USS *Tarawa*, an amphibious assault ship that Russell liked to refer to as "40,000 tons of twisted steel and sex appeal." The *Tarawa* had been in the Arabian Sea when the call for help came in. The heavily armed ship steamed straight to Yemen to aid the battered *Cole*.

Russell didn't usually pack heat, but now he carried a loaded, 9-millimeter pistol. He had volunteered to man a Yemeni tugboat and pull the crippled *Cole* out of Aden's harbor. He also brought along "somebody to do the shooting"—two sailors, each armed with M-16s. The three men now carefully searched every inch of the tug for weapons or more explosives. They even sent divers underneath to check for booby traps that might be hidden below the waterline. Yemen was crawling with Islamic militants who would love to double America's humiliation by launching a second brazen terrorist strike, this one against the *Cole* rescue operation.

Russell could feel the stares of Yemenis who had crowded along the shore to watch the rescue mission, which the Americans had dubbed "Determined Response." The Arab men wore traditional Yemeni robes with daggers tucked in their waistbands. Some pointed at the *Cole* and jeered. They were glad the American warship was finally leaving. The United States was considered too pro-Israel and anti-Palestinian for local tastes. Besides, the *Cole* was sitting on a prime fishing spot.

"We had to get her out of there," Russell said. "We went over and tied up to the Cole and actually pulled her away from the pier."

Russell maneuvered the tug behind the gaping wound on the port side. Another tug pushed from the starboard side. Two others were up front and began inching the $1 billion ship away from the pier.

By now it was nearly 9:30 A.M. and the shore was teeming with Yemenis, both men and women. They gathered in front of ramshackle buildings and blinked as a gigantic American flag was hoisted above the crippled destroyer, along with smaller flags that signaled it would have difficulty maneuvering.

Slowly, the hulking warship limped through the harbor. It passed the inlet where FBI investigators believed the suicide skiff, laden with explosives, had been launched the morning of October 12. As water lapped lazily in and out of the *Cole*'s yawning ulcer, the little armada puttered past al-Baraiqa, the village where two suspects were said to have constructed the bomb in a rented safe house.

There were still two hundred surviving sailors aboard the *Cole* and they stood at attention as their stricken ship made its unsteady exit. U.S. and Yemeni patrol boats zigzagged along the perimeter, wary of attack vessels disguised as fishing boats. A helicopter gunship hovered overhead. The *Cole*'s sound system defiantly blared "America the Beautiful" and "The Star-Spangled Banner." Even some Yemeni sailors couldn't help but snap to attention as they stood on a rotting pier and the deck of an idle Yemeni frigate.

Over the next several days, the *Cole* was loaded onto a Norwegian cargo ship for the long voyage back to the States. Some of its sailors embarked on the *Tarawa*, where they finally got hot showers and hot meals. They didn't talk much about the tragedy and Russell made a point of not broaching the topic. He even allowed investigators who were probing the attack to take over his office temporarily. As far as Russell was concerned, it was the least he could do.

It was early November and Russell was in the midst of a six-month deployment to the Western Pacific and Indian Ocean. The unexpected detour to Yemen was just part of the job to this career navy man. In fact, the unpredictability had a lot to do with the appeal of being in the armed services. Russell never knew exactly where he was headed next.

That's why he had made a point of voting for president so early that year. Russell, who lived in Jacksonville, Florida, had arranged for the Duval County Elections Office to send him an absentee ballot while at sea. The ballot had arrived October 1 as the *Tarawa* was docked in Thailand. It had come in a batch of mail that was delivered by truck during the ship's last day in port. By the time Russell opened the ballot, the *Tarawa* was steaming through the Indian Ocean toward the Arabian Sea.

"One of the things I've learned when you're deployed overseas is the time it takes the mail to get back," Russell said. "I don't care how quickly you throw it in the mailbox. It can take up to thirty days to get back to the States. So as soon as I got my absentee ballot, I got it witnessed, dated, and threw it back in the mailbox."

Thanks to the unpredictability of navy life, helicopters often must chase down ships in order to pick up and deliver mail. A chopper finally caught up with the *Tarawa* in the Middle East about a week after Russell dropped off his absentee ballot with the ship's postal clerk. The ballot, along with the rest of the ship's mail, was choppered north across the Arabian peninsula and dropped off in the tiny Persian Gulf archipelago of Bahrain. From there it was loaded aboard a military transport plane and flown to the United States, where it was dumped into the civilian postal system on the East Coast before finally making its way south to Florida. Russell's ballot arrived safe and sound at the Duval County Elections Office the day before the election, right about the time Russell was helping host the grief-stricken sailors of the *Cole*.

Russell took voting seriously. His reverence for this fundamental exercise of democracy had been instilled at Fairfax High School in suburban Washington, D.C. One of his teachers was a delegate to the Virginia state legislature.

"He showed us how important it is to vote," Russell recalled. "We were tasked in our senior year to write a bill to get something changed. Well, vehicle inspections in Virginia used to be every six months. We got it changed to a year. That's my claim to fame.

"Ever since then, I've voted. I haven't missed an election yet. Here's my cut on it: If you don't vote, you're voting. You're just saying you don't care what happens."

Like most navy ships, the *Tarawa* picked up the broadcast of Armed Forces Network, which provides sailors in far-flung locales with a taste of American television. In addition to the sports and movies shown by AFN, there was a nightly news feed made available by CNN. In the days after the election, Russell watched with amazement as his home state of Florida erupted into all-out political war over the presidency. He was incredulous that the "butterfly" ballot was roiling Palm Beach. Didn't those people know how to punch a simple hole in a piece of cardboard? And why hadn't they asked for new ballots? They obviously realized they had mistakenly voted for Buchanan or else they never would have subsequently punched the second hole for Gore. Surely they knew they had spoiled their ballots.

As the days stretched into a week and then into a second week, Russell's fascination turned to horror. CNN began reporting that Democratic lawyers had mounted an organized campaign to disqualify overseas ballots cast by members of the military. They were attacking several types of ballots, including those that arrived without a military postmark.

Russell hurried to the *Tarawa*'s onboard post office. He asked the mail clerks if his ballot had been postmarked. They told him no. The only absentee ballots they had bothered postmarking were the ones that sailors mailed in the final days before the election. The clerks had sent those via express mail. But the ballots mailed weeks ahead of time, including Russell's, had not needed a postmark. After all, federal law required that military overseas ballots "shall be carried expeditiously and free of postage." Russell got a sick feeling in his stomach. He had voted in every presidential election since he was old enough in 1980. He fervently hoped that his vote would be counted this time as well.

At 3:30 A.M. on Saturday, November 18, Russell was awakened by the *Tarawa*'s night duty officer. As he crawled out of his bunk, he was startled to hear the officer explain that Russell's wife, Mary, was on the phone. The officer had tried to tell Mary that her husband was sleeping, but she insisted he be awakened and brought to the phone. Mary had used the emergency number given to spouses of sailors. Something major must be wrong back home.

Russell was disoriented when he reached the phone and heard his wife's voice. He was still off the coast of Yemen, eight thousand miles from Jacksonville, and the phone connection had a distracting voice delay. Mary explained that she had just gotten home from taking their two children out to dinner when she received a phone call from a woman at the Duval County Elections Office. The woman told her that Russell's absentee ballot had just been disqualified at the urging of Democratic lawyers. A few minutes later, Mary had received a second call, this time from a man with the Republican Party. He confirmed that Russell's ballot had been disqualified, along with hundreds of others that the Democrats had protested. It was 7:30 P.M. on Friday in Jacksonville and the Republicans were in the midst of a fierce battle with the Democrats down at the Elections Office. In fact, they had been fighting since 9 A.M. that morning and looked like they were nowhere close to being finished.

"I was hot," Russell said. "Here I am, deployed overseas. I've done everything I can to cast my ballot properly. And I find out my vote doesn't count because of a lousy postmark—even though they received it before Election Day. Oh, I was torqued. Especially after that Palm Beach crap. They weren't confused about the ballot! And yet it looked like their votes were going to be counted. But to hell with the military.

"I commenced firing," Russell said. "Hard."

Years before Ed Fleming became a lawyer in Pensacola, Florida, he was a newspaper reporter for the European *Stars and Stripes*, which is owned by the Defense Department. The experience taught him many things, two of which came in very handy on Wednesday, November 15.

Fleming was among the small army of Republican attorneys who had mobilized to help Bush stave off Gore's desperate quest to overturn the election. On Wednesday morning, he received a phone call from the GOP's legal command center in Tallahassee.

"There was a rumor that there was going to be concerted, organized opposition to try to keep out the military votes, and so they asked me if I would monitor the situation here in northwest Florida," Fleming said. "I knew the county attorneys around here, so I called Tom Dannheisser, who's the county attorney in Santa Rosa County."

Dannheisser passed along a tantalizing piece of information to Fleming. He had just received a five-page memo—dated that day— from a Democratic lawyer outlining the entire Democratic game plan for disqualifying military ballots. Its author was Mark Herron, the lawyer who had lost his job at a Tallahassee law firm for enlisting in Gore's post-election army.

"Herron distributed what obviously was intended to be a confidential memo to their lawyers, to give them reasons to challenge the ballots," Fleming said. "But one of the attorneys that they hired locally to do that said: 'Well, gee, this seems good. I'll just send it to the county attorney in advance, so he'll know what points I'm going to make at the canvassing board meeting.' So he sent it to the county attorney of Santa Rosa. It was one of the dumber lawyers that had been retained by the Florida Democratic Party."

Fleming asked Dannheisser if he had received this memo in his capacity as county attorney. When Dannheisser said yes, Fleming said he was making an official request for the memo, which was now a public record. Dannheisser told Fleming to put the request in writing. Fleming complied and, by Thursday, he was holding the Gore team's "smoking gun." He pored over the document, which instructed Democratic lawyers to make all sorts of pettifogging objections to the military ballots, especially those that arrived without a postmark. Having spent several years as a Defense Department employee in Europe, Fleming knew that mail was often sent without a postmark. He began to formulate arguments he could make to counter the Democrats' antimilitary campaign.

"I sent the memo up to Tallahassee that afternoon and it all started from there," Fleming said with a chuckle. "I thought it was funny. Of course, being a former newspaper reporter, I knew that secrets went out the window with the advent of the Xerox machine. You never put anything in writing that you do not intend to get into the wrong hands, because Murphy's Law will come true. It will get into the wrong hands."

Upon receiving the Herron memo, the Bush command center in Tallahassee promptly blast-faxed it to Republican lawyers in all sixty-seven counties. The military ballots would be publicly tallied the next day by canvassing boards all across the state.

Nowhere would that battle of the ballots be fiercer than in Duval County, which was home to more military families than any other county in Florida. Tens of thousands of active duty sailors were based at massive installations like the Mayport Naval Station and the Jacksonville Naval Air Station. A huge chunk of the Atlantic fleet, including the USS *John F. Kennedy* battle group, called Duval County its home port. In fact, pretty much every sailor stationed along the East Coast at some point came through Jacksonville.

So it was no surprise that Duval had more absentee overseas ballots than any other county—618 of the 3,500 cast statewide.

Neither was it a surprise that five Gore lawyers showed up at the Duval County Elections Office at 9 A.M. Friday to disqualify as many of those ballots as possible.

Tom Bishop was one of the GOP lawyers who volunteered to counter the Gore assault in Duval County. He grew increasingly angry as he watched the Democrats, armed with the Herron memo, systematically disqualify large numbers of military ballots.

"They had their little cheat sheet they were using and they objected on every single possible ground they could, no matter how spurious," Bishop said. "It was so bad that there was rolling of the eyes by even some of the Democrats there who were watching their lawyers work."

Prior to November 17, the supervisor of elections checked the signatures on all ballot envelopes against signature cards on file at the elections office. He determined that only two absentee ballots could not be included because the signatures did not match.

But now the Democrats insisted that they be allowed to compare all signatures, one by one. For seven tedious hours, they bitterly argued that signatures on more than one hundred envelopes did not precisely match the signature cards—although some of the envelopes had been signed by sailors on rolling seas in hostile situations. Literally, the Gore lawyers objected if an "i" was not dotted or a "t" was not crossed in exactly the same manner as on the signature cards.

"You could clearly tell it was the same person's signature, but they would object because it didn't have a certain curlicue or didn't have a certain twist or it was smaller," Bishop said.

Even more infuriating were the attempts by Democrats to disqualify military ballots that had no overseas postmark. The ostensible logic behind this argument was that some voters might have marked their ballots a day or two after the election and then mailed them in. But the Gore lawyers took this argument to absurd lengths by actually disqualifying ballots that were received by the elections office before November 7. One of these ballots belonged to a sailor named John Russell, whose vote was unceremoniously thrown out.

"I don't know how somebody in the Sea of Japan or the Indian Ocean could have miraculously gotten it here on the 6th of November if it was supposedly mailed after the election," Bishop said. "The whole idea behind the foreign postmark is to make sure it's timely.

"All day long, there was a consistent pattern of doing everything they could to exclude ballots," he said. "It particularly stinks in the nostrils of a trial lawyer, like I am, because we have a certain thing that you learn when you're young at the bar, which is: You only make objections which are good for your client. What stunned me was that the Democrats had completely lost the big picture. They weren't going to win some of the objections, but they made them anyway. And even the ones where they could make an argument on the technical letter of the law, I couldn't believe this was the position the Democratic Party wanted to take on these ballots.

"They really wanted to knock these votes out on very hypertechnical reasons, even though they were the party who had been arguing for weeks about including and counting every ballot. So I thought it was a strange tactic. They were being really overly zealous advocates who weren't thinking at all about the big picture of what was right and wrong."

The Gore lawyers protested against ballots on which the return address of the attesting witness was incomplete. They also railed against ballots on which the foreign postmarks were smudged or even partially illegible. The Democrats would not back down, even when the Bush team hastily produced an affidavit from the chief postal clerk on the USS *John F. Kennedy*.

"It is not unusual for mail being sent by naval personnel, whether embarked on naval vessels or otherwise, to not have a postmark," wrote Chief Petty Officer Edgardo Rodriguez. "The ballots of military men and women should not be disqualified because of some technical issue arising under state law."

Even a letter from the deputy director of the Defense Department's military postal service did not sway the Gore lawyers.

"There are instances when time constraints do not allow for proper postmarking/cancellation of the mail," wrote Navy Captain E. M. DuCom. "The last flight may be departing the ship and the mail has to get on it. Personnel are working twelve to sixteen hours a day and then have to go on a four-hour watch during the night, so they are often scrambling to get their mailings done in a timely manner. No one is going to refuse to take a letter or ballot at the last minute because they do not have time to postmark it. It could be weeks before they see mail service again."

But the Democrats stood their ground. "Our goal was to challenge every vote that didn't appear legitimate," said Mike Langton, Gore's campaign chairman for northeast Florida.

By 7 P.M., the Democrats had lodged protests against 147 of the absentee ballots. The canvassing board agreed to hear formal arguments from both the Gore and Bush camps, but the lawyers spent another half hour bickering over who would go first. When it was finally decided that Gore lawyer Leslie Goller would go first, Circuit Judge Brent Shore, chairman of the Duval County Canvassing Board, expressed incredulity at her tactics. It was Shore's twenty-seventh wedding anniversary and he had promised to take his wife out to dinner, but now it looked as though he would spend the rest of the night listening to Democratic objections.

"I want to make sure that I understand your position," Shore said to Goller. "As I understand your position, if a service person in Germany avails himself or herself to free postage through the military, provides the absentee ballot on or before November 7th to be mailed in the normal course of through the military postal system, or otherwise, and they get the free postage, if that absentee ballot envelope, probably unbeknown to the person who mailed it, does not bear a postmark on it, even though it's otherwise proper, your position is that is an invalid ballot, and we should not consider it—is that correct?"

"That is our position," Goller replied.

Shore and the other board members spent the next three hours examining the 147 ballots the Gore lawyers wanted to toss. This was followed by hour after hour of endless wrangling, bad pizza, and stale coffee.

As the Republican lawyers argued, their political counterparts intensified the public relations war. GOP operatives tracked down the spouses of service members whose ballots had been disqualified. The spouses were urged to express their outrage to the local and national press. E-mails were sent to soldiers and sailors who were scattered in far-flung theaters, explaining that their votes had been tossed. The servicemen were invited to sound off about this outrageous disenfranchisement.

At 4:11 A.M.—more than nineteen hours after it began—the nightmarish battle over Duval's military ballots finally came to an end. Duval was the last of Florida's sixty-seven counties to complete the arduous task. When the canvassing board announced that the ballots of 149 soldiers, sailors, and airmen had been disqualified, a pair of jubilant Gore lawyers exchanged high-fives.

A Republican, visibly shaken by this sight, demanded to know how they could celebrate the disenfranchisement of U.S. military members risking their lives around the world. One of the Gore lawyers glibly replied: "A win's a win."

Of the Duval ballots that were counted, 318 went for Bush and 151 for Gore. Thus, Bush had netted 167 votes in Duval, his biggest single gain in the county-by-county tallying of overseas ballots. He netted another 493 votes in the other sixty-six counties, giving him a one-day total of 630 votes. Overnight, Bush's 300-vote lead had more than tripled to 930 votes.

Still, Republicans were angry that Gore's team had succeeded in disqualifying 1,420 ballots statewide—or more than 40 percent of the 3,500 votes cast. They vowed to go to court, if necessary, to resurrect as many of those ballots as possible in the coming days.

Particularly incensed was Dick Cheney, the former defense secretary who had overseen the Gulf War. Of all the dirty tricks attempted by Gore during the post-election struggle, Cheney considered this the dirtiest.

"I have strong feelings about the right of our people in uniform to vote—and they, perhaps, above all others," Cheney told the author. "They're out there putting their lives on the line for us. For the other camp to pursue a conscious strategy to try to disqualify their ballots, I thought, was bad form."

As for those ballots the Bush lawyers had managed to include, they attributed much of their success to their sneak peek at the Herron memo, which provided a virtual roadmap of the Gore strategy. But the Herron memo paid even greater dividends in the all-important public relations war.

In fact, Republicans had already begun leaking the memo to the media, which had little choice but to portray it as a calculated effort on Gore's part to disqualify the very soldiers and sailors he sought to command as president. On Saturday, the Bush forces decided to press their advantage.

"The vice president's lawyers have gone to war in my judgment against the men and women who serve in our armed forces," thundered Montana Governor Marc Racicot at a news conference. "In an effort to win at any cost, the Democrats have launched a statewide effort to throw out as many military ballots as they can."

Racicot, a fervent Bush backer, noted that Gore's bid to dis-qualify military votes came just as the *Miami Herald* was reporting that at least thirty-nine felons, including murderers and rapists, had managed to vote illegally. Most were registered Democrats.

"How can felons be allowed to vote, while the men and women in our armed forces cannot?" Racicot said. "That's simply not right."

Bush spokeswoman Karen Hughes was even more blunt.

"A targeted effort by the Democratic Party sought to throw out as many as a third of the overseas absentee ballots received since Election Day—many of them the votes of the men and women of our United States armed forces, who are serving the cause of freedom throughout the world," Hughes said. "No one who aspires to be commander-in-chief should seek to unfairly deny the votes of the men and women he would seek to command."

Gore was horrified. The TV networks and newspapers were going wild with the hypocrisy angle. For the first day since the post-election standoff began, there was no public statement from the vice president or press conference by his representatives in Tallahassee to counter the Bush offensive. The Democrats were being crucified and they knew it would only get worse if they stepped before the cameras.

The Bush team would not let up. They arranged for retired Army General Norman Schwarzkopf, the hero of the Gulf War, to issue a blistering statement.

"It is a very sad day in our country when the men and women of the armed forces are serving abroad and facing danger on a daily basis in places like Bosnia, Kosovo, or on ships like the USS *George*

Washington, yet because of some technicality out of their control they are denied the right to vote for the president of the United States, who will be their commander-in-chief," Schwarzkopf said. "These men and women do not have the luxury of getting in their cars and going to the post office to mail their ballots. They must depend upon a system that takes their ballot directly from their front line positions on a circuitous route to the ballot box.

"At the same time, because of other perceptions of irregularity, other ballots that have already been counted twice and are now being counted a third time," he added. "For the sake of fairness alone, these armed forces ballots should be allowed to be tallied."

The military ballot episode had turned into a fiasco for the Gore camp. The vice president was getting creamed in the press. He had no choice but to dispatch his running mate, Joe Lieberman, to do damage control on the Sunday morning political shows. Incredibly, the plan was for Lieberman to stick to his guns and actually try to defend the massive disqualification of military ballots. He was prepped on this strategy by no less an authority than Mark Herron himself, who spoke with Lieberman and other Gore officials on a conference call from Tallahassee late Saturday.

But when faced with the pointed questions of Tim Russert on NBC's *Meet the Press*, Lieberman began to waver from his prepared script.

"Will you today, as a representative of the Gore campaign, ask every county to re-look at those ballots that came from armed services people and waive any so-called irregularities or technicalities which would disqualify them?" Russert demanded.

"I don't know that I have that authority," Lieberman hedged. "I don't believe I do legally, or in any other way."

Although Lieberman was one of the most zealous crusaders in the post-election debacle, he was also a shrewd enough politician to realize, right there on the spot, that he had been sent on a fool's errand. He began to signal his ambivalence about the whole anti-military campaign. Asked whether he knew anything about Herron, Lieberman said no—even though he had been talking with him the night before! Lieberman also tried to distance himself from Herron's controversial memo.

"I checked with our campaign last night when I heard about this, because I was upset about it," said Lieberman, who was careful not to mention it had been Herron himself he consulted. "I've been told that the directions to our personnel were pretty much the same as the Republican people had, which is: Just make sure the law is followed. That's all."

Actually, the marching orders that were issued to Republican lawyers for the overseas absentee ballots were the exact opposite of the instructions to Team Gore. The Democratic lawyers were instructed to object whenever possible to every military ballot. By contrast, the Republicans had strict instructions to count every military ballot, even those in counties where the voters had marked the outside of their envelopes with a tell-tale "D," to signify Democrat. The Bush lawyers actually waged successful battles to count Gore votes.

While Lieberman acknowledged that "the benefit of the doubt" should be given to absentee military voters, he hastened to add that "it's got to be done by the law." In other words, he was continuing to defend the disqualification of military ballots on technical grounds, even if these were logically absurd. Still, the press gave him credit for softening his stance. Reporters would have been much less forgiving if they had known that Lieberman had consulted with Herron the night before. They would have been even less forgiving if they had been able to witness the angry reactions of Herron and the rest of Gore's high command as they watched themselves being betrayed on national television.

Besides, even if Lieberman had been able to bring himself to make a full-throated denunciation of the antimilitary campaign, it would have been meaningless. The ballots had already been disqualified. It was now safe for Lieberman to backpedal a bit. On Sunday, November 19, it appeared that while Gore might be losing the public relations battle over military ballots, he had won the war, sharply limiting what could have been a much bigger vote pickup for Bush.

That evening, cyber-journalist Matt Drudge posted the entire text of Herron's memo on his immensely popular web site, the *Drudge Report*. Millions of Internet users were able to peruse the five-page blueprint in its entirety. Although the liberal press scorned Drudge, his site was still considered must reading, and he had just given the story a major boost.

More military testimonials became public. One of the most powerful came from a naval flight officer who was serving aboard the USS *George Washington* in the Adriatic Sea. His name was Lieutenant Chad Krug. That's right, Chad. The Gore campaign was fighting tooth and nail to count every type of chad imaginable—dimpled, pregnant, hanging, swinging, and otherwise. But there was one type of chad that Gore most definitely did not want to count—Lieutenant Chad. The press ate it up.

"I must tell you that I have been watching the election proceedings as closely as I can, and I am very disappointed to find that my vote will be casually cast aside," Lieutenant Chad wrote. "It is ironic that some of the trash I have seen thrown in the streets of countries that I have visited is given more weight and respect than my absentee ballot.

"How did this happen? I dropped the envelope containing my ballot in the U.S. Post Office on board my ship, just as I am sure thousands of naval personnel did. I believe that dismissing these

absentee ballots is certainly wrong, and the Florida election officials should reconsider. I voted because I wanted my voice to be
heard. Isn't that what the democracy which I protect is really all
about?"

Republicans arranged for Chad's wife, Abby, to appear on
NBC's *Today* show. Katie Couric joked about the naval officer's
first name.

"Chad," she said. "Yes, that's right—Chad. Oy!"

Couric then showed her true colors.

"Republican officials contacted you and asked if you'd be willing to talk with members of the media, correct?" Couric asked
Mrs. Krug. "Did you have any trepidation about that, Abby?
Feeling that you might be brought into sort of a PR campaign by
either side?"

Couric then turned to another guest, Palm Beach County resi-
dent Seth Wirshba, who claimed he had been confused by the butterfly ballot into voting for two presidential candidates. Couric did
not ask Wirshba whether he had been contacted by the DNC's telemarketing firm, TeleQuest, as part of a "PR campaign" by Gore
lawyers. Instead, she complained that "his vote isn't counting either."
Couric had no way of knowing whether Wirshba's vote counted,
since it was impossible to trace ballots that had been cast in person
at Florida's polling sites. And yet she equated him with Lieutenant
Chad, whose disenfranchisement had been thoroughly documented,
thanks to the paper trail left by absentee ballots from overseas. Not
to mention the fact that Lieutenant Chad had done everything he was
supposed to do to cast his ballot properly. Anyone confused by the
butterfly ballot, on the other hand, had no one to blame but himself.

Sensing that the public's distrust of the press could inflame the
military ballot controversy even further, Republicans resurrected a
transcript of *Time* magazine's Margaret Carlson bashing overseas

military voters. On MSNBC's *Imus in the Morning* show, Carlson accused soldiers and sailors of choosing Florida as their home state because it had no income tax. She implied that their votes should therefore not be counted at all.

"Here we will have possibly a bunch of tax dodgers deciding the election," Carlson complained.

"I don't think," countered host Don Imus, "we want to refer to people serving in the military as tax dodgers, do you?"

"No, but they've chosen a state of convenience, like going to the Cayman Islands," Carlson insisted. "I mean, this is just taking this tax issue a little too far."

"People who are serving in the military, Ms. Carlson, are already grossly underpaid," Imus said. "Trying to take advantage of the tax laws in Florida, I think, can hardly be referred to as tax dodging. God, what the hell has happened to you?"

But Carlson insisted that service members are paid plenty. "When you put everything together, they do just fine," she said.

"No wonder people hate liberals, hate the press," Imus muttered.

Carlson's accusations struck a raw nerve among military families, thousands of whom were so underpaid they were forced to subsist on food stamps. But even those who were not on food stamps were outraged that the press would label them "tax dodgers."

Senior Chief Petty Officer Michael Gentry, who had been with the navy fifteen years, railed against Carlson in an e-mail that was distributed by Republicans.

"Voting is a serious matter to me and I am frustrated with those who... would so arrogantly call us 'tax dodgers,'" Gentry fumed. "I feel as if I have been slapped in the face and told my vote isn't important.

"Well, I beg to differ on this matter. This election, of all elections, may very well come down to that one vote that makes the difference. I and so many others like me who serve this great nation deserve to be heard!

"We expect our leaders to serve us with the same honor, courage and commitment that we serve them," Gentry concluded. "The U.S. military votes must count. The office of president affects those of us in the military more directly than any other citizen and counting our vote is simply the RIGHT THING TO DO! If they will count dimpled chad, but not the military vote that lacks a postmark—give me a break."

The damage to Gore's camp was incalculable. Public pressure became so intense that even Bob Butterworth, Gore's campaign manager in Florida, ran for political cover later on Monday. He very publicly issued a memo to the sixty-seven canvassing boards, asking them to reconsider the disqualified military ballots.

"Based upon news media reports, it appears that some of these ballots may have been rejected due to the lack of a postmark," Butterworth wrote. "This office urges supervisors and canvassing boards in any county which has received such ballots to immediately revisit this issue and amend their reported vote totals, if appropriate."

And yet Butterworth, like Lieberman, hastened to add that the ballots still had to comply with the technical letter of the law when it came to dates and postmarks and signatures. Gore's go-to guy in Florida just couldn't bring himself to unconditionally urge the counting of all military ballots. And, like Lieberman, Butterworth only softened his stance after the ballots had already been disqualified and it was too late to resurrect them.

At least Gore thought it was too late.

CHAPTER 8

STANDARDS DU JOUR

Despite Gore's success at disqualifying some 1,420 absentee ballots, enough military votes were counted on Friday, November 17, to more than triple Bush's lead from 300 to 930. As if that weren't enough bad news for one day, Gore learned that the recounts underway in Broward and Palm Beach counties weren't turning up nearly enough votes to eclipse Bush's newly swollen lead. And although the Miami-Dade canvassing board reversed itself on Friday by voting to proceed with a county-wide hand tally after all, board members warned they could not complete such a monumental undertaking until December, which seemed a long way off. And even if Gore survived that long, it seemed doubtful such a tally would be added to the official statewide returns. Democratic Judge Terry Lewis issued a ruling that same Friday that Katherine Harris had not abused her discretion by refusing to accept tardy counts.

But just when it looked as though Gore was out of options, lightning struck. The Florida Supreme Court, acting on its own volition, issued a ruling late Friday that blocked Harris from giving final certification of Florida's election results the next day. Having dipped their toes several times into the roiling sea of post-election controversy, the seven justices now jumped in up to their necks. They scheduled oral arguments from both sides for Monday.

Gore was jubilant. The ruling, at the very least, bought him some time. He now had all weekend in which to pull ahead in the hand recounts. Perhaps that would put him in the driver's seat for Monday's arguments. And Florida's Supreme Court was considered one of the most liberal, activist benches in the nation. It was the place where Gore had hoped the case would end up all along. He went on television again that night to make his pleasure known.

"The American people want to make certain that every vote counts," Gore said. "That is why I am pleased the hand counts are continuing. They are proceeding despite efforts to obstruct them. And that is why the decision just announced by the Florida Supreme Court preventing the Florida secretary of state from certifying the election results tomorrow is so important."

Gore's lawyers promptly filed briefs arguing that Katherine Harris had broken state laws by excluding tardy recounts from the certified election totals, and by issuing binding opinions that ruled out hand counts. The Florida Supreme Court justices read these arguments over the weekend and decided they agreed—even before they had heard the first word of oral arguments scheduled for Monday. In fact, they actually drafted their decision ahead of time. Bush lawyers were tipped off that the court would extend the certification deadline to Sunday, November 26. The oral arguments would be a mere formality.

Sure enough, as TV cameras rolled during Monday afternoon's oral arguments, the justices pretended that they hadn't yet made up their minds. They asked tough questions of both sides to demonstrate their ostensible evenhandedness. They even sat on their decision for more than twenty-four hours in order to give the impression that it was written only after carefully weighing the oral arguments.

Just before 10 P.M. on Tuesday, the Florida Supreme Court publicly unveiled what had been a foregone conclusion. In a forty-two-page ruling, the justices accused Harris of trying to disenfranchise voters by adhering to the deadlines set by Florida law.

"An accurate vote count is one of the essential foundations of our democracy," the unanimous ruling stated. "The will of the people, not the hypertechnical reliance upon statutory provisions, should be our guiding principle in the elections."

In other words, the court told Bush he was being too much of a stickler about Florida law. The important thing was to count votes, even if that meant bending the rules a bit. The court unilaterally—and arbitrarily—ruled that hand recounts must be added to the statewide totals if they were completed by Sunday, November 26. Never mind the state law that said all returns had been due on November 14. Never mind the state law that gave Katherine Harris sole discretion over whether to accept late tallies. Florida's high court unanimously swept away the legislature's carefully crafted election scheme and created its own—complete with a new calendar. Not a single justice dissented. While Gore had failed to post even a tentative lead over the weekend, the Florida Supreme Court now gave him another 115 hours to try. And just in case Bush had any crazy ideas about appealing the decision to federal court, the justices inserted a footnote that insisted the case contained no federal or constitutional issues. Suddenly, Al Gore was back in business.

"The Florida Supreme Court has now spoken," said Gore, who added that he was "gratified" by the court's "wise" decision. "We will move forward now with a full, fair and accurate count of the ballots in question. I don't know what those ballots will show.

I don't know whether Governor Bush or I will prevail, but we do know that our democracy is the winner tonight."

Although Bush had been trying to keep a low profile up until now, the decision by the Florida Supreme Court prompted him to take the gloves off.

"The court cloaked its ruling in legalistic language, but make no mistake: The court rewrote the law. It changed the rules. And it did so after the election was over," Bush said. "Manual recounts will continue in three selective counties with no uniform standards, no clear direction and, therefore, no fair or accurate result."

Although the decision by the Florida Supreme Court was a devastating blow to the Bush team, Republicans decided to make the best of a bad situation. Now that the court had extended the certification deadline, Bush lawyers concluded it was not too late to resurrect the military ballot issue after all. Moreover, the Florida Supreme Court had insisted that votes should not be disqualified by hypertechnicalities. Bush lawyers decided to turn that argument against canvassing boards that had thrown out military ballots for lacking postmarks and other such hypertechnicalities. On Wednesday, November 22, they filed a lawsuit against thirteen counties that had tossed ballots on hypertechnical grounds. Before the suit could even be processed, the Bush lawyers directly contacted the canvassing boards and demanded new hearings so that the issue of military ballots could be revisited.

The Florida Supreme Court "hypertechnical" ruling was not the only piece of fresh evidence wielded by the Republicans. They were now armed with Butterworth's memo urging the canvassing boards to soften their stance on military ballots. In addition, the Republicans had Lieberman's backpedaling words from the Sunday talk shows. The canvassing boards had little choice but to reconsider the issue. Gore lawyers showed up at these hearings, but found themselves in a supremely awkward position. It was difficult for the Democrats to continue arguing forcefully to disqualify military ballots now that the issue had become a political disaster for Gore. So the Democrats were a little sheepish at this second round of canvassing board meetings. And yet, incredibly, they continued to file hypertechnical objections to hundreds of ballots, refusing to withdraw them even in the face of overwhelming public opposition. Gore officials wanly tried to distance themselves from these continued objections, but by now it was clear that the vice president's own lawyers were explicitly directing the antimilitary effort. Herron was not some freelancer who just happened to have a personal aversion to military ballots. He had been directly hired by the Gore campaign and was so devoted to the vice president that he was willing to give up his job at a Tallahassee law firm to enlist in the post-election crusade. Mike Langton, one of the lawyers who vociferously objected to military ballots in Duval County, was no less than the chairman of Gore's northeast Florida campaign. Despite Lieberman's insistence that he never read the Herron memo, both he and Gore were intimately familiar with its contents.

The canvassing boards felt compelled to count at least some of the military ballots they had previously discarded. One of the ballots belonged to Lieutenant John Russell of the USS *Tarawa*. The process netted Bush another 176 votes.

Meanwhile, Gore was finding it surprisingly difficult to enact his two-pronged strategy for the hand recounts, which amounted to pressuring the canvassing boards to both proceed with the tallies and adopt the most liberal standards possible.

For starters, all four counties had hesitated to conduct full recounts. The GOP-dominated Volusia canvassing board relented only after being strong-armed by Butterworth. But even the Gold Coast boards, whose nine members included only one Republican, were reluctant to proceed. Broward and Miami-Dade, both of which initially rejected countywide tallies, were softened up by a series of Gore lawsuits and a barrage of political pressure from the Democratic Party. They finally caved after the Florida Supreme Court began issuing a series of short, pro-Gore rulings in the days before its sweeping overhaul of the electoral system.

Even the chairman of the all-Democrat Palm Beach County Canvassing Board, Judge Charles Burton, had voted against a countywide hand tally in the beginning. He had been outvoted only because the other two members of the board happened to be Gore loyalists. Carol Roberts was a feisty, openly partisan Gore supporter who at one point vowed to plow ahead with the recount even if that meant she had to go to jail. Democrat Theresa LePore supported the recount as a way of redeeming herself for designing the infamous butterfly ballot.

But even after the board voted 2-to-1 to proceed with the countywide tally, Palm Beach spent days waiting for the Florida Supreme Court to rule on whether it could legally proceed. Impatient for the vote counting to begin, Warren Christopher, Gore's top spokesman, and Alan Dershowitz, the vice president's advocate in the butterfly ballot case, each called Bruce Rogow, counsel for the Palm Beach board, on Thursday, November 16. Rogow, a registered Democrat and law professor in neighboring Broward County, was appalled by this naked power play. The pressure from Christopher, a former secretary of state, was particularly galling.

"There was nothing subtle about this," Rogow told the *New York Times.* "Warren Christopher does not call me every day to chat.

"But I found it inappropriate," he added. "These people care more about the spin than the law."

Rogow told the Associated Press that Christopher's call "was an effort to have me persuade my client in favor of starting the manual recount on Thursday. I told him no. I told him we'd have to wait."

He added: "I thought everyone got the message that the best thing to do was let me be a lawyer and not a politician."

Hours after Rogow rebuffed Gore's advances, the Florida Supreme Court gave Gore what he wanted anyway. But the strong-arm tactics continued even after the hand counts got rolling. In Broward and Palm Beach counties, Gore superlawyer David Boies resorted to a false affidavit in order to help convince the canvassing board to adopt a more liberal standard in counting ballots. The document erroneously asserted that an Illinois judge had ruled in 1990 that ballots must be counted even if there was no light visible through the dimpled chad.

Boies got the affidavit by calling a Democratic lawyer named Michael E. Lavelle at midnight on Tuesday, November 21. Lavelle swore out the statement the next morning. Boies used the affidavit in appearances before the Broward and Palm Beach canvassing board on Wednesday. When the falsehood was exposed by the *Chicago Tribune*, Lavelle hastened to swear out a second affidavit.

"My mistaken recollection was that the trial judge counted 'indented or dimpled ballots' where light did not shine through," Lavelle wrote. "In fact, the trial judge only counted 'indented or dimpled ballots' that light could pass through."

Lavelle faxed the second affidavit to Boies, but it was never forwarded to the canvassing boards, according to Burton Odelson, a GOP attorney monitoring hand counts on the Gold Coast.

Both Palm Beach and Broward adopted more liberal vote counting standards after receiving the false affidavit. But it was not the only pressure point brought to bear by Gore. In fact, the vice president had filed numerous lawsuits to force the boards to loosen their standards. The suits were filed even as Warren Christopher publicly championed the right of local boards to devise their own standards and even as Gore publicly praised the very people he was suing.

"I want to thank the citizen volunteers, no matter their political party, also the public officials involved in the canvass, all these people who have given enormous amounts of time in an extraordinary effort," Gore said on November 21, as his lawyers took these same citizens to court. "They're doing their jobs diligently and seriously, under difficult conditions, as Americans always do. They are rising to the occasion."

The constant pressure from Gore forces resulted in vote-counting standards that changed almost continuously, both from one county to another and within individual counties. Indeed, one needed a scorecard to keep up with the ever-shifting standards.

Palm Beach County was by far the most fickle of the lot. The board started out with one standard and then changed its rules no fewer than five separate times. These changes continued even after the wild swings during the sample recount on November 11. In the four-and-a-half days between completing the sample count and beginning the full count, Palm Beach officials came up with yet another standard. The board decided to count only chads on which two corners were detached because that was the standard adopted by the Broward canvassing board, which had already begun its countywide tally. Palm Beach officials wanted to be consistent with their neighbors to the south. But they didn't bother going back through the 4,695 ballots they had examined in the sample count to retroactively apply the new, stricter standard.

Then things got even more complicated. Before Palm Beach could begin using the two-corner rule it had copied from Broward, the Broward board changed its own rules. Bowing to pressure from Boies—and his false affidavit—as well as the barrage of lawsuits from Gore and overt political pressure from the Democratic Party, the Broward board agreed to jettison its strict two-corner rule and count dimples after all. Officials promised to go back through the ballots they had already counted and retroactively apply the new, more liberal standard. The move instantly added hundreds of votes to Gore's totals.

Palm Beach officials, having toughened their standards to be in agreement with Broward, now felt foolish. Broward had adopted the dimple rule already embraced by Miami-Dade officials. Suddenly Palm Beach was on its own again. Buffeted by the same legal and political pressures that were brought to bear against Broward, Palm Beach officials agreed to change their standard yet again. The board began counting dimples—but not all dimples. Palm Beach would only count dimples on ballots where there was a pattern of additional dimples in nonpresidential races. If a voter had clearly punched out chads in nonpresidential races, but only dimpled the presidential choice, that vote was not counted. Palm Beach had arrived at its fifth distinct standard.

All of these highly public rule changes left the nation utterly bewildered. America watched with a mixture of revulsion and fascination as exhausted, bleary-eyed counters squinted, yawned, bickered, laughed, held ballots up to the light, used magnifying glasses and even flashlights to divine the intentions of voters. Counters twisted ballots, dropped them on the floor, stepped on them, and repeatedly placed Bush votes into Gore piles. On some ballots, chads were taped over holes that had been punched by Bush voters. As the ballots were manhandled again and again, chads fell like rain on tables, floors, and judicial benches. The tiny rectangles of paper were tagged as police evidence, collected as souvenirs, stolen, fought over, and even eaten. In at least one case, a man who was working as a Democratic observer was subsequently put to work as an "impartial" vote counter. The only GOP member of the three boards, an

elderly woman with health problems, abruptly quit, forcing her
Democratic colleagues to scurry for another token Republican.

Statisticians pointed out that the Gold Coast recounts would
have to be 99.9999 percent accurate if they were to decide the election without leaving a statistical margin of error. As Americans sat
transfixed in front of their TV sets, few felt confident the counters
were getting it right even half the time.

CHAPTER 9

"A WHIFF OF FASCISM"

Matthew Szymanski felt silly. A handful of his colleagues were chanting "let us in," but it was halfhearted and disorganized and, well, weak. Like a self-conscious teenager in church, who dutifully mouths hymns in order to avoid getting a dirty look from his parents, Szymanski sheepishly chanted along with the rest of the Republican observers on the nineteenth floor of the Stephen Clarke government building in Miami. But when one of them piped up with a new chant—"no justice, no peace"—Szymanski refused to repeat it. It was just too ridiculous.

"Protesting was not part of my resume," said the constitutional lawyer from suburban Washington. "If they started singing 'Kumbayah,' I was out of there."

Indeed, the thirty-five-year-old Szymanski made an unlikely protester. He was wearing a charcoal, pinstriped business suit over a white, button-down shirt—"I always have my shirts pressed"—and a Chanel tie. Even his shoes screamed establishment—black wing tips, the official footwear of mild-mannered attorneys. Szymanski was so persnickety that even his fellow Republicans chortled when they noticed him carrying around a stack of three-ring binders, in which he had meticulously catalogued every scrap of litigation filed so far in Florida's post-election debacle. He amassed four of the binders in the first week after the election, before he was even asked to come to Florida and help the Bush team. The man was obsessed. His work was beginning to suffer. His billable hours were down. He spent hour after hour on the Internet, downloading the latest legal briefs from Florida and snapping them into his three-ring binders.

It was almost a relief when the call finally came from a friend on the Hill. Would he be willing to come to Florida and help the Bush team? Could he be ready to catch a flight the night of Wednesday, November 15? Szymanski ran it up the flagpole with the partners at his firm, who gave him their blessing. It wasn't a tough sell. Everyone was caught up in the drama being played out in Florida. Besides, there was a certain cachet to having someone from the firm down there in the middle of the action, perhaps even obtaining a little inside information.

But then the plans fell through and Szymanski didn't fly out on Wednesday night after all. Back at the office on Thursday and Friday, his colleagues razzed him mercilessly.

"People started saying, 'Did W. call lately?'" he recalled. "They were teasing me about it, like I was overplaying any presumed importance in this whole affair. So they joked for a couple of days, but then I got another call on Friday. And this time it was for real."

When he arrived in Miami early Saturday, he was assigned to the team of one hundred observers who would be witnessing the hand count on behalf of George W. Bush. Szymanski didn't know any of the other observers, although they all seemed to know each other. They were mostly "cause conservatives," the kind of people who were always at the front lines of political battles. By contrast, Szymanski had never even been in the Young Republicans Club. He was a lawyer in private practice in McLean, Virginia, who had a wife and two kids and a mortgage out in Loudon County. He felt like an outsider. And he could tell right away he was not considered part of the A Team.

The original plan had been for the observers to hit the ground running on Saturday morning by immediately monitoring the start of the countywide hand count. But then the Miami-Dade Canvassing Board decided to spend Saturday hearing arguments from both sides. And then the board decided to spend Sunday running all 653,963 ballots through the machines again to segregate the undervotes. So the hand count itself was postponed until Monday.

The delay gave Szymanski the opportunity he was seeking. He and the other observers were able to spend the weekend actually training for the recount. They learned that each ballot had rows with 24 chads each. One of the rows was for presidential candidates. Szymanski and the other trainees found it difficult to envision the precise layout, despite efforts by the trainers to describe it.

"They were all talking about the ballots and what you're supposed to be doing with the ballots, but we were saying, 'We can't visualize this,'" Szymanski said. "We wanted sample ballots. We wanted to *see* the things."

But the trainers had been trying for days to obtain a sample ballot or two from the Miami-Dade County Elections Office and had been repeatedly turned down.

Szymanski also spent a large portion of the weekend delving into his three-ring binders and formulating legal arguments for consideration by the senior Bush lawyers who were actually arguing the case before the canvassing board. He offered a procedural argument that ended up being accepted by the Bush lawyers. In fact, Szymanski's argument was the first of three arguments the senior lawyers made to the board on Monday. It was also the only one that prevailed.

"After that point, all of a sudden I was a player," he recalled. "I turned out to be part of the A Team."

That meant a spot on the first platoon of observers. Of the hundred Republicans, only fifteen were selected for the team that would set the tone for all the others. Matthew Szymanski had officially arrived.

But when he showed up for that first day of counting early Monday morning at the Stephen Clarke government building, Szymanski discovered that the canvassing board had adopted the most liberal standard possible for counting the 10,750 undervotes.

"Dimples, marks, I mean anything on a chad that could be perceived as an indication that the voter intended to punch that card, was counted as a vote," he said. Gore quickly began racking up big gains as board members personally examined the undervotes, one by one.

But Szymanski and the Republicans figured out a way to turn the liberal counting standard against the Democrats. As they sat down at card tables and began watching election workers hand recount the 643,213 ballots that the machines had actually recognized as legitimate votes, the Republicans made an exciting discovery. Some of the ballots that had been clearly punched for Gore also contained a dimple or ding or some sort of faint mark for one of the other presidential candidates. Granted, the Gore chads had been punched out so cleanly that the machine had no trouble counting these ballots as votes for the vice president. But time and again, Republicans noticed there were also dimples on chads for Bush or Buchanan or Green Party candidate Ralph Nader. It was as if the voter had begun to select one of the other candidates, but then withdrawn their stylus without fully dislodging the chad and instead voted decisively for Gore.

Republicans seized on these dimples as clear evidence of "over-votes," or ballots on which citizens had chosen two presidential candidates, thereby nullifying the whole effort. Never mind that one of the choices was clear as a bell and the other was, at best, dubious. If the canvassing board members, sitting over there by themselves and personally hand examining the 10,750 undervotes, were going to count dimples, then by God, the rest of the election workers, sitting over here at card tables and hand counting the remaining 643,213 ballots, were going to count dimples—even if that meant subtracting votes from Gore that had already been counted by machine. He who lives by the dimple dies by the dimple.

The board, not wishing to be seen as employing a double standard, had no choice but to go along with the Republican strategy. Szymanski and the other observers began disqualifying dozens of Gore votes.

"What we were doing was so important because we were able to throw out Gore ballots," Szymanski said. "It was mitigating what the board was doing as they were counting the undervotes."

The beauty of the strategy was that Democratic observers at the card tables dared not play the same game as the Republicans because it would only serve to eat up precious time. In fact, there were plenty of cleanly punched Bush votes that also contained dimples for Gore or one of the other candidates. The Democratic observers could have easily objected to these ballots and gotten them disqualified as overvotes. But they just let them remain as Bush votes.

"The Democratic observers were not objecting," Szymanski said. "They weren't lodging any objections because they wanted to speed it up and get through. They were racing against time.

"See, we were delay. It was in our interest to delay. We made objections even when we knew they'd be overruled because we wanted to delay. The Democrats were desperately avoiding delay.

"I counted three precincts as an observer. And as a floor manager I observed a whole bunch of other precincts. I do not recall one—not one—Democratic objection. We lodged hundreds.

"And another thing, the Democrats didn't send down their A Team," he added. "Some of the Democratic observers were more like bureaucrats. They were only mildly interested. They weren't on their toes. The Republicans had sent down lawyers, political types, high-level Hill staff, people who were taking the job seriously. We were wired and ready, highly motivated, highly focused."

By the end of Tuesday, the second day of counting, Gore had netted 157 new votes, thanks in large part to the board's examination of several thousand undervotes. But Szymanski was convinced those gains would have been doubled if he and the other Republican observers had not been feverishly disqualifying Gore over-votes at the card tables.

An even bigger question was whether the results of all this recounting would even be included in the certified results for Miami-Dade County. By 5 P.M. on Tuesday, November 21, Miami-Dade had already missed the deadline for finishing its recount by a full week. Florida Secretary of State Katherine Harris had said she would not accept tardy recounts and her decision had been upheld by a Florida Circuit Court judge. Although the Democrats were still frantically filing lawsuits in an effort to force Harris to accept late tallies, Republicans hoped they would amount to nothing.

"Monday and Tuesday, as far as we knew, were just academic exercises," Szymanski said. "Everybody understood the importance of it, but we all were wondering: Is any of this gonna matter?"

All that changed later on Tuesday evening. Szymanski had just returned to his hotel when the bombshell hit. The Florida Supreme Court ruled that Harris had to accept hand counts until Sunday, November 26. The Republican observers immediately convened a late-night emergency meeting in the ballroom of their Miami hotel.

"That's when everyone had their game faces on—I mean, you could hear a pin drop," Szymanski recalled. "And that's when we were advised by a lot of people that now it's for real."

So when Szymanski left his hotel the next morning to resume observing the hand count, he was more determined than ever to disqualify as many Gore votes as possible. The gravity of the previous night's Florida Supreme Court decision had sunk in and he began to sense that what he was doing was profoundly important.

But when he stepped out of the elevator on the eighteenth floor of the Stephen Clarke government building, he knew right away something was wrong. As he entered the cavernous room where the recount had been taking place, the first thing he noticed was that all the card tables were gone. In their place stood rows and rows of chairs, facing a table where the board soon began a public meeting.

To Szymanski's astonishment, the board abruptly voted to abandon the hand counting of all ballots that had already been tallied by machine. Board members explained they would not be able to meet the Florida Supreme Court's new deadline of November 26. Indeed, the board had been predicting for days that the task of hand counting all ballots in the county would not be completed until early December.

What happened next felt like a sucker punch to Szymanski. The board voted to finish counting the 10,750 undervotes. Board members reasoned there was enough time to tackle this relatively small batch of ballots, but not enough time to hand count the 643,213 ballots that had already been counted by machine. To make matters worse, this downsized recount would be moved to a small, enclosed "tabulation room" in the administrative offices on the nineteenth floor. There would be space for only one small team

of Republican and Democratic observers, and the media presence
would have to be drastically curtailed.

"They essentially told us to go home in shame," recalled
Szymanski, who stood in the front row of the board meeting, utterly
stupefied by the decision. "They hammered us. Figuratively, we
were doubled over. I saw a lot of Republican frowns. People were
really fretting. And I was just thinking: No way. This is so wrong.

"The statute says a manual recount has to be all ballots. The
word is *all*—it's very clear. I mean, the word *all* is there. If you're going
to do a manual recount, it has to be all ballots. All 650,000, not just
some 10,000 undervotes that the machine spits out. All or nothing."

Szymanski was particularly alarmed by the realization that
dimpled chads would now work exclusively in Gore's favor.
Dumbfounded, he headed down to the lobby, where he used his
cell phone to call a member of Congress. Soon another congressman joined the conference call and Szymanski was asked to stand
by so that he could explain what had happened to a radio talk
show host who was poised to go live on the air.

"But then my cell phone went dead," he recalled. "So I tried to
reach them on a public pay phone, but it was just—you know, I
was getting frustrated. I was using a credit card; I was trying to
make the calls; it was taking too much time; and I wasn't getting—
you know, sometimes you can run into the frustration of just not
being able to technically get it together. So that's when I went looking for a familiar face to find out where everybody was."

Szymanski learned that some of the observers had gone up to the
nineteenth floor to protest the board's decision. He jumped into an
elevator and headed up there, but was disappointed when he emerged
into the small hallway just outside the elevator door. There were
about thirty Republican observers—interspersed with a couple of
journalists—gathered around the door to the tabulation room, which

was now occupied by the canvassing board. Some of the observers were standing, others were sitting, and a handful was trying to sustain chants. The reporters were passing around a petition to protest their exclusion from the tabulation room. The Republicans, in a rare outburst of sympathy for the press, murmured "Let them in."

"A few people were sort of into it, but there was no synergy," Szymanski said. "People were kind of mealy-mouthed at that point. They were facing the tabulation room door and yelling, but it wasn't very loud. It wasn't heated. They were just sort of mumbling. I felt silly and out of place. I wasn't really energized for this."

Szymanski mouthed the words to some of the chants. "Let them in" gradually morphed into "let us in." But it didn't feel like much of a protest. Not like the angry, fire-and-brimstone protests that had been staged over the last two weeks by the Reverend Jesse Jackson all up and down the Gold Coast. Now, those protests had some spunk. By contrast, this sad little gathering in the hallway was in danger of fizzling out before it ever got rolling.

Then the elevator doors opened and out stepped a Democratic lawyer who had been highly visible throughout the recount process; a TV crew came over to interview him.

"There was a camera in his face and a journalist asking him questions and our people sort of thronged in a huddle around him," Szymanski said. "It sort of energized our crowd, because here was the enemy, the opposition, you know, a leader of the opposition, and we felt like we were really getting screwed. So some of our people were waving, wagging their fingers and yelling. It wasn't vicious or anything. It was just—it energized some people. And this is when people like started to get into it. No one interfered with the interview; it just created background noise.

"Then he walked to the elevator and some of our people were walking after him, still yelling and pointing. It was nothing obnoxious, but it was fair to say it was aggressive. And it wasn't the whole group and we weren't coordinated and there was no one directing us. It's just what some people did."

No one had laid a finger on the Democrat, who high-tailed it into the elevator and disappeared. But there was no denying that his little visit to the nineteenth floor had served to jolt the near-dead Republican protest back to life.

"That raised the level of interest," Szymanski recalled. "That made things more interesting."

But what really torqued the Republicans up was the sudden appearance of Joe Geller, chairman of the Miami-Dade Democratic Party. Geller emerged from the elevator just moments after the other Democrat had disappeared. Finding himself surrounded by unhappy Republicans, he proceeded directly to a trio of bankteller-style windows along one wall. He stopped at the window marked "Absentee Ballots."

"I'm not paying any attention to what he's doing, but he's standing at the window," Szymanski recalled. "As he walks away, one of our girls, Victoria—we called her Tory—she started yelling, 'He's got a ballot! He's got a ballot!' And this really energizes everybody."

Indeed, after being told for days that the elections office would not give out a single sample ballot—not even to Republican Congressman John Sweeney of New York who had asked and been denied three times—the Republicans were outraged to see this local Democrat given one automatically.

"It immediately disturbed a lot of us because we knew that he shouldn't have a ballot, no matter what kind of ballot it is—whether it's a sample ballot or real ballot or any kind of ballot," Szymanski said. "All we knew was that you weren't supposed to be able to get a ballot—any kind of ballot. And he walks out with a ballot!

"At that point, we're very disappointed, we're angry, we're outraged. We feel like we're being cheated. You know, the fix is in. So that charges everybody up."

Several Republicans got in Geller's face. They told him he was not supposed to have a ballot. They accused him and the other Democrats of stealing the election.

"He was shoving something into the inside pocket of his suit coat," Szymanski said. "I didn't see what it was, I just saw him stuffing something in. And he lowered his head and made a beeline for the elevators."

No one actually touched Geller. But his fleeting visit to the nineteenth floor had finally given the Republicans the passion they had been lacking.

"That's when it got loud," Szymanski said. "Even I was yelling at that point. The energy really electrified the room."

No longer weakly mumbling, the Republicans now lustily roared: "Let us in! Let us in!" They pounded on the doors of the tabulation room. Some beat on the walls. When a deputy sheriff opened and then tried to reclose the door, some Republicans held it open. When the deputy politely directed the Republicans to step back, they did and he closed the door. He and the other deputies seemed supremely calm, almost bemused by this Brooks Brothers uprising, one lawman even confessing to a not very active protester that it seemed pretty darn mild compared to the Elian Gonzalez protests.

Undaunted, the Republicans continued pounding and chanting. They were on a roll. Granted, with their tasseled loafers, strings of pearls, and conservative suits, they made an unlikely group of protesters. But they were furious that the entire election was, in their opinion, about to be stolen.

"It probably would have continued for some time, because it was kind of frenzied by then," Szymanski said. "But just as it reached its pitch, its crescendo, somebody opened the door and told us that if we'd shut up and be quiet, go back down to the eighteenth floor, the board would reconvene and make a decision. We didn't know what, so we quieted down and went down to the eighteenth floor.

"We thought they would rehear arguments or make some little procedural decision or, best case, we thought they would resume the full count," he said. "That was our best hope, the only thing we were thinking was within reach. We'd resume what we'd been doing Monday and Tuesday."

But when the board finally held its meeting, it went much further. Board members called off the entire recount—including the undervotes. Members reasoned that it would not be fair to carefully examine one batch of ballots while ignoring the rest. It had to be all or none. And since there was insufficient time to count all ballots, the Miami-Dade County Canvassing Board decided it would count none of them. In that spirit, they decided to not even count the 157 new votes Gore had netted over the last two days. The recount was suddenly over.

Now it was the Democrats who had been sucker punched. Although most of the Democratic observers had happily gone home after being dismissed by the board earlier in the day, enough remained to witness the momentous decision that had just deprived their candidate of the biggest single gain he had managed to amass in any of the four counties that had undertaken hand tallies. Worse yet, Gore had been pinning his hopes on Miami-Dade to provide him with hundreds more votes. For days, Democrats had been lusting after that stack of 10,750 undervotes as a "treasure trove" of new votes for Gore. Now the whole batch was suddenly off-limits.

Stepping back to survey the tattered landscape in the Florida recount wars, Democrats fairly despaired. Nearly two weeks after Gore first requested hand counts in Florida's four most promising counties, he had made precious little headway. Only Volusia County had finished its count, giving Gore a disappointingly small net gain of 98 votes. Counting was still underway in Broward, where Gore had picked up 137 votes. But in Palm Beach, which had once seemed so ripe for picking, Bush was actually ahead by 14 votes. And now Miami had called off its entire count.

The press was equally stunned. Reporters grilled Miami-Dade board members about whether they had been intimidated by the "Gucci goon squad." All three members emphatically insisted the protest had nothing whatsoever to do with their decision. In fact, they had begun to have second thoughts about the legality of a partial recount as soon as they gathered in the nineteenth floor tabulation room. Although not a single board member was a Republican, the Democratic Party said it was a monstrous lie that the board had not been intimidated.

"A whiff of fascism is in the air," declared Congressman Jerrold Nadler. The New York Democrat called the Republican protest on the nineteenth floor a "riot" incited by "a Republican rent-a-gang" that cowed the canvassing board into abandoning the recount.

"A mob threatened them, banged on their doors, roughed up people," Nadler said at a news conference, where he demanded a court order to force a resumption of the recount. "They succumbed to the mob violence and the intimidation."

Joe Lieberman, the vaunted "conscience of the Senate," agreed wholeheartedly. "This is the time to honor the rule of law, not to surrender to the rule of the mob," he thundered.

Although the entire GOP protest had begun as a show of support for the press, which was barred from the tabulation room, news agencies quickly turned against their new friends. There were skillfully vague accounts of Republican brutes "punching and kicking" Democrats. And yet not a single journalist was able to catch a glimpse of these acts in a building that was crawling with reporters and TV crews who filmed everything that was even remotely interesting. Liberal Democrats in Congress were reduced to citing the vague "news accounts" in a letter demanding a Justice Department investigation.

"I can categorically, under oath, say there was no violence," Szymanski said. "Anyone who states there was violence up there, that people were punched or kicked, is lying. Nobody ever felt threatened. We were a bunch of *yuppies*! C'mon! We weren't over-turning cars. This didn't intimidate anybody."

Even Gore himself joined in the histrionics. He said the entire election "would be over long since, except for this effort to block the process at every turn. In one county, election officials brought the count to a premature end in the face of organized intimidation."

For days, Gore was so incensed that he repeatedly telephoned "opposition researchers" at the Democratic National Committee to prod them into digging up the names of the Republican "riot-ers." The vice president of the United States was once again directly engaged in the politics of personal destruction. Al Gore, the man who wanted to be president, was obsessing, Nixon-like, over low-level lawyers and other GOP volunteers who had dared to raise their voices against him in Miami. He also began privately telling aides that Miami-Dade Mayor Alex Penelas had been suspi-ciously silent throughout the entire episode. He began calling oper-atives in Florida and demanding to know if Penelas had killed the recount. Although Penelas was a Democrat, he had broken with the party over the Elian Gonzalez case. Now Gore felt certain the Miami mayor had somehow sabotaged him behind the scenes. Although he had no proof, Al Gore now saw a conspiracy of both Democrats and Republicans trying to deny him the White House.

CHAPTER 10

O. J. WEIGHS IN

Although Al Gore asked the Florida Supreme Court to force Miami-Dade to resume its hand recount, not even the seven liberal justices of this activist bench were willing to go that far. The court had no compunction about usurping the discretionary authority of the Republican secretary of state, but it was not about to do the same to the Democratic canvassing boards. The seven justices unanimously turned Gore down on Thanksgiving, just two days after extending the deadline for manual recounts.

It was a crushing blow to the vice president. Of all the local, state, and federal courts that had become embroiled in the post-election debacle, none was friendlier to Gore than the Florida Supreme Court. If those seven justices weren't willing to force Miami-Dade's hand, then nobody would. At least not before Sunday, November 26, when Katherine Harris planned to finally certify Florida's statewide election results.

Without Miami-Dade's supposed "treasure trove" of undervotes, Gore fretted that Broward and Palm Beach would not give him enough new votes to overtake Bush before Sunday's certification.

This posed a major problem, since congressional Democrats were now openly grousing that the American public expected closure by the end of the long holiday weekend. So on Thanksgiving, Gore told his aides to spread the word that he would be contesting the certification with yet another lawsuit on Monday. Two days later, he let it be known that he would explain this lawsuit in a televised address on Monday. Gore was preemptively disabusing the American public of any expectation for closure over the holiday weekend.

Of course, there was always the slim possibility that Broward and Palm Beach counties would come up with enough votes by 5 P.M. Sunday to put Gore over the top. If that happened, Gore would become the certified winner and immediately demand that Bush concede. But Gore could tell by Thanksgiving that such a scenario was highly unlikely.

For one thing, it seemed doubtful that the canvassing boards would meet the Sunday deadline. In Palm Beach, county employees finished manually examining all 462,657 ballots at 6:25 P.M. on Wednesday. But they had set aside some 10,000 questionable ballots that still had to be adjudicated by the three-member canvassing board. Having already spent eight days plowing through 5,000 questionable ballots, the board now had four days in which to adjudicate 10,000 more. And since the three board members were the only people with the authority to count these ballots, there was no way to speed up the process with additional manpower. By the close of business on Wednesday, it was obvious to anyone with a rudimentary grasp of basic math that the board would have difficulty meeting the deadline. And yet, astonishingly, the board took Thanksgiving off.

"We'll be able to meet the deadline," board chairman Charles Burton confidently predicted. "We're making pretty good progress. We will put in whatever [time] is necessary."

Meanwhile, Broward election workers finished plowing through the county's 587,928 ballots by the end of Tuesday. Although the three board members had fewer remaining questionable ballots than their counterparts in Palm Beach, they opted to toil right through Thanksgiving. In fact, for more than a week, Broward officials had refused to allow themselves to be distracted by the jangle of conflicting court decisions and bewildering political developments exploding all around them. They simply put their heads down and kept counting, no matter how ferociously the maelstrom raged. They even had time to go back through those earlier ballots—the ones they had discarded because the chads were not detached by at least two corners—and retroactively apply the new, more liberal standard of counting chads that were merely dimpled, even if all four corners remained attached. As a result, the board met the deadline with seventeen hours and eight minutes to spare. At 11:52 P.M. on Saturday, November 25, Broward County finished its hand recount. It was the second county, after Volusia, to complete the undertaking, which had been requested sixteen days earlier by Gore. When the dust settled, Broward gave Gore a whopping net gain of 567 votes. Suddenly, a single county had slashed Bush's statewide lead by more than half.

By contrast, Palm Beach officials were easily distracted from the task of counting ballots. The board had wasted four and a half precious days awaiting legal guidance before it even began the countywide tally. Even after it got started, the board was forever getting sidetracked by public meetings, press conferences, and court appearances. Ironically, Gore himself caused some of the delays by pressing lawsuits that forced Burton to spend valuable time testifying in court. On Friday, Palm Beach officials belatedly realized their blunder. They never should have taken Thanksgiving off. By Saturday the board was in a full-fledged panic. It would have to pull an all-nighter just to have an outside chance of meeting the deadline.

By midnight on Saturday, Palm Beach officials found themselves in a familiar position—all alone among the four counties that had been requested to perform hand recounts. Volusia and Broward had completed the task, while Miami-Dade had acknowledged days earlier there was no point in trying to meet the impossibly tight deadline. The only place in Florida where ballots were still being tallied was Palm Beach County. As Saturday gave way to Sunday, the board still had 5,000 ballots to manually examine. That meant each board member had only a few seconds to scrutinize and make decisions on ballots that had already been singled out as the most difficult and questionable in the county.

At 2 A.M., board members were so frantic that they changed the rules yet again. They assigned two county workers to sort through the remaining ballots and make the "easy calls." For two weeks, only the board members themselves had the authority to adjudicate ballots that had been deemed questionable by lower level county employees. But now, fifteen hours before the deadline, the board was suddenly deputizing lower level county employees to reexamine these same ballots and award them to Bush or Gore. The *really* questionable ballots would be sent back to the board members. Under this new system, Gore's gains began to accelerate almost immediately.

Night gave way to morning and morning gave way to afternoon. At 12:35 P.M., Burton faxed a letter to Katherine Harris, seeking another deadline extension. He noted that the Florida Supreme Court, while setting the deadline at 5 P.M. Sunday, also allowed a back-up deadline of 9 A.M. Monday, in case Harris wasn't in her office over the weekend. But Harris had made it her business to come in on Sunday. She promptly denied Burton's request.

By now, the nation was transfixed by the televised spectacle of bone-weary board members desperately racing through impossibly large piles of ballots. The rumpled, red-eyed, raw-nerved bureaucrats reminded Americans of college students who stayed up all night because they had put off their studies for too long. Virtually no one believed the exhausted board members were giving as much careful attention to the last ballots as they had the first. In a process that had to be 99.9999 percent accurate in order to prevent the next president from being determined by a statistical margin of error, the Palm Beach County Canvassing Board seemed to have careened deeply into that margin.

At 4:25 P.M., Burton announced what had been obvious for days: The board would fail to meet the deadline. Board members decided to submit partial results that gave Gore a net gain of 180 votes. Harris immediately rejected these incomplete numbers, pointing out that Florida law required "all" ballots to be tallied in hand recounts. It was all or nothing. After two weeks of hard work, Palm Beach officials had nothing to show for it.

Rather than stop counting at 5 P.M., the board pressed on, saying it would submit complete, albeit tardy, numbers later in the evening. Finally, at 7:06 P.M., the count was over. Seventeen days after Gore had requested a recount, the board had missed the deadline by two hours and six minutes. Palm Beach, which had been the first of Gore's hand-picked counties to begin manually recounting votes, now became the last to finish.

The new numbers showed Gore posting an unofficial net gain of 215 votes. But the board, humiliated by its failure to meet the deadline, didn't bother turning in the full count that evening after all. Besides, the confusing lists of numbers didn't quite add up correctly. The board had begun its latest counting jag at 8 A.M. Saturday—more than thirty-five hours earlier—and was now too exhausted to reconcile discrepancies in the final results. Palm Beach would end up waiting another three days before finally submitting its numbers. During those three days, Theresa LePore conducted an audit that revealed Gore had actually netted only 188 votes, not 215. So she conducted another audit and the number fell even further to 174. Gore had actually netted fewer votes than he had from the partial recount that had been submitted before 5 P.M. Sunday. Gore's lawyers, however, ignored LePore's audits and kept insisting the vice president had netted 215 votes in Palm Beach County, even though that was never an official number.

Katherine Harris was not about to wait several days for Palm Beach County to get its numbers straight. In fact, she waited only twenty-seven minutes after the tardy conclusion of the Palm Beach count on Sunday to finally certify Florida's election returns. The ceremony was conspicuously public and intentionally formal so that the proceedings would carry an air of government-sanctioned legitimacy. There was much scribbling of signatures and passing back and forth of official-looking documents by Harris and the other two members of the Florida canvassing commission. It was as if the Magna Carta were being signed as TV cameras rolled.

"On behalf of the state canvassing commission, and in accordance with the laws of the state of Florida, I hereby declare Governor George W. Bush the winner of Florida's electoral votes for the president of the United States," declared Harris, decked out in a red dress and matching lipstick, as if to tweak her catty detractors. "Our American democracy has triumphed once again, and this is a victory in which we can all take a great deal of pride and comfort. The true winner in the election is the rule of law."

Cheers exploded from the hundreds of Bush supporters gathered outside the statehouse building where Harris sat. They were echoed a thousand miles west, outside the Texas governor's mansion in Austin. At long last, Bush had officially, certifiably won Florida, with a margin of 537 ballots, and was awarded the state's twenty-five electoral votes, giving him 271 nationwide—or one more than necessary to become president. Florida's votes had been counted once, twice—in some cases three or four times—and each time the result had been the same. Bush came out ahead.

Gore knew that the TV images of jubilant Republicans in Florida and Texas would reinforce the impression, first created by the networks for more than two hours on Election Night, that Bush was truly the forty-third president of the United States. Gore had to do something to get those images of celebrating Republicans off the TV. And he knew just the person to do it. Joe Lieberman was hurried before the TV cameras to dismiss the certification as meaningless.

"This evening, the secretary of state of Florida has decided to certify what by any reasonable standard is an incomplete and inaccurate count of the votes cast in the state of Florida," Lieberman complained from a hotel near the White House. "Vice President Gore and I have no choice but to contest these actions."

By this time, the Bush team was no longer squeamish about calling on Gore to step aside. Later that evening, James Baker addressed reporters in Tallahassee.

"I can certainly understand the pain and the frustration of losing an election so very, very narrowly, but it is time to honor the will of the people," Baker said. "It is time to let the orderly process of transitioning go forward."

Baker's empathy was withering. The game was so far gone that the Bush team was now openly pitying Gore. They felt his pain. How very Clintonesque. Bush was now making excuses for Gore, which was far worse than attacking him. The message was unmistakable: Poor Al Gore is in denial. Cut him a break. He can't help it if he's a "Sore Loserman."

Even Florida Commissioner of Agriculture Bob Crawford, a Democrat, called for closure.

"It's over," said Crawford, a member of the state canvassing board who signed the certified results. "You know, Yogi Berra once said, 'It's not over till it's over.' Well, it's over, and we have a winner. And it's time to move on."

Most of the nation agreed. That same day, a poll by ABC News and the *Washington Post* showed that 60 percent of Americans thought Gore should concede the election and let Bush become president. Only 35 percent thought he should not concede. Other polls showed virtually identical results. The next day, NBC News conducted a poll that showed 61 percent of Americans thought Bush had legitimately won the presidency. Some Democrats privately fretted that Gore's refusal to concede was doing permanent damage not just to himself, but to the entire party. And even if Gore somehow managed to win at this late stage, he would have severe difficulty governing for one term, let alone two. He would be considered illegitimate by virtually every Republican in America and a fair chunk of Democrats. Bob Dole went on TV to report that Republicans might even boycott a Gore inauguration. The GOP-controlled Congress would bitterly block his every initiative, resulting in a doomed, one-term presidency. Democrats began grousing that they would be better off ceding the White House to Bush and then attacking his legitimacy as a way of winning back the Congress in 2002.

But Gore had no intention of stepping aside. The man who just days earlier had vowed to "abide by the result" of the recounts and "take no legal action to challenge the result," was already approving a lawsuit that would be filed the next day, contesting the entire election on a variety of fronts.

In Gore's mind, he had merely lost round one of a two-round fight. Indeed, Florida law allowed the loser of an election two chances to reverse the outcome. The loser could "protest" the results prior to certification and then "contest" the results afterward. Having now lost the protest, Gore simply proceeded with the contest.

Some Democrats privately reproached Gore for having spent so much time on the protest phase that he didn't leave himself enough time to mount a proper contest. After all, the election was nearly three weeks old. The standoff had dragged on far longer than anyone could have imagined and the public was clamoring for finality. And even if Gore continued to ignore the polls, he couldn't ignore the calendar. The Electoral College would meet on December 18 to officially cast its ballots for president. The federal deadline for challenging any slate of electors was December 12. Since Bush had already won Florida's twenty-five electors, the names of those Republican stalwarts were on their way to the National Archivist in Washington. If Gore were to have any hope of challenging these electors with a slate of his own, he would have to somehow overtake Bush's certified, 537-vote lead in the space of fifteen days. That meant Gore would have to file his lawsuit, go to trial, make his case, refute any evidence put on by Bush, win a judgment that would restart hand counts in selected counties, and actually get those ballots counted—all in the space of just over two weeks. In all likelihood, this would have to be accomplished even more quickly because there was a good chance Gore would lose at the Circuit Court level and be forced to appeal to that friendliest of benches, the Florida Supreme Court. Time now became Gore's number one enemy.

Of the four hand recounts the vice president had requested, only two—Volusia and Broward—had been completed in time to be accepted by Katherine Harris. So Gore focused on the other two counties—Palm Beach and Miami-Dade—in his new lawsuit.

Specifically, he demanded that the court force Harris to accept Palm Beach's tardy results, which Gore insisted would give him an additional 215 votes. Never mind that this number was unofficial and inflated. Gore was going for the largest numbers possible. He also asked that a more liberal counting standard be retroactively applied to some 3,300 ballots the Palm Beach board had rejected. Gore estimated that would net him another 800 votes.

As for Miami-Dade, Gore's lawsuit demanded that the court— or an agent of its choosing—finish counting the 10,750 "under-votes." Gore estimated that he would net another 600 votes from this pile. In addition, since Miami-Dade employees had hand tallied only 20 percent of the county's 653,963 ballots in general, Gore asked the court to count the remaining 80 percent—although he refrained from estimating how many votes this would net him.

Finally, Gore pulled a new plaintiff into the stew of post-election litigation. He sued Nassau County, at Florida's northeastern tip, claiming election officials there cheated him out of 51 votes. Gore had picked up the 51 votes during Nassau's mandatory recount, immediately after the election. But county officials later discovered they had failed to recount a batch of ballots that heavily favored Bush. When these ballots were put back into the mix, Gore's 51 votes disappeared. Gore did not dispute these facts, but rather sought to trip up the board on technicalities. Specifically, he charged that no one had filed an official request with Nassau to revise its certified numbers. Secondly, Gore said the board's meeting to revise the count was illegal, since one of the board members could not attend and sent a substitute instead. Gore's willingness to cite technicalities in order to snare 51 votes was a measure of how desperate he had become. Indeed, less than a week earlier, the vice president had hailed the Florida Supreme Court for denouncing Katherine Harris's "hypertechnical" adherence to the law.

In sum, Gore estimated that he was entitled to 1,666 votes from Nassau, Miami-Dade, and Palm Beach counties. His twenty-four-page lawsuit was filed in Leon County Circuit Court in Tallahassee at 12:11 P.M. on Monday, November 27. The case was assigned to Judge N. Sanders Sauls, a cagey Democrat given to amusing southern colloquialisms.

Gore lawyer David Boies sought a dramatically accelerated trial schedule. In fact, he wanted the trial to begin as early as Tuesday afternoon—a scant twenty-four hours after the suit was filed—and certainly no later than Wednesday. Judge Sauls, while agreeing to take extraordinary measures to expedite the case, nonetheless gave the Bush team until Friday to file its response to the suit. That meant the trial would not actually commence until Saturday, December 2—a mere ten days before the electors had to be seated.

To speed things along, the Gore team suggested Sauls count only the most promising batches of ballots—namely, the 10,000 "undervotes" from Miami-Dade and the 3,300 "dimpled" ballots that had been rejected by the Palm Beach board. Although these represented just 1 percent of the 1.1 million ballots from these two counties, Gore was willing to forgo the remaining 99 percent in the interest of expediency.

"There are ways to expedite this," Boies pleaded to Sauls during a pretrial hearing Tuesday. "And I can't think of a legitimate reason not to begin the counting on Thursday, at least with respect to the Dade County ballots."

This prompted the usually low-key Bush lawyer Barry Richard to rise in anger against Gore's hurry-up offense. Richard, a Tallahassee Democrat, was incredulous that Gore wanted to count ballots even before the trial was held. "My client is entitled to a hearing before Mr. Boies's client gets relief," Richard snapped to the judge. "Every time your honor gives him another thing, he's back on his feet asking for one more thing you've already denied him—twice.

"We've already truncated this proceeding so that my client has little or no time to prepare for a hearing. Mr. Boies [is] asking this court to give him everything he's requested, which is to begin another ballot recount before he has provided one iota of evidence or permitted my client to have one hour of hearing on whether or not he's entitled to that recount."

Sauls acknowledged he had already cut in half the normal period of ten days in which the defendant can reply to the plaintiff. "I can't strip you of every right that is known to everybody to accommodate [Gore]," he told the Bush lawyer.

"We can't wait until Saturday," Boies protested to the judge. "We're going to have to appeal that decision, because it is our view that waiting until Saturday is tantamount to denying [the entire lawsuit]."

As Boies argued for expediency in the court of N. Sanders Sauls, Gore himself was making the same case in the court of public opinion.

"This morning, we have proposed to the court in Tallahassee a plan to have all the ballots counted in seven days, starting tomorrow morning, and to have the court proceedings fully completed one or two days after that," Gore told reporters who were summoned to the lawn of his residence at the U.S. Naval Observatory in Washington. "I believe this is a time to count every vote and not to run out the clock. This is not the time for delay, obstruction and procedural roadblocks."

Gore and his lawyers insisted that if they were precluded from counting ballots until after the lawsuit was settled—which would not happen until the following week—there would not be enough time to complete the task by December 12. But Sauls countered that the ballots in question had not even been shipped yet from the Gold Coast to his Tallahassee courtroom.

"I've essentially denied your beginning to count something we don't have right now," Sauls told Boies.

Bush lawyers warned that it would be unfair to count only some of the ballots from the two counties, as the Gore team was requesting. They argued that Sauls had to count all ballots, or none at all. It was a striking role reversal. Previously, Gore had sought the largest possible universe of ballots to recount, while Bush had tried to narrow that universe as much as possible.

The argument spilled into additional pretrial hearings on Wednesday, when the Bush lawyers succeeded in convincing Sauls that if he was going to take possession of some of the ballots from Palm Beach and Miami-Dade, he would have to take possession of all of them—all 1.1 million of them. By getting the judge to treat the ballots as an all-or-nothing proposition, the Bush team was hoping to ensure that any legal victory by Gore would degenerate into a losing race against time: counting 1.1 million ballots before December 12.

Boies, sensing the case slipping away from him, pleaded with the judge at least to allow the smaller group of ballots to be sent to Tallahassee immediately, even if that meant that a second convoy would bring the bulk of the punch cards later.

"Your honor, we are, of course, paying for the expense," Boies reminded the judge. "Since they're prepared to bring it up and we're paying for the expense, it seems to me that there's no legitimate reason not to have them come up."

"I'm going to leave it to them," Sauls said, gesturing to the squawk box on his bench to signify election officials from Miami-Dade and Palm Beach, who were participating in the hearing via conference call. "What do you all want to do down there? Do you want to send up two times or do you want to do it once? It's your call."

"One time, from Miami," said Miami-Dade election official Murray Greenberg.

"One time it is," the judge concluded. "All right, that's it— one time."

Gore was forced to appeal this and other rulings by Sauls to the Florida Supreme Court. The trial had not even started and already the vice president was taking an overtly adversarial role against a Democratic judge. Even the high court thought this was too much, and summarily refused to hear Gore's pretrial appeals.

On Thursday, the post-election struggle reached new heights of absurdity. As TV choppers hovered overhead and a police escort cleared the path on Ronald Reagan Turnpike, a Ryder rental truck was loaded with all 462,657 ballots from Palm Beach County and headed north toward Tallahassee. The twenty-four-hour cable news channels covered every inch of the otherwise mundane journey with a breathless excitement not seen since O. J. Simpson led police on a low-speed chase in his white Bronco. In fact, Simpson himself watched the ridiculous TV coverage in his South Beach, Florida, home and then emerged to compare the spectacle with his own journey six years earlier, when he was accused of brutally murdering his estranged wife and her lover.

"All I could think of was: Now I know what people went through when they were trying to watch the basketball game and my Bronco was going up the freeway," Simpson observed. "It's boring."

The talking heads begged to differ. "It's historic," gushed one CNN correspondent. The carnival atmosphere only intensified the next day, when Miami-Dade sent its 653,963 ballots north in another convoy.

The ballots were locked in a vault in the Leon County Clerk's Office. Judge Sauls, exasperated by the constant pretrial bickering between the Bush and Gore lawyers, muttered: "Is there any possibility of locking Mr. Boies and Mr. Richard in that vault?" At another point, he likened the flurry of frivolous motions and counter-motions to "being nibbled to death by ducks."

Sauls was not alone in tiring of the spectacle. America had had a bellyful. Each day brought another round of hair-raising stories of voting irregularities. The *Miami Herald* revealed that ballots had been illegally cast by at least 445 Florida felons, nearly 75 percent of whom were registered Democrats. The newspaper had checked only twelve of the sixty-seven counties. If the pattern held up statewide, more than 5,000 felons had cast ballots. That meant Gore probably posted a net gain of 2,500 votes from felons alone. That was 50 percent more than all the votes Gore was demanding in his lawsuit before Judge Sauls. Yet in the crush of daily developments, the *Miami Herald* bombshell merited barely a mention by the rest of the press.

On Saturday, Sauls commenced the trial, saying he hoped the whole thing would take only twelve hours. But the Gore lawyers, after flirting with the idea of calling no witnesses in order to save time, decided to produce two witnesses whose testimony consumed seven hours. They were, at best, weak witnesses. The first was a long-winded statistician named Kimball Brace, whom Gore lawyers touted as a national expert on voting machines. Although Brace argued that Gore should get credit for dimpled ballots, he admitted under cross-examination that a dimple could be produced by a voter who did not intend to vote for the candidate. Bush lawyers also ridiculed Brace's contention that "chad buildup" in voting machines had stymied would-be Gore voters.

The second witness was a nervous Yale statistician named Nicholas Hengartner. Speaking through a thick, Eastern European accent, this non-U.S. citizen suggested that Democrats in America were more likely to be deprived of their votes than Republicans because they tended to use older, less reliable voting machines. He didn't mention that Gadsden, one of the most Democratic counties in Florida and the only one where blacks outnumbered whites, used optical scanners, which were more modern than the old punch-card machines. And Gadsden's mandatory recount had turned up more previously undiscovered votes than sixty-two other counties.

At one point during his testimony, Hengartner acknowledged mistakes in his own sworn statement in the case. Citing a particular passage, he said: "That doesn't make any sense. I apologize."

The Bush team then called Charles Burton, the ubiquitous chairman of the Palm Beach County Canvassing Board. Under direct examination, Burton acknowledged for the record that the hand count in Palm Beach was conducted by himself and two other Democrats. He also said he initially opposed the countywide hand tally because of shifting standards on whether a dimple counted as a vote.

Judge Sauls directly questioned his circuit court colleague, showing wide deference to his fellow jurist. He asked Burton if there had been any scientific basis for the board to go ahead with the countywide tally after the sample count showed a net gain of 19 votes for Gore. Burton said no. At the conclusion of his gentle questioning, Sauls told his fellow judge: "I salute you as a great American."

Evidently not getting the hint, Gore lawyer David Boies then rose and peppered this favored witness with adversarial questions. For example, he got Burton to acknowledge that he ultimately came to support full hand recounts.

The trial recessed after nine and a half hours and resumed the next morning for a rare Sunday session. Bush lawyers put their own statistician, Laurentius Marais, on the witness stand to challenge the assertion that Democrats used older, less reliable voting machines. But Boies was ready—or thought he was.

"You have testified that certain statistical analyses that link lead paint with injuries to children didn't meet your standards for statistical scientific analysis, correct?" Boies asked.

"No, sir," Marais replied.

"You didn't do that?" said Boies, who appeared taken aback.

"No."

"Um, well sir, what did you testify?"

At this point, Bush lawyer Phil Beck interjected: "Your honor, I'm going to object to the relevance of this. In any event, if time is short, why is he quizzing him about other—"

"Your honor, I think it goes to his credibility," Boies shot back. "And I think it goes to the way he performs statistical analysis."

Sauls ruled it was "irrelevant" to include "testimony from some other case," especially one that had "absolutely no materiality" to the Gore suit. Boies tried to recover.

"Would the court permit a comparison of the way he approaches... the scientific statistical analysis in other cases with the way he's done it here?" the Gore lawyer ventured.

Sauls again refused. The usually unflappable Boies seemed momentarily flummoxed by the setback. As he hesitated, Beck jumped into the void.

"I'm going to ask the court to admonish Mr. Boies about his obligation not to go down that route unless he has a legitimately held belief that there is a difference in methodology," Beck scolded. "Because otherwise, all he's doing is grandstanding and saying that this man testified in cases that Mr. Boies thinks will be unpopular with the public. And that's not right."

"Your honor, I'm not grandstanding," protested Boies, who nonetheless agreed to "abandon" that line of questioning.

Beck had struck a nerve. Boies was a media darling who spent almost as much time talking to the TV cameras as he did talking to judges. He was a super-lawyer, a celebrity who had developed a cult-like following in the press—much to the delight of Gore's political team. Although plenty of lawyers on both sides of the fight had privately groused that Boies was a grandstander, this was the first time someone actually said it to his face in open court.

Bush lawyers spent much of the day eliciting testimony from GOP attorneys who described the chaotic conditions and changing rules of hand recounts they had observed in both Palm Beach and Miami-Dade. At every opportunity, the Bush team pounded home the theme that the process had been hopelessly flawed.

Finally, the witness stand was occupied by a woman named Shirley King, chairman of the Nassau County Canvassing Board. She had planned on retiring after a long and unblemished career when she had suddenly been named as a defendant in Al Gore's lawsuit for allegedly depriving him of 51 votes.

King denied Gore's assertion, and explained that during the mandatory, statewide recount, she had accidentally failed to run several hundred ballots through the machine. This particular batch of ballots had been overlooked because they were stored upside down in ballot boxes, which concealed the red stripe along one edge that signaled to poll workers that they were presidential ballots. When King realized the error, she made the sure that the County correctly tallied all ballots, a process that erased Gore's contested 51 votes. King seemed truly remorseful for her temporary mistake.

"I wanted every vote to count," she explained.

Sauls seemed utterly captivated by her story and became protective and even solicitous of the witness. He pronounced her another "great American." Gore's luck was running from bad to worse. The judge who would decide his lawsuit had now publicly lionized two of the people Gore was suing.

The trial concluded at 10:44 P.M., after twenty-three hours of debate and testimony. Sauls gave the lawyers a world-weary look.

"At this time, counsel, I must tell you: A case well tried—and argued," the judge said. "And I suppose what I should do at this time is I'll take it under submission. And I'll give you a decision in the morning. The court will stand in recess."

On Monday, December 4, Sauls rendered his verdict. He decisively rejected every aspect of Gore's suit.

"The court finds that the plaintiffs have failed to carry the requisite burden of proof," Sauls said. "Plaintiffs shall take nothing by this action. And the defendants may go hence without delay."

In other words, Gore was denied every vote, both counted and uncounted, that he had sought in the counties of Nassau, Palm Beach, and Miami-Dade. It was a crushing repudiation of the vice president's efforts.

"Boy," said liberal commentator Paul Begala, who had helped Gore prepare for the presidential debates during the campaign. "Judge Sauls handed my team the biggest ass-whippin' since the Texas-Oklahoma game." Begala, a native Texan, was referring to the Sooners' blowout of the Longhorns, 63-14.

And yet the devastating setback in the courtroom of Judge N. Sanders Sauls turned out to be the least of Al Gore's problems that day.

CHAPTER 11

KIDNAPPING ELECTORS

Bob Beckel was tired of politics. The fiercely partisan liberal Democrat had been at it since the early 1970s, when he protested the Vietnam War and worked on George McGovern's presidential campaign. In those days, Beckel had felt real passion about the business. He believed he was making a difference. Sure, McGovern had lost in a landslide, but Beckel went on to join the National Committee for an Effective Congress, the liberal political action committee founded by Eleanor Roosevelt in 1948. He became interested in an emerging political strategy known as "targeting." In those days, liberals were short on money, so Beckel and others began questioning the practice of pouring precious resources into entire states when it was clear that at least certain portions of those states were going to vote Republican anyway. He began to study the voting histories of individual counties and even precincts, categorizing each as being dominated by GOP, Democrat, or swing voters. Over time, Beckel and his colleagues simply wrote off the Republican precincts and limited their work in Democratic precincts to get-out-the-vote drives. That freed up most of the money and other resources for the all-important swing precincts, where elections were won and lost. The political practice of targeting had been born.

Beckel used this new tool in dozens of political campaigns that successfully exploited public disillusionment in the wake of the Watergate scandal and President Nixon's resignation. Then came the heady days of the Carter administration, when Beckel was tapped to become the youngest deputy assistant secretary of state in history. Later he took a post in the White House itself. And when it came time for Carter's reelection bid, Beckel was dispatched to Texas to fend off a primary challenge from Massachusetts Senator Ted Kennedy.

But his biggest break of all came in 1984, when Beckel was hired to run Walter Mondale's entire presidential campaign. Looking back on that experience, Beckel liked to joke that he had the distinction of doing two things—one good and one bad—that will forever be remembered by historians. The first was to convince Mondale to ask Democratic challenger Gary Hart the following question during a primary debate: "Where's the beef?" The line, borrowed from a commercial for Wendy's hamburgers, eviscerated Hart because it crystallized suspicions that he was all flash and no substance. Oh, and there was also that one bad thing Beckel had done. "I managed the largest loss in the history of American politics," he deadpanned.

Such was the self-deprecating wit that kept Beckel gainfully employed after Mondale's forty-nine-state defeat to Ronald Reagan. By the time Reagan ran for reelection in 1984, Beckel had decided it was safer to talk about politics than actually participate. He became a talking head. His quick wit and acid tongue soon earned him regular appearances on ABC and CNN. He began co-hosting CNN's *Crossfire Sunday*. Naturally, he argued from the left. After Reagan settled in for his second term, Beckel formed his own political consulting firm, Bob Beckel and Associates. Although he gradually eased out of the talking head business, he became popular on the speaking circuit. Year after year, he crisscrossed the nation to give speeches at trade meetings, corporate retreats, visiting nurses associations, any group that ponied up the speaker's fee. He was often paired with a conservative speaker, who was invariably less funny than Beckel. In fact, even conservative audiences couldn't help but like this husky, irreverent partisan who jokingly referred to himself as "the last liberal white guy in America."

Still, the constant grind of traveling from one town to another, giving essentially the same speech day after day, took its toll on Beckel. It was a lucrative business, but the old passion had faded. He had been milking his one famous line—"Where's the beef?"—for sixteen years and began wondering how much longer he could continue. At age fifty, he was entertaining serious thoughts about getting out of the political game altogether.

But as Beckel stayed up late to watch the incredible drama unfold on Election Night 2000, he began to feel those old passions stir for the first time in years. He was fascinated to see a Florida election official go on television in the wee hours of the morning and announce the last remaining counties to be tallied.

"I thought: That's an old scam I used to pull," Beckel said. "You'd hold back a couple counties. You'd call the county guys and say, 'Don't report until I tell you to.' I mean, at least the guy could have said, 'I'm not sure what's out.'

"Well, that got me to thinking about it," Beckel said. "I began thinking that this might be worth taking a look at. Just my own curiosity."

An idea began to take shape in Beckel's mind. While his interest in political rhetoric had waned, he had never lost his passion for the statistical minutia of precinct-by-precinct politics. By now,

computer modeling had taken political targeting to a level of sophis-
tication Beckel had never dreamed possible a quarter century earlier.
In fact, he had been quietly employing this vastly refined tool to conduct private polling and in-depth analyses of voting patterns. Beckel
had remained something of an expert in the political nuances of not
just states, but individual counties and even precincts. Suddenly, to
his astonishment, it looked as though a handful of his beloved
precincts and counties would determine the entire presidency. It was
precisely the opposite of Mondale's forty-nine-state blowout.

"I literally made the decision at 5 o'clock in the morning," he
said. "I decided that I wanted to take a targeted look at the votes.
I decided to look at these precincts, particularly black precincts in
Florida, and the Palm Beach precincts, and look at the voting patterns—going back over the last three presidential elections,
precinct by precinct."

Beckel was particularly mesmerized by the fury over the "butterfly" ballot. Palm Beach County residents were insisting they had
been confused into voting for both Gore and Buchanan. While
Beckel recognized immediately that there was no way to salvage
ballots on which voters had chosen two presidential candidates, he
nonetheless sensed the political opportunities.

"If you vote twice, it's too bad. That's just the way it is, even
though clearly the intent of those people was to vote for Gore. But
I wanted to know how many of those people there were. How
many had made a mistake like that," he said. "I mean, you just
can't make a legal case for the overvotes. But you can make a
moral case, which is really what I was doing. I was trying to make
a moral case for it."

Beckel's embryonic idea was now growing wings and claws. If
Bush's lead in Florida held, he would have 271 of the nation's 538
electoral votes—exactly one more than he needed to become pres-

ident. But if Beckel could somehow convince three Bush electors to defect, Gore would become the forty-third president of the United States. Even if Beckel could flip just two Bush electors, the race would become deadlocked, with each candidate holding 269 votes. There would be a terrific uproar, of course, but the election would have to be resolved by the House of Representatives. Although the GOP-dominated House would certainly support Bush, perhaps it wouldn't come to that. Perhaps Gore could figure out a way to resurrect enough votes before then to win.

Beckel knew more about the obscure topic of presidential electors than most Americans. After all, he had actually seated a slate of electors in the 1984 election. He knew that both parties chose electors primarily on the basis of loyalty. It would be extremely difficult to convince even a single elector to defect. In fact, many states had passed laws making such defections illegal. Although Beckel considered those laws unconstitutional, now was not the time to fight that esoteric battle. Besides, there were plenty of states in which flipping electors—while politically taboo—was not prohibited by law.

Perhaps Beckel could locate a few weak links in Bush's chain of electors. Then he could make a compelling case that Gore had won not only more votes nationwide, but should have won more votes in Florida. Beckel would appeal to their basic sense of fairness.

"If you could make the case that a significant number of people intended to vote for Gore over Bush in Florida, and if you sent a study—a real statistical study, affirmed by three good political scientists—to electors in states where Bush won, where the electors are not bound by law, then I'm sure there would be electors, Republican electors, who are perfectly decent people, who've had a history of being fair and compassionate people, who might be at least willing to read it," Beckel said. "It was so close. All it would take would be two electors.

"By early afternoon, it occurred to me: Shit, if this study comes out the way I think it's gonna come out, I'm gonna send it to Bush electors," Beckel said. "So within eight hours the whole idea came together in my head."

Now Beckel's idea was fully formed, fangs and all. It was an incredible long shot, but the potential payoff was undeniably sweet. Bob Beckel, the man who had lost forty-nine states to the Republicans, would single-handedly deliver the White House to the Democrats. Perhaps this was Beckel's shot at redemption.

"The chances of that happening, in my own mind, were about five hundred to one," he acknowledged. "But I just had to. I mean, from my own conscience, I just had to do it."

Almost immediately, Beckel faced a problem. If he sent out a mass mailing to all 271 Bush electors, his plot would certainly be exposed and demonized by the GOP. After all, most electors were party stalwarts who served in state legislatures or had similarly high-profile positions in the GOP. These guys would take one look at Bob Beckel's effort to flip electors and run screaming to the press. The backlash against Gore might be severe. No, these high-profile Republicans were not Beckel's target audience. He needed to go in under the radar and pick off the weak or vulnerable members of the herd. He had to hone in on relatively obscure Republicans who were not hard-wired into the party hierarchy.

"I was gonna call friends of mine in these targeted states, people that I knew, and simply say: Look, of these electors here, which ones—'cause they all don't have titles on their names—which ones are, you know, state reps, state senators, people who just wouldn't even begin to look at my study, so I wouldn't send it to them."

Beckel figured that once he was armed with such information, he could separate the wheat from the chaff when it came to targeting electors.

"I've seated electors before, so I know a little bit about this," he said. "You do try to put your brother, your mother, anybody you can on that you know is going to be with you. But there are states where the state chairman or the governor, if he's in your party, will say: 'By the way, Mary Rose down the road here has been an elector for twenty years, you know. Put her on, will you, 'cause she's a loyal Republican and blah, blah, blah.'"

The Mary Roses of the electoral college became Beckel's target audience. They would become his "faithless electors."

"Then, of course, the problem became getting all the information and how you do that while keeping the thing completely quiet," Beckel said. "And I thought: There's just no way that anybody's going to know about this. Certainly, I didn't mention it to my wife, I didn't mention it to anybody."

By Wednesday afternoon, Beckel was already researching some of his targeted precincts in Florida. But he had to interrupt his work in order to give a long-scheduled speech in Washington with Rich Bond, former chairman of the Republican National Committee.

"Bond was in a furious mood and so was I," Beckel recalled. "I jumped on Bush and he got really angry. But I never, ever mentioned my plan. All I said was, 'Look, Rich, whether you ever want to believe this or not, George Bush did not win the state of Florida, in my view. And who knows? Maybe some electors will have a change of conscience.' That's all I said."

But in the superheated political atmosphere that had already taken hold that first day of the post-election struggle, Beckel's comments were fighting words to Republicans in the audience. Rumblings of a Democratic plot to flip Bush electors began to spread in GOP circles. Oblivious to the fact that he had already tipped his hand, Bob Beckel discretely resumed work on his new project.

"The next day I retained a statistics firm from the Midwest—on my own dime," he said. "The reason I wanted to keep this thing quiet was because I knew how explosive it was. I shouldn't say that. I thought I knew, but I never really understood. I've never seen anything like this—the passions on this thing."

Beckel managed to work on his project in secrecy for about a week. He had made contact with one hundred people who agreed to send feelers out to potentially vulnerable electors. Then Beckel received a phone call from the *Wall Street Journal*. A reporter named Tom Hamburger wanted to know about Beckel's "study."

"I said to Tom, 'Where'd you get that?' and he said, 'Well, you know, I've got sources, Bob,'" recalled Beckel. "And instead of taking a deep breath and saying, 'I'll get back to you,' I said: 'Tom, I've known you for a long time. That's a damn good piece of reporting. I am doing a study, that's true.'"

Beckel went on to explain his project, hoping it would be portrayed in the best possible light.

"It is information gathering on my part, using my own network," he told Hamburger. "I call on mostly Democrats, but some Republicans, too, and ask, 'Who are these electors and what do you know about them?' I just wanted to know who these electors are."

Beckel emphasized that he had not yet contacted the electors directly. "I wouldn't do that without first informing the Gore campaign."

By the time the interview was over, the damage had been done. On Thursday, November 16, the front page of the *Wall Street Journal* had a story headlined: "Gore resolves to stay on offensive as Democratic aides rally to his cause." The story revealed that Beckel had "begun a quiet intelligence-gathering operation that could aid a last-ditch Gore strategy in the Electoral College." The story went on to explain that Beckel, who had "close ties" to

Warren Christopher, Gore's point man in Florida, "has been check-
ing into the background of Republican electors, with an eye
toward persuading a handful of them to vote for Mr. Gore."

Readers came away with the impression that Beckel was digging up dirt on the personal lives of Bush electors in order to black-
mail them into defecting to Gore's team. After all, this was
precisely what the Clinton-Gore team did during impeachment,
encouraging surrogates to dredge up long buried secrets about
members of Congress, Democrat and Republican alike, who were
critical of the White House.

As soon as he read the story, Beckel knew he was in trouble.

"I never should have used the word 'background,'" he said. "It
came out like I was looking into the background of electors, as
opposed to the background of the laws of the states.

"But you know, I look back on this now and I say to myself:
'You've been around too long to make these dumb mistakes like
that.' But, like everybody, we were exhausted."

Beckel insisted he never had any intention of blackmailing
electors with personal dirt.

"I would no more do that than shoot my neighbor's kid," he
said. "The whole idea was abhorrent to me. But when I read it that
way, I don't blame the other side for being furious. I'd have been
furious too if I read that."

The story broke on the same day that Florida Secretary of State
Katherine Harris conditionally certified Bush as the winner—pend-
ing adjustments from overseas absentee ballots, which were due
the next day. With Harris poised to definitively certify Bush as the
winner just two days thence, Beckel's plot triggered alarm bells
within the Bush camp. After all, by this time Gore's own press
secretary, Chris Lehane, had publicly observed that half the states
have no laws against faithless electors.

At first, Beckel's plot was largely overshadowed by the crush of other developments that day. It was day nine of the post-election debacle and the public was becoming accustomed to a nonstop torrent of plot twists, each one more stunning than the previous. In this sort of maelstrom, the Beckel story might very well have fizzled out. But then he went and poured gasoline on the whole incendiary mess.

"I'm trying to kidnap electors," Beckel announced to Neil Cavuto of Fox News Channel on Friday, November 17. "Whatever it takes."

Beckel later insisted he wasn't trying to be provocative. He had simply come to believe that it was his patriotic duty as an American to find faithless electors.

"When the Founders developed the whole concept, the idea was that electors, early on, were lobbied. Very hard. And if you weren't going to be able to contact electors, why not just have numbers? Why go through this ritual, right? And so not only wasn't there anything technically wrong, it was perfectly legal."

But in the year 2000, the American public found the quest for faithless electors deeply troubling. Beckel blamed GOP partisans for fomenting public opposition to his plan.

"When dyed-in-the-wool, hard-core, Republican Bush supporters heard that an elector could switch, they just assumed that a liberal Democrat—and the Democrats are the Clinton people and the Gore people—were gonna break the law and do anything they could to get their vote. And so there was paranoia rampant about it.

"It was picked up by I can't tell you how many local TV and newspapers and run. And it was just exactly the wrong story at exactly the wrong time. So I think that's what inflamed it. I don't think it had anything to do with me. It had to do with the perception that we're out there intimidating people, threatening people. And the second thought in the mind in that kind of person is:

Typical of the Clinton-Gore crowd—anything to win. So I was all of a sudden lumped in with Gore. And I've never liked Gore that much. I haven't spoken to Gore in years."

Beckel insisted he wasn't working for the Gore campaign.

"Not in any way," he said. "In fact, they were furious with me. They sent word back through my guys that work for me that the national crowd was furious with me. And then Gore came out, very gratuitously one night, in one of those evening statements, saying: 'And by the way, I'll accept no elector from George Bush.' It just got me more pissed off."

Still, Beckel acknowledged he had provided advice to the Gore camp in the closing days of the campaign. Furthermore, the Gore team was actively flirting with the idea of flipping electors, even as the vice president publicly tried to distance himself from the plot. In fact, Gore had even retained an authority on the Electoral College to advise him on his prospects.

"Gore is three electors away from a victory, two away from a tie," the expert told Frank J. Murray of the *Washington Times*. "Some might defect."

By now, more Democrats than just Beckel were on the quest for faithless electors. Web sites sprang up overnight, urging Democrats to bombard electors with phone calls, letters, faxes, and e-mails. The names and addresses of electors were plastered all over the Internet. Four electors in particular were singled out for intense lobbying because they were thought to be vulnerable. But even the other electors were barraged with tens of thousands of pleas. For every call or letter or fax from a Democrat who was urging defection, the electors received two more from Republicans who implored them to stand firm.

Gore officials took comfort in historical precedents. As recently as 1960, six Alabama electors who signed pledges to vote for

John F. Kennedy voted instead for Senator Harry Byrd, a Virginia Democrat. That same year, an Oklahoma elector was persuaded to switch from Richard Nixon to Byrd.

However, the furor over Democratic efforts to raid Bush electors only served to strengthen the resolve of Republicans who had pledged to vote for the Texas governor. The Republican Party, sensing it had Democrats on the run over an explosive issue, decided to press its advantage. On Wednesday, November 15, Republican National Committee Chairman Jim Nicholson drafted an e-mail entitled "Help Stop Democratic Electoral Tampering." It urged recipients to "express your outrage at [Beckel's] low-handed tactics." On the day before Thanksgiving, the e-mail was sent to hundreds of thousands of Republicans across the nation.

"I got a call from my office on Wednesday afternoon, saying that the phones were ringing off the hook, the faxes were coming in about my project," Beckel recalled. "I didn't think much about it. I thought, well, maybe it's a latent reaction to one of my TV appearances or something.

"And then Friday, after Thanksgiving, I went into the office and literally every line was lit up. Ten lines and they were all lit. The fax machine was backed up a thousand something. The postman came in looking like Santy Claus.

"It got nasty, I tell you. I got 15,000 faxes, 10,000 letters, 2,000 phone calls, 132 death threats. They picked up a guy in Harrisburg, Pennsylvania, with my picture and a bullet hole through it—with a gun. So it was just brutal. They got into my garage at my office and wrote 'You're dead.' I had to go into protective custody."

Beckel, his wife and their children fled to what he called a "safe house" in Maryland. But he kept working to find faithless electors. By now it was obvious that no Bush elector would actually switch sides and vote for Gore. So Beckel began searching for a few who would merely abstain. Four abstentions would be enough to throw the election into the House. Five would give Gore the lead, 267-266, although it was doubtful he could be elected president without a full contingent of 270. Still, Gore would then be able to argue he received more votes in both the Electoral College and the popular election. It would be a public relations triumph, if nothing else. Beckel redoubled his efforts, eventually moving his family back home under the watchful eye of a twenty-four-hour security force.

"My wife, as you can imagine, she just didn't understand this. Ohhh, God. I mean, we'd been through this with the right-to-life people, the gun people, but in smaller numbers. Nothing like this.

"Fortunately, they hadn't found the home number, which I was very surprised at. After about four weeks, five weeks, when I hadn't gotten a call at home, and everything had cooled down, I finally got down to just overnight security."

However, things took a turn for the worse one day as Beckel took his daughter to a neighborhood restaurant.

"My wife comes into McDonald's with a look on her face that was frightening—which my daughter, fortunately, did not see. And she said I need to talk to you for a second. So we stepped over to the side and she said there's a phone call at home on the recorder and it says: 'Beckel, you're gonna die. But you're gonna watch your wife and kids die before you.'

"You can imagine what that did. That sent them back to western Maryland to the safe house that we had out there. Three times I had to do that. It was just horrible."

While his family life deteriorated, so did the atmosphere at his own office. Two top Democratic staffers quit in protest at Beckel's attempt to tamper with the electoral system.

On Thursday, November 30, Beckel got the chance to publicly lambaste Jim Nicholson for the e-mail during a joint appearance on ABC's *Good Morning America.*

"The Constitution gives me a right to send a piece of mail to an elector," Beckel said. "This is an incendiary time, Jim, and I will tell you: I'll take my responsibility for this project and understand how sensitive it is. But I didn't organize a massive campaign. You did. These people have a right to contact me. But you asked them to contact me by suggesting I've done something illegal. It's wrong, Jim."

It took Beckel well into December to complete his project. To give it credibility, he pointed out that Bush had been cheated out of thousands of votes in the western panhandle when the TV networks prematurely and erroneously called Florida for Bush. But he argued that those gains would be outweighed by votes Gore should have received in Palm Beach County and elsewhere in the state where voters were confused by ballots. Beckel enclosed a letter, asking the electors to examine their consciences and consider abstaining. He also pointed out that this was his first contact with them. He disavowed other Democratic efforts to lobby the electors. Seeking to establish common ground, he also pointed out that he, like the electors, had been subjected to a barrage of harassment in recent weeks.

But the electors held firm. Not one broke ranks. Ironically, their resolve had been fortified by the earlier uproar over Beckel's bombast. Many of them had received calls directly from the Bush camp, which made them all the more determined to resist Beckel's overtures. The Democratic strategist had unwittingly played a major role in galvanizing Republicans to rally around Bush. His plan had backfired. Bob Beckel, the man who had lost forty-nine states to Reagan, had also blown his shot at redemption.

"But I'll say this: I was on my way out of politics altogether. I mean, I got tired of the whole damn thing," Beckel confided. "This got me reenergized, I can tell you that. I mean, as soon as I get some of these bandages off, I'm back in their swingin'."

CHAPTER 12

"MAY HAVE EVEN BEEN SLIGHTLY FAVORABLE"

O n Wednesday, November 22, George W. Bush finally reached for the heavy artillery. He asked the U.S. Supreme Court to step into the Florida imbroglio and end the madness. It was a profound escalation of the battle, the political equivalent of going thermonuclear. And yet it received surprisingly scant attention from the press. For one thing, the request was overshadowed by the daily crush of earth-shattering developments that by now had become routine in this sprawling, all-consuming story. But more important, the Democrats and the press had always poohpoohed the notion that the standoff would be decided in the federal court system. They insisted the whole fight was a state matter that would ultimately be resolved by the Florida Supreme Court.

There was no small measure of wishful thinking in this attitude. After all, the Florida Supreme Court was a liberal, activist bench whose members were all Democratic appointees. Several justices, including Chief Justice Charles T. Wells, had been active contributors to the Democratic Party before their appointment to the bench. Since there were no conservatives on the bench, there was no competing school of ideological thought; no healthy dissension or devil's advocate to expose weaknesses in majority opinions; no robust debate in which all sides of an issue were thoroughly vetted. In fact, the court almost always ruled unanimously. It was downright creepy. So it was not surprising that Gore kept insisting these seven liberal justices should be the final arbiters of the presidency.

By contrast, the U.S. Supreme Court was a mixed bag of liberals, moderates, and conservatives. There was plenty of robust debate and healthy dissension on any number of weighty issues. The court often split 5-to-4 on important decisions, although there was no telling which way the split would fall in many cases. While the press characterized the U.S. Supreme Court as stridently conservative for the purposes of the Florida story, the court was not conservative enough, for example, to overturn *Roe* v. *Wade*, which legalized abortion. The truth of the matter was that Democrats feared their case simply wasn't strong enough to stand up in the U.S. Supreme Court, if it went that far. So they ridiculed suggestions that the court would even take the case and encouraged the press to do the same. The conventional wisdom became almost monolithic: Federal courts were loath to stick their noses into state controversies. The U.S. Supreme Court would be especially reluctant to wade into this contentious quagmire. It was the longest of long shots.

So, from the very beginning of the post-election struggle, the media focused most of its attention on the Florida state court system, which was deluged with scores of Gore lawsuits. Besides, whenever Bush sought relief from a federal court, he came up empty handed. Federal courts in Miami and Orlando had rejected Bush arguments from the very first days of the battle. While the Eleventh Circuit Court of Appeals in Atlanta was sufficiently intrigued by the case that all twelve justices considered its merits, the court ultimately told Bush to try again later, after the dispute had been thoroughly adjudicated by the Florida Supreme Court.

And so it seemed unremarkable when Bush, having suffered a severe setback at the hands of the Florida Supreme Court, appealed its sweeping, pro-Gore ruling directly to the U.S. Supreme Court. As far as the Democrats and press were concerned, Bush was merely tilting at windmills yet again. The poor guy was practically delusional. There was simply no way on God's green earth that the nation's highest court—which was notoriously reluctant to entangle itself in politically superheated brawls—would accept the Florida case.

At the time Bush made his request, Katherine Harris was still four days away from certifying the statewide results, thanks to the deadline extension by the Florida Supreme Court. Although Miami-Dade County had just called off its hand recount, Broward and Palm Beach counties were still frantically tallying ballots. Bush feared these counts would put Gore over the top before certification, so he asked the U.S. Supreme Court to halt them.

"The unequal, constantly changing, and standardless selective manual vote recount under way for the past two weeks in Florida is a patently unfair process that is having an impact far beyond Florida's borders, and that cries out for correction by this court," Bush lawyers said in their filing.

The Republicans argued what they had been arguing all along in both the federal courts and the Florida Supreme Court—that selective hand recounts were unconstitutional. The logic was fairly straightforward: Since the tallies had turned up previously undiscovered votes for both candidates in all four counties selected by Gore, it seemed reasonable to assume that there were additional undiscovered votes in most, if not all, of the remaining sixty-three counties. And yet those votes would remain undiscovered because Gore had not requested hand recounts in those other sixty-three counties. As a result, voters in the four selected counties were more likely to have their ballots counted than their neighbors in the rest of Florida. That meant a vote in Volusia, Broward, Palm Beach, or Miami-Dade counties carried more weight than a vote in the other counties. In America, every person's vote was supposed to count the same as every other person's. Thus, the hand tallying of ballots in selected Democratic counties was a violation of the Fourteenth Amendment's "equal protection" clause because it diluted the impact of votes in other counties.

This was not the only federal or constitutional issue raised by the Florida fiasco. Bush also argued that the Florida Supreme Court had usurped the authority of the state legislature to select presidential electors. After all, the U.S. Constitution explicitly grants state legislatures the sole authority to choose electors. In fact, in the early years of the republic, state legislatures chose electors directly—without bothering to hold popular elections. Technically, the only reason residents of Florida or any other state got to vote in presidential elections was because the legislatures had specifically constructed such popular contests as their way of selecting presidential electors. But if the legislatures preferred, they could return to choosing the electors themselves. In other words, twentieth-century Americans were able to vote for president only because they were granted permission by their state legislatures. Nowhere in the Constitution are ordinary citizens given the authority to choose electors. And nowhere in the Constitution are courts given such authority. So Bush argued that the Florida Supreme Court, by sweeping away the legislature's election laws and substituting its own scheme, had violated the Constitution.

Finally, Bush argued that the Florida Supreme Court violated a federal law that bars states from changing their election rules after the election. When voters went to the polls on November 7 in Florida, state law required that their votes be certified on November 14, subject only to the addition of overseas ballots. More than a week after the election, the Florida Supreme Court unilaterally changed the law by extending the deadline until November 26. While that might have been defensible if it had been done prior to Election Day, changing state election rules after the fact clearly violated federal law.

Bush lawyers used unusually colorful language in their twenty-eight-page petition to the U.S. Supreme Court. They said the Florida Supreme Court's ruling "opens the door to an electoral catastrophe." Moreover, "some Florida officials were bent on paving the road to chaos that the state supreme court has now endorsed." The Florida recounts were a "circus."

"In plain contravention of the requirement of the Constitution of the United States and federal law, the state supreme court has embarked on an ad hoc, standardless, and lawless exercise of judicial power, which appears designed to thwart the will of the electorate as well as the considered judgments of Florida's executive and legislative branches," the lawyers fumed.

Publicly, Gore's lawyers continued to roll their eyes at Bush's childish and delusional insistence on running to the U.S. Supreme Court. But privately, the lawyers were alarmed by this dramatic escalation of legal warfare. One day after Bush asked the high court to step in, Gore asked it to butt out. In briefs filed Thursday evening, Gore lawyers called Bush's request a "bald attempt to federalize a state court dispute." They went on to warn: "This court's interference with the normal processes by which questions of state law are resolved, and… the president and vice president of the United States are chosen, would only diminish the legitimacy of the outcome of the election."

It was yet another role reversal. The Democrats were uncharacteristically arguing that states—not the federal government—should hash out their own disputes. The Republicans—who normally champion states' rights over federal intervention—were now begging the feds to get involved. Some conservative purists openly criticized Bush's strategy, even as they acknowledged it might be his only hope of securing the White House.

The verbal broadsides hurled by the Bush and Gore legal teams in their filings to the U.S. Supreme Court were largely overshadowed by the more pressing developments of the week. On Wednesday, the day Bush filed his petition, the news of the day was Miami-Dade calling off its hand recount in the face of GOP "rioters." On Thursday, the day Gore filed his reply, the press focused on the Florida Supreme Court's refusal to force Miami-Dade to resume the recount.

It wasn't until Friday, when the U.S. Supreme Court announced it would take the case, that the world suddenly sat up and took notice. Moving with uncharacteristic speed, the court announced it would hear ninety minutes of oral arguments in one week—starting Friday, December 1. It asked both sides to provide briefs by Tuesday and replies by Thursday. The whole thing struck terror into the hearts of Gore's legal team, who nonetheless put on a brave face.

"I will predict that the United States Supreme Court is not going to reverse the Florida Supreme Court," Gore lawyer David Boies boasted in Tallahassee.

But the nation's high court sure seemed interested in wading into the dispute. In an extraordinary move, it asked both sides for advice on what, if anything, it should do in the event that Bush turned out to be right about the Florida Supreme Court having violated federal law. The court seemed intrigued by the dispute, which heartened the Bush team.

The media's focus on the U.S. Supreme Court turned out to be fleeting. In the week between accepting the case and actually hearing the arguments, the high court was shunted to the back pages again by the ever more colossal developments of the day. In fact, one of those developments seemed to indicate Bush wouldn't need the U.S. Supreme Court after all. On Sunday, two days after the high court agreed to take the case, Bush was certified the winner of Florida after all. Although he had failed to shut down the recounts in Palm Beach and Miami-Dade, he still came out on top. Only when Gore filed a new lawsuit to contest the election results did the Bush team realize it might still need the U.S. Supreme Court as a firewall.

But during the last days of November, the world paid far more attention to a down-home county judge named N. Sanders Sauls than it did to the mightiest court in America. After all, at least Sauls allowed TV cameras into his humble courtroom in Tallahassee.

By contrast, the U.S. Supreme Court maintained its aversion to cameras—although it allowed the proceedings to be audiotaped and then played back after the hearing concluded. But the lack of moving pictures to animate the esoteric legal arguments prompted ABC and CBS to quickly cut away from the audio feed. The twenty-four-hour cable news channels, however, played the whole thing, giving viewers an earful of the rarified legal debate.

Bush's lead attorney, Theodore B. Olson, spoke for less than a minute before the first justice interrupted. Soon questions were flying from all the justices except Clarence Thomas, who maintained a studied silence.

At length, it became apparent that the court's two moderates—Justices Anthony M. Kennedy and Sandra Day O'Connor—were troubled by the Florida Supreme Court's wholesale rewriting of election laws.

"I mean, it had to register somehow with the Florida courts that that statute was there and that it might be in the state's best interest not to go around changing the law after the election," O'Connor said.

Kennedy added: "What we're talking about is having laws with sufficient specificity and stability that people can rely on them in advance and not have them changed after the fact."

But this change did not seem to bother liberal justices Ruth Bader Ginsburg and Stephen G. Breyer.

"I do not know of any case where we have impugned a state supreme court the way you are doing in this case," Ginsburg admonished Olson.

Breyer, a personal friend of Al Gore, wondered aloud whether the court could even "make a difference to the outcome of the election," since Bush was certified as the winner after asking the high court to take the case.

Gore's lead attorney, Harvard law professor Laurence Tribe, accused the Bush team of "disenfranchising people, which is what this is all about. Disenfranchising people isn't very nice."

The court rendered its verdict at noon on Monday, December 4. The nine justices unanimously granted Bush's request to nullify the Florida Supreme Court's entire decision. The high court archly described the ruling by the state supreme court as riddled with "obscurities and ambiguities." As politely as possible, the justices said their Florida counterparts had ignored the federal law against changing the rules after an election. Finally, the U.S. Supreme Court all but accused the Florida justices of thumbing their noses at the U.S. Constitution, which expressly authorized state legislatures, not courts, to determine the method of choosing electors. The repudiation was so complete that the U.S. Supreme Court saw no need to delve any further into the constitutional questions raised by Bush's petition. After all, those questions now seemed moot.

"The judgment of the Supreme Court of Florida is therefore vacated," the nine justices wrote.

"Vacated" is the legalistic word judges use when they mean "obliterated from the face of the earth." The highest court in the nation had summarily wiped from the books the entire forty-two-page ruling by the highest court in Florida. The vaunted ruling that had accused Katherine Harris of trying to disenfranchise voters with her "hypertechnical reliance upon statutory provisions" suddenly was no longer the law of the land. The Florida court's unilateral extension of the certification deadline, which had given the very breath of life to Gore's dying bid to seize the presidency, had been one gigantic legal mistake that was now retroactively rendered null and void. The U.S. Supreme Court invited its junior varsity counterpart in the Sunshine State to take another crack at producing even a shred of justification for its ruling, but the invitation was more of an academic exercise. Al Gore's one sweeping court victory was no more.

Gore, who had publicly hailed the Florida Supreme Court's ruling as a "wise" decree that made "democracy... the winner," changed his tune after it was repudiated.

"Well, I think the U.S. Supreme Court ruling was neutral," Gore told reporters, warming to his own spin. "May have even been slightly favorable to us."

But the ruling was not even remotely favorable to Gore. It retroactively declared the Florida Supreme Court's extension of the certification deadline illegal. Since Broward County had made use of that illegal extension to give Gore a net gain of 567 votes, it was entirely arguable that those votes no longer existed, at least in a legal sense. While the U.S. Supreme Court did not explicitly instruct Katherine Harris to subtract those 567 votes from Gore, that was certainly the logical effect of the ruling. Harris felt it was a moot point, since Bush was still in the lead anyway. But if Gore had somehow managed to overcome Bush's 537-vote lead, Bush could now argue that Gore should be deprived of the 567 votes he netted in Broward's tardy hand recount.

In fairness, Gore could certainly argue that the military ballots that were belatedly accepted by a dozen canvassing boards after their early "hypertechnical" rejection should be disqualified again, since they were counted after the original absentee deadline of November 17. But that would have meant a loss of only 176 votes for Bush. If both candidates' late ballots were retroactively subtracted, Bush would still end up with a net gain of 391 votes more than his certified, 537-vote lead.

But Katherine Harris, having already been savaged by the Gore camp and the press, was not about to announce that she was summarily throwing out the military ballots and the fruits of an eleven-day recount in Broward County. Since Bush was still ahead, she decided to leave well enough alone.

Besides, three hours after the U.S. Supreme Court vacated the Florida Supreme Court's sweeping, pro-Gore decision, Leon County Circuit Judge N. Sanders Sauls decisively crushed every element of Gore's lawsuit contesting the certified results of Florida's election. Not even Al Gore could spin this second devastating defeat of the day into something "slightly favorable" or even "neutral." Instead, he immediately appealed the Sauls ruling to the bench that had just been subjected to an unprecedented public humiliation—the Florida Supreme Court.

CHAPTER 13

AL GORE, POLITICAL KAMIKAZE

On the afternoon of Monday, December 4, it became obvious that Al Gore could not possibly become president. Despite nearly a month of fierce combat, Gore had lost virtually every battle of the post-election war. He lost the initial vote count. He lost the mandatory statewide recount. He lost the manual recounts in his handpicked Democratic counties. He lost before the U.S. Supreme Court, which vaporized the Florida Supreme Court's pro-Gore ruling. He lost his appeal before Circuit Judge N. Sanders Sauls. In short, the vice president had now decisively lost both the protest and the contest phases of the post-election struggle. His entire effort had been an abject failure.

And yet, as grim as the last twenty-seven days now looked, the next eight looked even grimmer. No matter what Gore might be able to accomplish by December 12, the deadline for seating electors, Bush possessed four enormous trump cards that would surely prevent the vice president from prevailing in the end.

The first was Katherine Harris, the Florida secretary of state and honorary chairman of Bush's Florida campaign. Any new votes that Gore might find in the next eight days would not really count unless they were certified by Harris, the state's chief elections officer. Harris had already certified Bush as the winner and sent the names of twenty-five Republican electors to the National Archivist in Washington. Her authority to certify a winner had been upheld by county judges in Tallahassee and the U.S. Supreme Court in Washington. The only court that had challenged Harris's discretion was the Florida Supreme Court, whose ruling was subsequently "vacated" by the U.S. Supreme Court. Even if the Florida court tried to force Harris to accept new votes that Gore might unearth in the next eight days, it seemed unlikely such a ruling would stand. In fact, having already been vindicated by both lower and higher courts, Harris would be well within her rights to defy any new ruling by the Florida Supreme Court. Sure, it would set up an unprecedented showdown between the executive and judicial branches of Florida's government. But by this point in the post-election struggle, unprecedented showdowns were a dime a dozen.

The second trump card possessed by Bush was the U.S. Supreme Court itself. In the event that the beleaguered Katherine Harris would not have the stomach to stand up to the Florida Supreme Court, the U.S. Supreme Court would almost certainly administer another slap-down. After all, the high court had already demonstrated its willingness to rein in the judicial activism of the Sunshine State's seven liberal justices. If the Florida Supreme Court were to insist on embarking on yet another adventure in rewriting state law, the U.S. Supreme Court would be forced to intervene—if for no other reason than to defend its own imperative. To refrain from intervening would be tantamount to letting the lower court get away with flouting the highest court in the land. Like it or not, the U.S. Supreme Court now had a dog in this fight. It was not about to stand idly by while that dog got mauled.

The third and perhaps most powerful trump card was the Florida legislature, which by this point had clearly signaled it would step in and restore Bush's electors, if necessary. In fact, the GOP-dominated legislature was already preparing for a special session that would reappoint the Bush slate in the event it was dislodged by a Gore court victory. Even Florida Minority Leader Lois Frankel, a devoted Democrat, acknowledged the reality of the situation.

"Republicans want George Bush to win and will make sure that happens," she lamented.

Republicans, meanwhile, pointed to the Constitution: "Each state shall appoint, in such manner as the legislature thereof may direct, a number of electors." There was further explication in *The Federalist*. "Without the intervention of the State Legislature, the President of the United States cannot be elected at all," wrote James Madison, the father of the Constitution, in Federalist 45. "They must in all cases have a great share of his appointment and will, perhaps, in most cases, of themselves determine it." In Federalist 68, Alexander Hamilton said the selection of electors is left to state legislatures in order "to afford as little opportunity as possible to tumult and disorder."

Bush supporters now pointed to the "tumult and disorder" in Florida as justification for the legislature's intervention. GOP lawmakers would enforce their constitutional right to choose electors—if Gore forced their hand by trying to circumvent the slate already certified by Katherine Harris. The legislature's action, grounded in the Constitution, was certain to be upheld by the federal courts, including the Supreme Court.

Besides, Florida lawmakers had a very real fear that if they did not act, they risked disenfranchising all 6 million voters in the state. That's because if Gore managed to displace Bush's slate of electors with a slate of his own, or if both candidates ended up fielding competing slates of electors, the U.S. Congress might simply ignore Florida when it came time to ratify the Electoral College vote on January 5. Republicans on Capitol Hill were already warning they would not accept a Florida slate of electors for Gore. That might prevent the state's 6 million voters from having any voice at all.

In fact, the U.S. Congress was Bush's fourth trump card. Although both parties on Capitol Hill genuinely dreaded the prospect of being forced to adjudicate the presidency, this "doomsday scenario" was becoming more plausible with each passing day. Both the Democrats and Republicans drafted plans on how to handle what would be an even stickier political problem than impeachment. A slate of Gore electors would certainly prompt an objection from at least one House member and one senator. That would be enough to send the matter to both chambers for separate votes. Although the Gore slate would be rejected by the Republican majority in the House, the Senate was split 50-50, with Joe Lieberman still among the Democrats. Ironically, such a tie would be broken by Gore, who as vice president remained president of the Senate until January 20. With Gore and Lieberman guaranteeing Senate support of the Gore slate and the House supporting the Bush slate, the deadlock would be broken by the governor of Florida, who happened to be Bush's brother, Jeb. In politics, it is hard to find a surer bet than your own brother.

By this stage of the post-election struggle, Democratic strategist Bob Beckel had abandoned his hopes of convincing a handful of Bush electors to defect and instead was urging them to merely abstain. But even if Beckel succeeded, Bush would surely end up winning in the long run. That's because if neither candidate won the 270 electors necessary for election, the contest would be decided by the House alone, as prescribed by the Twelfth Amendment. Instead of each House member getting one vote, each state delegation would get one vote. Since the Republicans controlled twenty-eight of the fifty state delegations, Bush would win.

All four of these Bush trump cards were on the table and in plain sight to Gore on the afternoon of Monday, December 4. But instead of acknowledging the obvious and releasing the nation from its protracted political purgatory, Gore chose to redouble his efforts and fight blindly onward with his scorched-earth warfare. There are two possible explanations for this political suicide mission.

The first is that Gore genuinely believed he could prevail against the Florida secretary of state, the U.S. Supreme Court, the Florida legislature, and the U.S. Congress. But this explanation flies in the face of everything that is known of Gore's ballyhooed intellect and considerable political skills.

The second explanation is much more plausible. Gore knew he could not win, but decided to inflict as much damage as possible on the inevitable Bush presidency. He figured he might as well go out in a blaze of glory, undermining the legitimacy of the coming Republican administration. Besides, to give up now would mean Gore would have to face that most painful of realities—the sudden death of his political career. Any hope of becoming the automatic front-runner for the Democratic Party in 2004 had died in those first weeks of the post-election debacle. Gore might as well play out the string for the next eight days, regardless of the toll it would take on the nation. He would become a political kamikaze, sacrificing his future presidential ambitions for the long-term benefit of the Democratic Party. In fact, he was quietly encouraged to carry out this strategy by labor and civil rights leaders, who hoped to salvage something from the Florida fiasco by inflicting maximum damage on Bush.

So Gore's decision on December 4 to continue fighting was fundamentally different from his decision on November 9 to officially protest the outcome of the election. It was a decision somewhat modulated by the counsel of moderate Democrats who wanted to limit their own kamikaze risk by demanding that Gore affix an end point to his agonizing quest. The vice president reluctantly agreed. For the first time in nearly a month, Gore's team publicly promised to make the Florida Supreme Court its final battleground. The public took this to mean that if Gore lost the appeal of Judge Sauls's ruling, he would concede. The vice president, however, had other ideas. He may have been on a kamikaze mission, but he wasn't above grasping at straws on the way down.

On Tuesday, December 5, Gore reiterated that he would take his fight no further than the Florida Supreme Court. But he also embraced two additional cases in the Florida courts. These sought to throw out more than 20,000 absentee ballots in Seminole and Martin counties. It was an extraordinary move from a man pledged to a mantra of "count every vote." Even the plaintiffs acknowledged that these cases involved only a fraction of absentee ballot *applications* where Republican officials had filled in missing information. While it was debatable whether even this act was improper, the upshot of the case was that 20,000 innocent absentee voters in Seminole and Martin counties were in danger of being summarily disenfranchised. Republican operatives had not touched a single *ballot* and only a small minority of the *applications*. But because it was impossible to trace domestic absentee ballots to individuals, the Democrats argued that all 20,000 ballots had to be tossed. Conveniently, the net result would be a swing of several thousand votes in Gore's favor—more than enough to overcome Bush's 537-vote lead.

Gore's public support of these lawsuits came just hours after the Florida Supreme Court announced that it *might* take Gore's appeal of Judge Sauls's ruling. "The court has not actually taken the case," cautioned court spokesman Craig Waters, but it was under consideration. The court's ambivalence startled the Gore team, which had assumed acceptance of their appeal was a certainty. Suddenly, the Seminole and Martin cases loomed as necessary alternatives to get a hearing in the Florida Supreme Court, if the court refused to accept the Sauls appeal. Without them, Gore faced "sudden death."

"Those two cases are likely to travel the same route as the case that went into Judge Sauls's court and will end up in the Florida Supreme Court," Gore said of the Seminole and Martin suits. "All of the current controversy will end up being resolved, one way or another, in the Florida Supreme Court."

Gore officials now privately hoped that resolution would be a dramatic, last-minute victory via the Seminole and Martin cases. The press had been buzzing for days about the potential of these "sleeper" lawsuits to deliver the White House to Gore. While acknowledging their political unpopularity, the Gore team viewed these suits as a potentially cleaner legal victory than trying to overturn Judge Sauls's ruling against them.

To preemptively soften up his critics, Gore talked about the details of the cases in an attempt to establish sympathy for the plaintiffs, one of whom had strong connections to the vice president. Gore alleged that Republicans—but not Democrats—had been allowed inside the election headquarters in order to help fill out some of the absentee applications in Seminole County.

"The Democratic Party chair was denied the opportunity to even look at the list of applications," Gore complained. "The Republican Party workers were allowed to roam around unsupervised inside the office and bring their computers in and fix all of the ballot applications for one side, even as the Democrats were denied an opportunity to come in, denied a chance to even look at the application.

"Now that doesn't seem fair to me," Gore said. "And apparently in Martin County, they were able to go in and take all the applications home with them."

Gore emphasized that "more than enough votes were potentially taken away from Democrats because they were not given the same access that Republicans were."

Left unsaid was that the candidate who wanted to count dimpled chads and double-voted butterfly ballots for himself, now wanted to disqualify the votes of 20,000 people, because roughly 2,000 ballot *applications* had been completed by members of the Republican Party.

While Gore made a point of offhandedly mentioning that he was technically "not a party" to the suits, he might as well have been one. In addition to publicly praising the suits, Gore had accepted more than $100,000 in cash and favors from Harry N. Jacobs, the plaintiff in the Seminole case. Both Gore and Lieberman had met during the campaign with Jacobs, a fiercely partisan Democrat who once commissioned his own TV ad to attack Bush's running mate, Dick Cheney.

Jacobs admitted in a sworn deposition that before filing the lawsuit he had sought advice from Mitchell W. Berger, a Fort Lauderdale attorney and Gore fundraiser who was intimately involved in the vice president's recount efforts. Jacobs also testified that he had consulted other Democratic operatives and was a longtime acquaintance of Bob Poe, chairman of the Florida Democratic Party.

And yet Jacobs, like Gore, publicly clung to the fiction that his lawsuit had nothing to do with helping the vice president.

CHAPTER 14

"SEVEN JUSTICES OF THE COURT AGREE"

I t was widely speculated that the Florida Supreme Court, having just been publicly chastened by the U.S. Supreme Court, would not want to venture back into the post-election briar patch. But on Tuesday, December 5, the day after Gore asked the seven justices for more help, the court announced it would hear arguments from both sides on Thursday, December 7. The court emphasized that it had not officially decided to take the case, but would entertain arguments on that question at the hearing. Simultaneously, lawyers were expected to argue the merits of the case itself, as if the court had agreed to adjudicate the whole mess. The press essentially ignored this distinction and treated the announcement as if the court had officially accepted the case. Gore lawyers made no attempt to mask their desperation.

"Now is the last chance for a legal judgment to be rendered in this case," the Gore legal brief said. "In but a few more days, only the judgment of history will be left to fall upon a system where deliberate obstruction has succeeded in achieving delay."

During oral arguments, Gore lawyer David Boies even offered to limit the recount to the 9,000 or 10,000 unexamined undervotes from Miami-Dade. But several justices challenged him to demonstrate why they should wade back into the post-election quagmire. And even the justices who seemed most sympathetic to Gore acknowledged there was little time to count ballots before Tuesday, the deadline for seating electors.

"We're here today, December 7," said Justice Barbara Pariente. "What is the time parameter for being able to complete a count of those undervotes?"

"We believe these ballots can be counted in the time available," Boies assured her. "Obviously, time is getting very short. We have been trying to get these ballots counted, as this court knows, for many weeks now."

Justice Harry Lee Anstead pointed out that it would take much longer if the recount were expanded to include all 1.1 million ballots that had been trucked up to Tallahassee from the Gold Coast.

"We're now here on December the 7th, with December the 12th, you know, fast approaching," Anstead said. "How can we resolve an issue like that at this late date?"

"There's never been a rule that says you have to recount all the ballots in an election contest," Boies replied, evidently forgetting the Florida law that specifies "all" ballots must be recounted.

It was obvious from the justices' questions that they were still smarting from their trip to the woodshed.

"You would agree that when the United States Supreme Court has said that there is plenary power in the appointment of electors in the state legislature, that that means that they've got full power?" Chief Justice Charles T. Wells asked Boies.

The Gore lawyer nimbly replied that while the legislature has "the power to determine the manner of the selection," it had already exercised that power by creating election laws, which were now subject to judicial interpretation.

"The legislature has provided this court with the authority to interpret these laws," Boies insisted. "Whenever the legislature passes a law, what the legislature is doing is passing a law that is going to be interpreted by the courts."

Bush lawyer Barry Richard argued the court should not even accept the appeal. "This is nothing more than a garden-variety appeal from a final judgment by a lower court that [conducted] an entire, full evidentiary hearing," he fairly spat.

"We had an absolute failure on the part of the plaintiffs here," Richard added. "This court gave the plaintiffs the opportunity to have a trial to prove their case, and it was an absolute failure, in the record of this case, to establish an abuse of discretion by any of the challenged canvassing boards."

Boies implored the justices to let the Gore team cobble together enough votes from a patchwork of counties to overtake Bush's 537-vote lead.

"There is now an undisputed record that the 215 net ballots that were counted in Palm Beach County should be included, that they're legal votes, and that the 168 net ballots for Vice President Gore and Senator Lieberman that were counted in Miami-Dade County should be included," Boies said.

But the justices pointed out that these adjustments would not be enough to put Gore over the top. They suggested the Gore team wanted to make up that difference with a fishing expedition among the 9,000 to 10,000 Miami-Dade undervotes.

"Why wouldn't we conclude here that, at most, all that you have demonstrated in the trial court is a possibility that there may be a difference in the outcome?" Anstead said. "Because, as you have conceded, no one has looked at the 9,000 votes that you're talking about."

Like a math student taking an oral examination, Boies began furiously crunching numbers in an effort to close the gap.

"We've shown that 215 and the 168—and that gets you up to 383," Boies said. "At that point, you're down to 100 votes, your honor."

Actually, that would bring Bush's lead to 154 votes. But in reality, it would only reduce it to 195 votes, because Gore's true Palm Beach gain had been only 174 votes, not 215, though Boies continued to use the inflated number in his arguments to the Florida Supreme Court. The man who had used a false affidavit to help convince the Broward and Palm Beach canvassing boards to accept dimples was now using a false vote count to convince the Florida Supreme Court of his case.

Gore's and Bush's attorneys were reluctant to remind the justices of their humiliation at the hands of the U.S. Supreme Court. But Katherine Harris's lawyer showed no such compunction. In fact, he was downright blunt.

"I think, Mr. Chief Justice, that what you need to do is: You need to be careful—in terms of constructing statutes or remedies— not to do anything that would constitute a change in the law," Joseph Klock admonished Wells. "The fact is, the court can't change the law."

"But you're not suggesting that the interpretation or construction of a sentence is a change of law, are you?" asked Justice R. Fred Lewis.

"But Justice Lewis, there is just so much baggage the word 'interpretation' can carry on its back before it becomes more of a change than it is an interpretation," Klock lectured. "Going from seven days to nineteen days—that's a lot of baggage for the word to carry."

Such exchanges only served to reinforce expectations that the court would turn away the appeal. Why risk getting burned again?

After all, the court had not yet responded to the U.S. Supreme Court's first extraordinary rebuke. Why risk a second rebuke? Even many Democrats were pessimistic about Gore's chances as the court adjourned without bothering to announce whether or when it would rule on the merits of the case.

The Gore team's mood darkened even further the next day, when Leon County Judges Nikki Clark and Terry Lewis dismissed the Gore-endorsed lawsuits in Seminole and Martin counties that would have disqualified thousands of absentee ballots and vaulted Gore into the lead. Democrats were now openly acknowledging Gore had reached the end of the line. All that was left was a formal rejection of Gore's appeal by the Florida Supreme Court. Reporters who had been in Tallahassee for more than a month were so confident there would be closure by the end of Friday that they actually booked flights to take them back to Washington the next morning.

And then the sky fell in. At 4 P.M., the Florida Supreme Court dropped the mother of all bombshells. By a 4-to-3 decision, the court gave Gore everything he had asked for and more. It gave him 215 votes from the tardy hand recount in Palm Beach County, even though the canvassing board had found only 174 votes. It gave him 168 votes from the aborted hand recount in Miami-Dade, even though the rest of the ballots were never recounted. In fact, rather than order the remaining votes tallied, the court simply demanded a hand recount of the 9,000 to 10,000 undervotes that had not yet been manually examined. Finally, in the shocker of all shockers, the court ordered "a manual recount of all undervotes in any Florida county where such a recount has not yet occurred. Because time is of the essence, the recount shall commence immediately."

The Florida Supreme Court had given Gore far more than he had ever requested—or even dreamed possible. In one bold stroke of judicial activism, the four liberal justices had thumbed their noses at the U.S. Supreme Court and opened a Pandora's box of unimaginable mischief from one end of the Florida peninsula to the other. Suddenly, Bush's 537-vote lead was slashed to a mere 154. And surely it was only a matter of time before Bush's lead would be eclipsed altogether. After all, the four justices had summarily ordered brand new hand recounts throughout the entire state. There were more than 40,000 undervotes in more than forty counties. A nation that had been appalled by the spectacle of chaotic, standardless hand recounts in a mere four counties now braced for the madness to multiply tenfold.

"Only by examining the contested ballots, which are evidence in the election contest, can a meaningful and final determination in this election contest be made," wrote Justices Anstead, Lewis, Pariente, and Peggy A. Quince.

But unlike the earlier decision by the Florida Supreme Court—where the justices were, as usual, unanimous—this new decision caused an enormous and unprecedented rift among the court's members. Chief Justice Well wrote a stinging dissent in which he declared he "could not more strongly disagree" with the majority opinion.

"The prolonging of judicial process in this counting contest propels this country and this state into an unprecedented and unnecessary constitutional crisis," Wells wrote. "There is a real and present likelihood that this constitutional crisis will do substantial damage to our country, our state, and to this court as an institution."

Up until this point in the post-election struggle, Democrats had dismissed talk of a constitutional crisis as the overheated rhetoric of Republican alarmists. But now such warnings were emanating from the Democratic chief justice of one of the most liberal, activist courts in the nation, the only bench in the entire post-election fiasco that had been hailed as "wise" by no less than Al Gore himself. Wells had been an active contributor to the Democratic Party before his ascension to the bench and had wholeheartedly agreed with the court's earlier, pro-Gore ruling. Yet now even Wells was warning, in the strongest language imaginable, that the madness was spiraling out of control and threatening to harm not just the court, but the entire nation.

"This contest simply must end," he wrote. "It is inescapable that there is no practical way for the contest to continue for the good of this country and state."

Bush would later call the ruling his biggest setback in the post-election struggle.

"I was all poised—and posed," he told the author. "Laura and I were in the governor's mansion living room. The Florida court was to meet and everybody was confident they'd rule the right way. And there I was, all ready. And they ruled against us."

Meanwhile, Democrats cheered the split decision and rejoiced that victory was, at long last, within their grasp. "This is great!" Gore told an aide in Washington. "Amen!" shouted his campaign manager, Donna Brazile. "Let the counting commence!" hollered campaign chairman William Daley.

And yet, even as the Gore team celebrated, a host of enormous obstacles quickly came into focus. How would these votes be counted? Who would count them? What would be the standards? And could it all be completed by the deadline for seating electors, which was just three days away?

The Florida Supreme Court, while having no compunction about throwing open Pandora's box, was quick to jump out of the way, leaving all messy, logistical questions to Judge Sauls, who didn't think the case had any merit to begin with. The four justices ordered Sauls to handle the new counts in any way he saw fit. As for standards, well, that was for others to figure out.

"In tabulating what constitutes a legal vote, the standard to be used is the one provided by the legislature: 'A vote shall be counted where there is a clear indication of the intent of the voter,'" the majority wrote. It was a cop-out of staggering proportions. After all the madness of the past month, the Florida Supreme Court was practically guaranteeing out-and-out anarchy by leaving it up to the local canvassing boards in scores of individual counties to determine the definition of a valid vote. There had been no fewer than six separate standards among the three Gold Coast counties that conducted manual recounts. God only knew how many standards would be devised by more than forty additional canvassing boards.

Although the ruling was handed down at 4 P.M. on a Friday afternoon, when government employees all over Florida were heading out of their offices, the court decreed that "because time is of the essence, the recount shall commence immediately."

Judge Sauls, who could see this particular train wreck hurtling down the tracks, promptly recused himself from the case. The nearly impossible task of organizing and overseeing the recounts fell to Terry Lewis, the Democratic judge who had twice ruled against Gore by insisting Katherine Harris had not abused her discretion in rejecting tardy hand counts. Lewis gamely called a late night hearing in his Tallahassee courtroom and essentially asked the Bush and Gore lawyers how in the world he should proceed.

At the conclusion of the freewheeling hearing, which was televised, Lewis decreed that all counties must send him their plans for recounting undervotes by noon the next day, which was Saturday. He publicly announced his fax number, figuring most election officials were watching the proceedings on TV and this would be the quickest and most efficient way of spreading the word. But the judge's fax machine immediately became clogged with countless "blast faxes" sent by furious Americans who were also watching the proceedings on TV. The machine remained clogged all night and into the next day, preventing most counties from submitting their plans.

Lewis said he hoped to have all recounts completed by 2 P.M. on Sunday. But when it came to setting standards for what constitutes a vote, Lewis, like everyone else in Florida, simply punted. He referred to the Florida Supreme Court's vague reference to divining "the intent of the voter." In other words, the local canvassing boards would each have to figure out their own separate definitions of what constitutes a valid vote.

Lewis invited representatives of both parties to observe the hand recounts. But in a break from the rules of the earlier tallies, Lewis would not allow these observers to lodge immediate objections to individual decisions made by the ballot counters. That would take up too much time.

Panic gripped election officials from the panhandle to the Everglades. Many counties had not segregated the undervotes from the rest of their ballots and had no computer software that would allow them to do so.

"It will be somewhat like finding needles in a haystack," said Bradford County election supervisor Terry Vaughan.

Other counties were able to run the ballots through machines to segregate the undervotes, only to discover more undervotes than when they conducted the first machine count. This was precisely what had happened earlier in Miami-Dade.

Bush representative James Baker could only shake his head at the burgeoning chaos.

"This is what happens when, for the first time in modern history, a candidate resorts to lawsuits to try to overturn the outcome of an election for president," Baker lamented. "It is very sad. It is sad for Florida. It is sad for the nation. And it is sad for our democracy."

That evening, Bush asked the U.S. Supreme Court to once again step in and put a halt to the chaos the Florida Supreme Court had unleashed. At 9:18 P.M., Bush lawyer Theodore B. Olson submitted a forty-two-page brief to Justice Anthony M. Kennedy, who handled all emergency measures from the Eleventh Judicial Circuit, which includes Florida. Olson told Kennedy it was essential that the nation's high court jump back into the controversy "in order to preserve the integrity of the electoral process for president and vice president of the United States and in order to correct the serious constitutional errors made by the Florida Supreme Court."

On Saturday morning, election officials all over Florida began the tedious task of separating undervotes from ordinary ballots and hand counting them, one by one. The standards varied from county to county, but Republican and Democratic observers were barred from lodging individual protests. Almost immediately, arguments erupted over whether to count chads in all their many incarnations—dimpled, pregnant, hanging, swinging, and otherwise. Soon Bush's 154-vote lead began to shrink even further.

But at 2:45 P.M., the U.S. Supreme Court once again stepped into the fray. It ordered an immediate halt to all recounts and announced it would hear oral arguments in the case on Monday, December 11. But this time, the high court would do more than just obliterate the handiwork of the Florida Supreme Court. This time, the high court would actually tackle the constitutional questions raised by Bush.

Although the U.S. Supreme Court had been unanimous in its initial repudiation of the Florida Supreme Court, it now issued a 5-to-4 decision to stop the recounts. The majority opinion was written by Justice Antonin Scalia.

"I will not address the merits of the case, since they will shortly be before us," Scalia wrote. "It suffices to say that the issuance of the stay suggests that a majority of the court, while not deciding the issues presented, believe that the petitioner has a substantial probability of success."

Gore was devastated. The hand counts for which he had fought so hard were suddenly halted just as they were getting started. One of his lawyers, Ron Klain, said Bush's lead had already dropped below 100. Victory had been within reach, perhaps just hours away. And now the highest court in the land had all but sealed Gore's doom. Scalia was openly telegraphing the final decision, even before oral arguments had been heard.

"The counting of votes that are of questionable legality does in my view threaten irreparable harm to petitioner, and to the country, by casting a cloud upon what he claims to be the legitimacy of his election," Scalia wrote. "Count first, and rule upon legality afterwards, is not a recipe for producing election results that have the public acceptance democratic stability requires."

The justices in the minority made precisely the opposite argument.

"Preventing the recount from being completed will inevitably cast a cloud on the legitimacy of the election," wrote Justice John Paul Stevens, whose dissent was joined by Justices Ginsburg, Breyer, and David H. Souter. "The majority has acted unwisely."

The next day was Sunday, December 10, just two days before the deadline for seating electors. Congressional Democrats on the Sunday morning talk shows acknowledged this was the end game. They had long since tired of the damage Gore was doing to himself, the party, and, yes, the nation. Besides, the Democrats on Capitol Hill were not eager to have the election mess land in their own laps. Washington was full of doomsday scenarios in which Congress would be forced to choose the next president. The scars from impeachment a couple of years earlier still hadn't completely healed. The last thing Congress needed was another constitutional crisis to adjudicate. No, it was better to let the U.S. Supreme Court take the heat on this fiasco. Already there were dire warnings in the press that the high court would sully itself as a partisan bench if it ruled for Bush. That was just as well with the Democrats in Congress. Perhaps they could make some political hay by railing against the conservative cabal on the high court that appeared ready to install Bush as president. It would give them something to run against in the midterm elections of 2002.

Still, some Democrats were unwilling to surrender. They urged Gore to fight on, even if the high court ruled against him. Former New York Governor Mario Cuomo said if the justices slam dunked Gore, the next step "could be to convince some electors previously thought to be committed to Bush. You only need three to make Al Gore president, even if he loses Florida. Think about that."

Cuomo issued this threat on CNN as Democratic strategist Bob Beckel was putting the finishing touches on his "study" to convince electors to defect.

"I hope all Americans understand that even if the Supreme Court does what it's threatening to do—which is to say we're not going to let you look at the ballots; we're going to say George Bush is the winner—that will not make him the president," Cuomo said. "After the Supreme Court would have beat Gore, there's no guarantee that three or four electors who were previously supposed to vote for Bush wouldn't turn around, out of anger and confusion perhaps, and say, 'We're going to go with Al Gore.'"

This was precisely the sort of scorched-earth warfare that offended so many Americans. It also set off new alarm bells in the Bush camp. Having come this far, the Republicans no longer put anything past the Democrats.

"We are in touch with our electors," James Baker warned. "We hope very much that they will remain faithful. We believe they will."

Baker added: "If they think they can swing some of them, they're going to try. On the other hand, maybe we ought to be considering doing the same thing with theirs. What's fair for one side, it seems to me, is fair for the other."

It would be one of the lasting legacies of the post-election struggle—the Republicans had finally learned to be every bit the street fighters the Democrats were. One of the unintended consequences of Gore's protracted and desperate bid to overturn the election was that it emboldened previously timid Republicans to take swift, decisive, and cutthroat actions.

On Monday, December 11, for the second time in ten days, the U.S. Supreme Court entertained arguments in the Florida fiasco. The historic case was now officially titled *Bush v. Gore*. Having lost the first round, Gore lawyer Laurence Tribe was unceremoniously benched at the last minute and replaced with David Boies, who at least had posted a couple of victories at the Florida Supreme Court. Never mind that Boies had never appeared before the U.S. Supreme Court, where Tribe had argued no fewer than thirty times. The move was emblematic of Gore's entire campaign. For nearly two years, he had shuffled campaign chiefs as if they were baseball managers. Bush, on the other hand, had stubbornly stuck with his tight-knit circle of Texas advisers, even when the Washington punditocracy had called for heads to roll in the wake of his defeat to John McCain in the New Hampshire primary. True to form, Bush now stuck with Theodore Olson as his voice at the U.S. Supreme Court. Both Olson and Boies wore conservative suits and ties, although Boies insisted on wearing his trademark black sneakers into a court so staid that some counselors still donned morning coats.

Even the justices who had argued against jumping back into the fray now seemed to agree that Bush's constitutional rights had been trampled by the selective and standardless hand recounts.

"Why shouldn't there be one objective rule for all counties, and if there isn't, why isn't it an equal protection violation?" Souter asked Boies. "I think it's behind what's bothering Justice Kennedy, Justice Breyer, me, and others is: We're assuming there's a category in which there just is no subjective appeal. All we have are certain physical characteristics. Those physical characteristics, we are told, are being treated differently from county to county."

Justice O'Connor seemed to agree.

"Why isn't the standard the one that voters are instructed to follow, for goodness sakes? I mean, it couldn't be clearer. I mean, why don't we go to that standard?" she said.

"I think there are a lot of times in the law in which there can be those variations, from jury to jury, from public official to public official," Boies countered.

But Kennedy kept trying to pin Boies down. He asked him point-blank: "Do you think that in the contest phase there must be a uniform standard for counting the ballots?"

"I do, your honor, I think there must be a uniform standard," the lawyer said. "I think there is a uniform standard. The question is whether that standard is too general or not. The standard is whether or not the intent of the voter is reflected by the ballot. That is the uniform standard throughout the state of Florida."

"That's very general; it runs throughout the law," Kennedy shot back. "Even a dog knows the difference in being stumbled over and being kicked. You know it."

He added: "From the standpoint of the equal protection clause, could each county give their own interpretation to what 'intent' means, so long as they are in good faith and with some reasonable basis finding intent? Could that vary from county to county?"

"I think it can vary from individual to individual," Boies acknowledged.

"So that even in one county, it could vary from table to table—I'm counting these ballots, you're counting this one?"

"I think on the margins, your honor, whenever you're interpreting intent, whether it is in the criminal law, in administrative practice, whether it is in local government, whenever somebody is coming to—"

"But here you have something objective," Kennedy interrupted. "You're not just reading a person's mind. You're looking at a piece of paper. And the supreme courts in the state of South Dakota and in other states have told us that you will count this if it's hanging by two corners or one. This is susceptible of a uniform standard. And yet you say it can vary from table to table within the same county."

To speed things along, Boies offered to narrow the hand counts to those counties that favored Gore. This sudden abandonment of the Florida Supreme Court's statewide ruling startled Chief Justice William H. Rehnquist.

"I thought the Supreme Court said you had to do it all—in the interest of fairness," Rehnquist protested. "I thought you agreed with me on that a moment ago."

"I did, I did, your honor," Boies backpedaled. He was only making a helpful suggestion to save time.

Olson argued that the Florida Supreme Court had made a "major, major revision" of state law with its latest pro-Gore ruling. He called it a blatant violation of Article II of the U.S. Constitution, which explicitly gives state legislatures sole authority to choose electors.

"The judiciary in every state, under that argument, could overturn, rewrite, revise and change the election law in presidential elections, notwithstanding Article II, at will," Olson said.

Katherine Harris's lawyer, Joseph Klock, unintentionally provided comic relief to the otherwise tense proceedings by addressing Justice Stevens as Justice William J. Brennan, who died in 1997.

"Justice Brennan, the difficulty is that under—I'm sorry," he said, realizing his blunder as laughter erupted in the court. Klock plunged ahead with his argument, reproaching himself for trying to use the justices' names.

"That's why they tell you not to do that," he said.

But within moments, he did it again when addressing Justice Souter.

"No, Justice Breyer, what I'm saying is—," Klock began.

"I'm Justice Souter. You've got to cut that out."

When it came time for Scalia to grill Klock, he made a point of introducing himself.

"Mr. Klock? I'm Scalia," he deadpanned, drawing even bigger laughs.

"Yes sir, I'll remember that," said the chastened Klock. "It will be hard to forget."

Once the proceedings were over, the court realized it had little time to issue a decision. After all, the next day was Tuesday, December 12, the deadline for seating electors. In fact, even if the Supreme Court had ruled immediately, from the bench, in Gore's favor, it would be difficult to imagine him winning the presidency in the space of a day.

As if to guarantee no frantic, last-minute grab for votes, the court did not issue its decision until 10 P.M. on Tuesday, December 12—just two hours before the deadline for seating electors without danger of congressional challenges. TV news correspondents and producers literally sprinted out of the U.S. Supreme Court building with the decision clutched in their hands and began trying to make sense of the historic document on live television. The five-week drama was ending the same way it had begun—with the networks confusing its viewers. Indeed, some talking heads initially held out hope that the decision was somehow good news for Gore. Once again, the media had it wrong.

"This is a complicated situation," intoned CBS's Dan Rather as he puzzled over the ruling. "What it does not do is, in effect, deliver the presidency to George W. Bush."

Hoping against hope, Rather added: "It keeps alive—keeps alive—at least the possibility of Al Gore trying to continue his contest."

But the ruling did just the opposite. It drove a stake right through the heart of Gore's last, desperate grasp for the presidency. No fewer than seven justices of the United States Supreme Court declared unequivocally that the Florida recount—Gore's only hope of overturning the election—was unconstitutional.

"We find a violation of the equal protection clause," the majority opinion said. "When the state legislature vests the right to vote for president in its people, the right to vote as the legislature has prescribed is fundamental; and one source of its fundamental nature lies in the equal weight accorded to each vote and the equal dignity owed to each voter."

So much for the conventional wisdom, repeated endlessly by Democrats and the press, that the Florida flap raised no constitutional issues. Seven members of the U.S. Supreme Court had just declared the Constitution had been violated. The argument Bush had been making all along was true—selective, standardless hand recounts gave more weight to some voters than others.

"Having once granted the right to vote on equal terms, the state may not, by later arbitrary and disparate treatment, value one person's vote over that of another," the court said. "The recount mechanisms implemented in response to the decisions of the Florida Supreme Court do not satisfy the minimum requirement for non-arbitrary treatment of voters necessary to secure the fundamental right."

Boies's tap dance with Kennedy about shifting standards came back to haunt the Gore lawyer.

"As seems to have been acknowledged at oral argument, the standards for accepting or rejecting contested ballots might vary not only from county to county but indeed within a single county from one recount team to another," the court said. "Palm Beach County, for example, began the process with a 1990 guideline which precluded counting completely attached chads, switched to a rule that considered a vote to be legal if any light could be seen through a chad, changed back to the 1990 rule, and then abandoned any pretense of a *per se* rule, only to have a court order that the county consider dimpled chads legal. This is not a process with sufficient guarantees of equal treatment."

So much for Bob Nichols's insistence to all those reporters on that first chaotic day of that first chaotic recount that the Palm Beach Board hadn't changed its vote-counting standards. No less an authority than the U.S. Supreme Court affirmed what millions of Americans had felt in their stomachs from the start—the hand recounts were a farce.

"The state supreme court ratified this uneven treatment. It mandated that the recount totals from two counties, Miami-Dade and Palm Beach, be included in the certified total," the court continued. "Yet each of the counties used varying standards to determine what was a legal vote. Broward County used a more forgiving standard than Palm Beach County, and uncovered almost three times as many new votes, a result markedly disproportionate to the differences in population between the counties."

Having waded into the finer points of pregnant chads, the highest court in the land plowed ahead with its relentless indictment of the unconstitutional absurdities of the Florida recount.

"That brings to analysis yet a further equal protection problem. The votes certified by the court included a partial total from one county, Miami-Dade. The Florida Supreme Court's decision thus gives no assurance that the recounts included in a final certification must be complete," the court said. "The press of time does not diminish the constitutional concern. A desire for speed is not a general excuse for ignoring equal protection guarantees."

No longer did the court try to cloak its rebuke of the Florida Supreme Court in polite legalese. It savaged the state court for failing to set standards for its latest recount order.

"That order did not specify who would recount the ballots. The county canvassing boards were forced to pull together ad hoc teams comprised of judges from various circuits who had no previous training in handling and interpreting ballots. Furthermore, while others were permitted to observe, they were prohibited from objecting during the recount."

So much for Judge Terry Lewis's late-night punt on guidelines for statewide hand recounts. But the high court blamed the Florida Supreme Court for passing the buck down to the hapless circuit court.

"We are presented with a situation where a state court with the power to assure uniformity has ordered a statewide recount with minimal procedural safeguards. When a court orders a statewide remedy, there must be at least some assurance that the rudimentary requirements of equal treatment and fundamental fairness are satisfied."

The situation in Florida was branded nothing short of hopeless.

"It is obvious that the recount cannot be conducted in compliance with the requirements of equal protection and due process without substantial additional work. It would require not only the adoption (after opportunity for argument) of adequate statewide standards for determining what is a legal vote, and practicable procedures to implement them, but also orderly judicial review of any disputed matters that might arise."

All of these things, obviously, could not transpire in the two hours remaining before midnight. The court pointed out that federal law "requires that any controversy or contest that is designed to lead to a conclusive selection of electors be completed by December 12. That date is upon us, and there is no recount procedure in place under the state supreme court's order that comports with minimal constitutional standards. Because it is evident that any recount seeking to meet the December 12 date will be unconstitutional for the reasons we have discussed, we reverse the judgment of the Supreme Court of Florida ordering a recount to proceed.

"Seven justices of the court agree that there are constitutional problems with the recount ordered by the Florida Supreme Court that demand a remedy," the majority concluded. "The only disagreement is as to the remedy."

Indeed, there were no fewer than four dissenting opinions, each with various justices agreeing with this portion or that of each particular dissent. But the overwhelming majority of justices—seven out of nine—agreed that Gore's tortured quest to overturn the election had blatantly trampled the U.S. Constitution, the very document a president swears to uphold. The U.S. Supreme Court did not arrive at this landmark decision capriciously. Nor, as the Democrats and press would soon argue, did the justices plunge into this tar pit to make some sort of right-wing power grab.

"None are more conscious of the vital limits on judicial authority than are the members of this court, and none stand more in admiration of the Constitution's design to leave the selection of the president to the people, through their legislatures, and to the political sphere," the court said. "When contending parties invoke the process of the courts, however, it becomes our unsought responsibility to resolve the federal and constitutional issues the judicial system has been forced to confront.

"The judgment of the Supreme Court of Florida is reversed."

Once the meaning had sunk in, once Dan Rather knew that Al

Gore's goose was cooked, the press characterized the court as "bitterly divided." This ignored the fact that only two justices found the Florida recount constitutional: John Paul Stevens, eighty, the court's oldest and most liberal member, and Ruth Bader Ginsburg, appointed to the bench by Bill Clinton. Ginsberg, interestingly, had actually been Clinton's second choice for the appointment; his first was Mario Cuomo, the man currently urging Bush electors to defect. Ginsburg's husband, Martin, contributed $1,000 to the Clinton-Gore campaign in 1992.

All seven of the remaining justices—Rehnquist, O'Connor, Kennedy, Scalia, Thomas, Souter, and Breyer—confirmed Bush's claim that the Constitution had been violated. Breyer was a Clinton appointee and a personal friend of Al Gore and yet even he could not ignore the obvious—the recounts were a sham.

Still, Democrats and the press stubbornly refused to portray the Supreme Court's ruling as a 7-to-2 decision. They seized on the fact that two of the seven justices in the majority—Souter and Breyer—still held out hope for a timely remedy. These two liberal justices felt the December 12 deadline could be stretched closer to December 18, the day the Electoral College would vote for president. The other five justices in the majority felt there wasn't enough time to fix the monumental problems with Florida's recount. They took their cue from the federal law that insists electors must be in place six days before they vote.

And yet, the myth was already taking root. The landmark ruling in *Bush* v. *Gore* would forever be described by Democrats and the press as a 5-to-4 vote. It allowed them to characterize Bush's victory as that much more slender, his legitimacy that much more tenuous. It allowed Gore and his embittered allies to boil the whole presidential election, in which 100 million Americans had cast ballots, down to the malevolent whim of a solitary, right-wing justice. The mythmakers invariably cast either Justice Scalia or Justice Thomas, the court's most conservative members, as the one who diabolically tipped the scales in Bush's favor.

Ten weeks after the Supreme Court's decision, the *New York Times* ran a front-page, revisionist account of the ruling. "Their opinion later caused some confusion by its reference to 'seven justices of the court' who 'agree that there are constitutional problems with the recount,'" the story editorialized. "That was true, but it was also beside the point, because by then the only question was whether there was a remedy for those problems, in the form of a restructured but continuing recount. On that question, the vote remained 5-to-4."

But the main decision, the one that ruled on the constitutionality of the Florida recount, was 7-to-2. Only on the infinitely narrower issue of whether there was sufficient time for a remedy—which was a question of mundane logistics, not sweeping constitutionality—did the court split 5-to-4. Given that the decision came just two hours before the expiration of the December 12 deadline and only six days before the Electoral College actually voted, the hopes of the two swing justices—Justices Souter and Breyer—for a timely remedy were unrealistic in the extreme.

The most widely quoted passage of the landmark *Bush* v. *Gore* decision was not: "We find a violation of the Equal Protection Clause." The press was not eager to give credence to the majority's lofty language about assuring "the equal dignity owed to each voter." There was no clamor to repeat the seven justices' call for the "rudimentary requirements of equal treatment and fundamental fairness." And certainly the least popular line was: "seven justices of the court agree."

No, the quote that made the most headlines was taken from a dissenting opinion written by the most liberal justice of all.

"Although we may never know with complete certainty the

identity of the winner of this year's presidential election, the identity of the loser is perfectly clear," huffed Stevens. "It is the nation's confidence in the judge as an impartial guardian of the rule of law."

CHAPTER 15

SEVEN MINUTES OF MAGNANIMITY

Once the talking heads finally figured out that the historic *Bush* v. *Gore* ruling amounted to the vice president's death knell, Democrats felt free to say what their hearts had been telling them for weeks—it was time for Gore to concede. Suddenly, the vice president and his inner circle of advisers were no longer able to enforce the strict party discipline that had kept Democrats united, at least publicly, in defense of Gore's quest. The high court ruling proved downright cathartic for senior Democrats and even some of Gore's own lawyers, who suddenly felt liberated from any lingering delusions of victory.

"That's checkmate," concluded Representative James P. Moran, Virginia Democrat. "It's over."

Senator Robert Toricelli, New Jersey Democrat, slipped into the past tense while describing on MSNBC how Gore had "served our country very well. This is a very difficult evening for him and clearly the race for the presidency has come to an end. And George Bush is going to be the next president of the United States."

Laurence Tribe, the Harvard lawyer whom Gore had benched in favor of media darling David Boies, now was able to have his revenge.

"I think the gracious thing is to accept—even if one disagrees with—the decision of the Supreme Court," Tribe declared on NBC. "I'm sure that Vice President Gore has the kind of reverence for the Supreme Court as an institution that he will really not undertake to be less than complete and gracious in his acceptance of this result."

Another Gore lawyer, Dexter Douglass, was more blunt: "It sounds like we lost."

Even Edward Rendell, general chairman of the Democratic National Committee, went on national television to acknowledge the obvious.

"Gore should act now and concede," Rendell said flatly. "And I believe he will."

But Al Gore was not yet ready to face reality. In fact, he was seething as he watched his fellow Democrats sell him down the river on TV before the Supreme Court decision was an hour old. He desperately tried to round up all these stray Indians and lock them back on the reservation. He dispatched his closest advisers, whose numbers had dwindled as the ordeal dragged on, to silence the blasphemers. The rage of the inner circle was almost palpable. The vice president himself began e-mailing talking points to his remaining loyalists.

"The Democratic Party does not think Gore needs to concede," snapped the DNC's Joe Andrew, who as national chairman was responsible for the organization's day-to-day operations. "This is his decision to make. We stand united behind him."

Andrew said it was "outrageous" for his own general chairman, Rendell, to call on Gore to step aside. "It was completely inappropriate for anyone who has a title in our party to in any way imply that Al Gore should concede," he said.

Mark Fabiani, Gore's deputy campaign manager, was even more bitter.

"We've come to expect that from Rendell," Fabiani hissed to the *New York Times*. "He seems to be more interested in getting his mug on TV than in loyalty."

As for Gore having handpicked Rendell to chair the DNC in the first place, Fabiani muttered: "Sometimes you make personal mistakes in this business."

Chastened, Rendell tried to take back his televised comments, insisting on the air they had been taken "out of context." But the damage was done.

Even Laurence Tribe was hauled to the woodshed by Gore's enforcers. He called CNN just before midnight to sheepishly backpedal from the fatalistic comments he had uttered on NBC.

So this is what it had come to. The Democrats, in absolute disarray, were turning on each other with a ruthlessness that made even the post-election war against Bush seem tame by comparison. Clearly, the strain and exhaustion of the past five weeks were taking a toll. Gore's followers were reduced to political cannibalism.

Having dispatched his enforcers to silence the likes of Ed Rendell and Larry Tribe, Gore began consulting with his lawyers. He called Boies, who had already gone home to New York, and Ron Klain, who was still in Florida. He talked late into the night with Warren Christopher, the lawyer and diplomat who had been comfortably asleep in his Los Angeles bed when he first answered Daley's call five weeks earlier. Gore and his legal team spent hours poring over the Supreme Court decision for any glimmer of hope that could be transformed into yet another appeal. Gore wondered aloud whether the Supreme Court decision could be parlayed into some sort of massive outcry from the black community, providing political cover for one last assault on Bush. The Reverend Jesse Jackson, who had been advising Gore throughout the post-election debacle, implored him to use "every means available" to fight on, promising a "civil rights explosion." Other aides privately reproached the Supreme Court for what they called a blatantly partisan ruling. There was even discussion about whether the December 12 deadline could be pushed to December 18, when the Electoral College would actually vote. After all, plenty of states missed the December 12 deadline for seating electors. On the other hand, none of those states was as close or contentious as Florida.

In order to keep his options open and salvage what remained of loyalty in the Democratic Party, Gore instructed Daley to issue a bland statement at about 11:30 P.M. "Al Gore and Joe Lieberman are now reviewing the 5-4 decision issued tonight by the Supreme Court of the United States. The decision is both complex and lengthy. It will take time to completely analyze this opinion. We will address the court's decision in full detail at a time to be determined tomorrow."

The spin was already beginning. Daley had made a point of referring to the ruling as "the 5-4 decision." Headline writers in newsrooms all across America dutifully parroted this "5-4 decision" for the next day's editions.

The Bush team had long ago sworn off any thoughts of celebration until Gore actually conceded. Still, the Republicans had to say something before the night was over. So James Baker strode to the podium at the statehouse in Tallahassee and addressed reporters. "This has been a long and arduous process for everyone involved on both sides," Baker said. He added that the Bush team was "pleased and gratified" by the court's ruling, but he declined to take questions. This was not the time to get drawn into a lot of word games with journalists about whether Bush was gloating or angry or relieved or whatever. The subtext of Baker's short message was clear: Bush was giving the vice president some time to concede on his own. The last thing the Republicans needed was to *demand* a Gore concession, which would only serve to harden Democratic resolve and perhaps delay the outcome even further.

Gore kept agonizing, Hamlet-like, until after 2 A.M., finally instructing his legal team in Tallahassee to pull another all-nighter and draft one last batch of briefs. He figured he had conceded too early once before and wasn't going to repeat the mistake. He would sleep on it.

But the next morning, when the vice president looked over his lawyers' handiwork, he acknowledged it was pretty far-fetched. The lawyers wanted to go back to the Florida Supreme Court and try to convince the justices that the deadline for seating electors could actually be pushed to December 18, even though Boies had already told the court it could not. At the same time, the lawyers would somehow persuade the justices to issue uniform statewide standards for recounting ballots. Then, after the Florida Supreme Court agreed to all this, the lawyers would ask the U.S. Supreme Court to essentially rescind its pro-Bush ruling. Gore lawyer Ron Klain practically begged for permission to pursue this legal "strategy" for the next six days. When Gore demurred, some lawyers in Tallahassee actually wept. The scene was reminiscent of that first morning, five weeks earlier, when Gore aides cried after learning there was no room for them on the maiden planeload of operatives bound for Tallahassee. The bizarre crusade was ending as it began— with the tears of true believers. The jihad was over!

Gore then summoned Daley, the man whose father was said to have stolen Illinois for John F. Kennedy four decades earlier. Perversely relishing his own role as the Rasputin of American politics, Gore told Daley that he had changed his mind and was going to make one last lunge for the presidency. Daley was momentarily mortified. Gore hastened to explain that he was only kidding.

At 10 A.M., twelve hours after the landmark Supreme Court decision, Daley issued a statement: "The vice president has directed the recount committee to suspend activities." The press was told to expect a prime time concession. But Gore realized he would not be able to deliver it from his nineteenth-century mansion at the Naval Observatory. He was supposed to host a Christmas party for three hundred people, including rock singer Jon Bon Jovi, that had been planned for months. He would have to duck out of the bash and head over to his vice presidential office in the Old Executive Office Building, which is next door to the White House.

That afternoon in Tallahassee, Jesse Jackson held another angry rally to declare that Bush has "stolen" the election.

"He'll be the president legally, but he does not have moral authority," Jackson told a reporter after the rally. "Because his crown did not come from the people—it came from the judges."

Other Democrats were similarly embittered. Some on Capitol Hill begged Gore not to use the words "concede" or "concession" in the speech he was about to deliver. Instead, they implored him to say that he was merely "withdrawing" from a race he didn't really lose. They said the election was, at worst, a tie, and beseeched Gore not to give Bush the satisfaction of knowing he had truly won.

But Gore ignored the advice. He'd finally had enough of fighting dirty. At 9:02 P.M., he stepped before the cameras and, to everyone's surprise, took the high road.

"Good evening," he began. "Just moments ago, I spoke with George W. Bush and congratulated him on becoming the forty-third president of the United States. And I promised him I wouldn't call him back this time."

It was a wry reference to his retracted concession five weeks earlier. At least Gore was showing a self-deprecating sense of humor. And he had referred to Bush as "president" right out of the gate.

"I offered to meet with him as soon as possible so that we can start to heal the divisions of the campaign and the contest through which we've just passed," Gore continued. "I say to President-elect Bush that what remains of partisan rancor must now be put aside, and may God bless his stewardship of this country."

Technically, the onus all along had been on Gore alone to put aside the partisan rancor, since he had been the antagonist. Bush had spent the last thirty-six days strictly playing defense. But the part about blessing Bush's stewardship was a nice touch.

"Neither he nor I anticipated this long and difficult road. Certainly neither of us wanted it to happen. Yet it came, and now it has ended—resolved, as it must be resolved, through the honored institutions of our democracy."

Gore was still trying to level the playing field, to equate himself with Bush as blameless in the Florida debacle. He was portraying himself as an innocent bystander, coping as best he could with a great trauma that had been foisted upon him while he was minding his own business. "It came," Gore insisted, as if a meteor had struck the earth. But it was Gore, not some mysterious force of nature, that had caused the post-election nightmare.

"The U.S. Supreme Court has spoken. Let there be no doubt: While I strongly disagree with the court's decision, I accept it. I accept the finality of this outcome."

The man who had stubbornly denied the finality of the election for thirty-six days, pressing the fight for weeks after it became obvious he could not possibly win, was now patting himself on the back for accepting finality. He could have accepted finality on the afternoon of Thursday, November 9, when the mandatory recount showed he would not pull ahead and the butterfly ballot controversy offered no suitable remedy. He could have accepted finality on the afternoon of Monday, December 4, when Judge Sauls and the U.S. Supreme Court dealt him back-to-back defeats and Bush was left holding all the trump cards. The truth of the matter was that finality had arrived a long time ago. It just took a minor eternity for Gore to accept it.

"This has been an extraordinary election, but in one of God's unforeseen paths, this belatedly broken impasse can point us all to a new common ground, for its very closeness can serve to remind us that we are one people with a shared history and a shared destiny."

Translation: Traumatizing the nation by dragging it to the brink of a constitutional crisis was actually a good thing. After all, it reminded everyone of their shared destiny.

"There is a higher duty than the one we owe to political party. This is America and we put country before party."

Al Gore, who just weeks earlier had drawn his four concentric "circles of responsibility," safely ensconcing himself in the first circle, his supporters in the second, the Democratic Party in the third, and the nation in the last, was now preaching the virtues of putting "country before party." If Gore had put country before party thirty-six days earlier, the country would have been spared the entire wrenching ordeal.

"As for what I'll do next, I don't know the answer to that one yet," Gore said. "I know I'll spend time in Tennessee and mend some fences, literally and figuratively."

This was taken as a poignant acknowledgment of Gore's failure to carry his home state of Tennessee, which he had represented for sixteen years in Congress. If Gore had won in Tennessee, he would not have needed Florida to win the White House. In any event, his pledge to return to his rural homestead proved empty. Gore moved directly from his mansion at the Naval Observatory to a private house in suburban Washington, the city he always considered home.

"Some have asked whether I have any regrets. And I do have one regret—that I didn't get the chance to stay and fight for the American people over the next four years, especially for those who need burdens lifted and barriers removed."

In other words, he had no regrets about single-handedly traumatizing the nation for thirty-six days.

"As for the battle that ends tonight, I do believe, as my father once said, that no matter how hard the loss, defeat may serve as well as victory to shake the soul and let the glory out."

The man who once claimed to have invented the Internet was now crediting his father for Edward Markham's poem, "Victory in Defeat."

"In the words of our great hymn, 'America, America,' let us crown thy good with brotherhood, from sea to shining sea."

Mercifully, Gore refrained from breaking into song.

"And now my friends, in a phrase I once addressed to others, it's time for me to go," he said, tweaking a line he had used against the elder President Bush in 1992. "Thank you and good night.

"And God bless America."

Gore had barely stepped away from the podium when the media gushing began in earnest. ABC's Peter Jennings actually choked up on the air. So did Chris Matthews, the Democratic host of MSNBC's "Hardball." Virtually every journalist in America tripped over himself to praise the address as spectacularly gracious, nothing short of "the speech of Gore's political life." In reality, it had been the speech of Gore's political death.

It was as if Gore's seven minutes of magnanimity somehow made up for the previous thirty-six days of relentless political selfishness. The cad who had tried to disenfranchise GIs serving overseas and civilians living in Seminole and Martin counties was suddenly celebrated as a perfect gentleman. The ruthless politician who had personally directed a smear-and-destroy campaign against Florida's secretary of state for daring to uphold the law was now practically likened to Lincoln at Gettysburg. The Nixon-like figure who had obsessed over his enemies, real and imagined, ranging from the Democratic mayor of Miami-Dade to the Republican "rioters," was hastily enshrined on the loftiest pedestal of statesmanship.

In the space of a few moments, all was forgiven by an adoring press, which had never held Gore responsible for trying to achieve the outcome that most of them had wanted anyway. And yet Gore never apologized for what he had done to the nation or its institutions. He never said he was sorry for preemptively savaging Bush's legitimacy by insisting that he, Gore, would have won if only all the votes had been counted. In this respect, as in so many others, Gore was truly Clintonesque.

The post-election debacle was the defining moment of Al Gore's twenty-four-year career in politics. For five weeks, he was unquestionably the most powerful person in the United States. In fact, he wielded more raw, unadulterated influence over the nation for those thirty-six days than he probably would have as president for four or even eight years. For that matter, he was more powerful than Bush or Clinton or any other president in an era when the influence of the White House was gradually being diluted by the forces of globalization. For one blinding burst of chaos at the close of the twentieth century, a solitary man held sway over the entire American political process. Gore alone had the capacity to keep the standoff going. Gore alone had the capacity to end it. Bush was left forever awaiting Gore's next move. Bush, as the *de facto* winner who had never fallen behind in the Florida contest, could not be expected to concede. As far as most Americans were concerned, the question wasn't even on the table. By contrast, the public pressure on Gore to step aside was immense from the outset and grew only stronger as the standoff dragged on. But he single-handedly kept the nation on tenterhooks for five long weeks. It was his moment of maximum influence. Gore the loser—not Bush the winner—dictated the entire agenda.

And yet the post-election mess was widely portrayed as a struggle between two men who bore equal responsibility for this unprecedented period of political angst. In the early going, the press vaguely intoned that one of them would have to step aside for the good of the nation. The implication was that Bush had just as much an obligation to concede as Gore. But Bush had won the election and Gore had lost, even when the votes were recounted many times. Gore was always the antagonist, even when it became painfully obvious that he could not possibly prevail. And yet the press steadfastly refused to assign any moral or ethical weight to the relative positions of the two combatants. Journalists found it much more convenient to take the simplistic approach: Since there were two people seeking the presidency and neither one of them would concede, then they must be equally culpable in subjecting the nation to this harrowing ordeal, right? This posture had the added benefit of seeming vaguely impartial. Yet if the positions of Gore and Bush had been reversed, would the press have provided as much cover to the Texas governor for thirty-six days?

When it finally ended, Democrats resolved to turn Gore's defeat into a powerful political weapon. They decided to never let go of the Florida story, but rather to constantly repeat and even embellish it until it had attained the status of legend. Bush had stolen the election, pure and simple, the Democrats argued. He had been aided in this colossal theft by right wing extremists on the U.S. Supreme Court and racist stormtroopers in Jeb Bush's political machine, who systematically barred blacks from the polls. It was important to inject race into the storyline, even though there was virtually no evidence that blacks were turned away, because the Democrats desperately needed to reclaim the moral high ground after Gore's unseemly power grab. So they tried to transmogrify the Florida election into some gigantic civil rights abomination. They ranked it up there with no less than slavery, lynch mobs and the assassination of Martin Luther King Jr. The most strident elements of the Democratic Party practically branded President Bush a white supremacist.

"For Blacks, Nov. 7 Carries Taint of 1960s Injustices," blared a front-page headline in the *Los Angeles Times* eight days after Gore conceded. What the story lacked in evidence, it made up for in rumor and innuendo.

"Many African Americans have a sick feeling in their stomach about a Bush presidency," the story asserted.

"For more than a month, they've been hearing stories about election day shenanigans—dark tales about missing ballot boxes and suspicious highway checkpoints—all seemingly part of an effort to keep blacks from voting for Al Gore.

"Throw in the very public action of the U.S. Supreme Court— compared by some to the infamous 1857 Dred Scott decision that returned a slave to his master—and the 2000 election adds up to an injustice of historic proportions in the eyes of many blacks."

In February 2001, Terry McAuliffe began his tenure as chairman of the Democratic National Committee by flogging the Florida fiasco. President Clinton's best friend came right out and accused Bush of stealing the election, in part by erecting roadblocks to blacks who had intended to vote for Gore.

"Let's not forget, Al Gore won that election," McAuliffe incited the party faithful. "If Katherine Harris, Jeb Bush, Jim Baker, and the Supreme Court hadn't tampered with the results, Al Gore would be president."

While Democrats were embittered by Florida, Republicans were emboldened. Gore's audacity during those thirty-six days had a galvanizing effect on the GOP. Never known as a particularly activist collection of people, conservatives suddenly found themselves staging impassioned, spontaneous demonstrations from Miami to Washington. Having hungered for the White House for so long, only to see it nearly snatched from their grasp by yet another Clinton-Gore scam, Republicans finally roused themselves from their slumber and began waging the kind of hand-to-hand political combat that Democrats had long ago mastered. It took a shock as big as Florida to bestir the sleeping giant. But once awakened, the GOP renounced its complacency and vowed never again to be lulled into thinking it could take the White House without cracking a sweat. Close calls have a way of changing one's outlook on politics. And Florida was the ultimate close call. It was also a searing, defining experience for an entire generation of conservatives, a great battle from which they emerged victorious. Florida was something they would tell their grandchildren about.

Journalists would also regale their offspring and anyone else who would listen with tales of their role as chroniclers of this historic episode. Naturally, they would ignore their simultaneous role as Al Gore's chief enablers. Having made the whole post-election debacle possible in the first place through their bogus and biased coverage on Election Night, journalists spent the next thirty-six days rationalizing every Gore offensive, no matter how odious. Afterward, they did their best to fan doubts about Bush's legitimacy. News organizations began recounting ballots themselves, often adopting more liberal standards than the canvassing boards had employed. Whenever these tallies showed Bush gaining ground, they were downplayed by the press. Whenever they showed Gore overtaking Bush's lead, they received extensive coverage. Never mind that seven justices of the U.S. Supreme Court had ruled that selective hand recounts were unconstitutional. The important thing was to cast aspersions on Bush's legitimacy.

While some news organizations limited their recounts to a few counties or just the undervotes in a single county, several large news consortia actually went to the trouble of recounting all 6 million ballots in all sixty-seven counties of Florida. This ambitious undertaking had one goal—to demonstrate, once and for all, that Bush had indeed stolen the election. But even if these recounts, which were not complete when this book went to press, were to reaffirm Bush's win, they would still be meaningless.

After all, if hand recounts in selected counties dilute the impact of votes in uncounted counties, then hand recounts in selected states dilute the impact of votes in uncounted states. If the media consortia truly wanted an accurate recount, they would hand tally all 100 million ballots in the nation. Perhaps then Bush would win some of the states he narrowly lost, such as New Mexico.

But even such a colossal undertaking would amount to nothing more than an academic exercise. These meandering journeys down hypothetical paths are known in the news business as "what-if" stories. But a truly fair and objective press would entertain other, more plausible "what-ifs."

For example, what if Florida felons had been prevented from casting thousands of illegal ballots that overwhelmingly favored Gore? And what if the networks had not robbed Bush of 10,000 votes in the western Panhandle by prematurely and erroneously giving Florida to Gore? Finally, what if the networks had not deprived Bush of the popular vote victory nationwide by declaring the election over when it was still very much in play?

But none of these "what-ifs" got much play in the press, since they would only serve to reaffirm the legitimacy of Bush's victory.

So reporters returned again and again to just one hypothetical—the endless recounting of ballots in Florida.

In the midst of the standoff, a journalist asked Gore whether Bush was trying to steal the election. Instead of simply saying no, Gore cleverly replied that he had chosen not to use that word. The implication was clear: Of course Gore believed Bush was trying to steal the election, although the vice president was too polite to resort to such incendiary rhetoric. Gore's top aides and followers, however, had no such aversion to employing the politically charged word. They frequently accused Bush of stealing the election both during and after the Florida standoff.

Did Al Gore try to steal the election? That depends on the definition of the word "steal." The dictionary defines it as the taking of someone else's property, especially by unjust means. By that definition, it can certainly be argued that Gore tried to steal the election. After all, Florida's 25 electoral votes always belonged to Bush. In order to take them away, Gore resorted to measures that were ruled unconstitutional by seven justices of the U.S. Supreme Court. He even sought the disenfranchisement of brave GIs serving overseas and innocent civilians living in Seminole and Martin counties. He secretly consulted an Electoral College expert in hopes of discovering faithless electors. Finally, he resorted to the politics of personal destruction, directing a smear-and-destroy campaign against Florida's secretary of state for daring to uphold the law. All the while, he openly placed his own interests above those of the nation, as his concentric "circles of responsibility" so graphically illustrated.

If these are not unjust means, then what are?

Still, Democrats had every reason to believe the thievery rap would cling to Bush more than Gore. After all, such political revisionism had succeeded in the past. Most Americans, for example,

believed Clarence Thomas rather than Anita Hill during the ugly
Senate confirmation of the U.S. Supreme Court justice. But by the
time the Democrats and their allies in the press had finished demo-
nizing the high court's only African-American, the polls had
flipped. More Americans, in retrospect, came to believe Anita Hill
rather than Clarence Thomas. The myth had taken root in the
national consciousness.

Similarly, Democrats hoped more Americans would ultimately
come to believe that Gore, not Bush, had been rightfully elected
president. Florida would become the new battle cry, the bogeyman
to replace former House Speaker Newt Gingrich, whose usefulness
as a political whipping boy had waned in the years since he had left
office. With the GOP now controlling the House, the Senate, and
the White House for the first time in nearly half a century, demor-
alized Democrats desperately needed to vilify someone or something—as long as it was Republican. They openly predicted the
Bush administration would be hobbled from the outset by questions
of legitimacy. Even Republicans braced for the worst.

But then something unexpected happened. During Bush's first
months in office, most Americans closed ranks behind their new
president. The nation seemed relieved that it would no longer be
subjected to an endless stream of increasingly sordid scandals. While
Clinton had stumbled at the start of his administration and dis-
graced himself at the end, Bush demonstrated a sure-footedness that
reassured Republicans and Democrats alike that an adult was now
in charge. The new president deftly cultivated a bipartisan bon-
homie that silenced most cries of illegitimacy. To be sure, the liberal
base of the Democratic Party remained determined to exploit the
Florida fiasco in future elections. But it seemed entirely possible the
strategy would backfire. Many moderate Democrats, not to mention
virtually the entire American mainstream, were anxious to move on.

"I always felt that our nation, once we got beyond all the counts, recounts, five different counts, or whatever it was, revotes, would be anxious to seek a higher ground," Bush told the author. "That there is such a goodness about America, that that would enable me and others who are there for the right reasons in Washington—Republicans and Democrats, by the way—to prove the skeptics wrong. To seize upon the inherent spirit of America and move forward. And so, in kind of an interesting way, the house divided turned out to be an opportunity to unite.

"The country wants a different tone in Washington—I sensed that," he added. "The country doesn't want to go back to the days of divisiveness and bitterness."

Even liberal Democrats like Massachusetts Senator Ted Kennedy affirmed Bush's legitimacy and marveled at his success in restoring civility to Washington. They likened the new Bush era to the days when President Ronald Reagan and House Speaker Tip O'Neill enjoyed a close personal friendship, even while disagreeing over public policy.

"I believe that there's a spirit, a positive, can-do spirit that is now beginning to take hold in the nation's capital," Bush said. "I believe we can have an honest discussion on issues, and an honest disagreement, without name-calling and finger pointing and needless divisive rhetoric, which discourages people around the country. I'm so pleased with the progress being made—not for my sake, but for the sake of our country."

Amazingly, the Florida ordeal had served to strengthen the new administration, not weaken it. The press, which had confidently predicted Bush and Cheney would get off to a shaky start, was once again proven wrong.

"It's been a hell of a ride," Cheney told the author as he sat in the ornate office where Gore had delivered the concession speech that ended the standoff. "Who could have scripted something like that? Nobody could."

Bush was equally philosophical about the thirty-six-day ordeal.

"I was in an interesting perspective," he said. "I had just finished running the ultimate political marathon and was coming down, kind of adjusting from a grueling process. And so was the vice president, don't get me wrong. I mean, he put his heart into it as well. I'm the kind of person, though, when I felt like I'd given it my all, and expended every ounce of energy, that there was nothing more I could do.

"And, you know, I wished it would have ended," the president confided. "There were moments during the period of time that I wish it would have ended. But that's just not the way it worked out. And I'm a more patient person for it, by the way. Really."

Maybe we all are.

ACKNOWLEDGMENTS

I am indebted to many people, especially my wife, Becky, who first encouraged me to take on this project. She and our children, Brittany, Brooke, Ben, Billy, and Blair, gamely tolerated my absence for forty-six consecutive days after the election. Even more admirably, they put up with my presence for the next sixty-seven days as I wrote the manuscript at home. Meanwhile, my mother, Teresa Sammon, provided daily prayers that were much appreciated.

Publisher Al Regnery, who proposed this undertaking in the early days of the post-election debacle, provided moral support and the unfettered freedom to write what I saw fit. Regnery's eagle-eyed editors, Harry Crocker and Emily Dateno, expertly honed and sharpened the manuscript.

This book would not have been possible without the cooperation and support of the reporters and editors of the *Washington Times*, especially Editor in Chief Wes Pruden, Managing Editor Bill Giles, Deputy Managing Editor Fran Coombs, and National Editor Ken Hanner. I am particularly grateful to my partner, White House correspondent Joe Curl, for holding down the beat while I was AWOL.

And I received invaluable assistance from Joe Szadkowski, director of the *Times*'s superb library, and his crack staff of researchers.

I also wish to thank Brit Hume and my other friends at Fox News Channel for their support and patience. The same goes for Llewellyn King and Linda Gasparello at *White House Weekly*.

Finally, I owe a special debt to the aides and supporters of Al Gore who spoke with me throughout the pre- and post-election struggles, both on and off the record. Without naming names, I thank them for their insights. Ditto to the many GOP lawyers, politicians, and strategists who provided invaluable assistance. And I'm grateful to President Bush and Vice President Cheney for taking the time to answer my questions for this book.

INDEX